An autobiography by:

CHRISTY CANYON

First Edition

Library of Congress-in-Publication Data

Canyon, Christy.
    Lights, Camera, Sex! an autobiography / by Christy Canyon –1st ed.

Cover Photos Courtesy of Vivid Video

Printed in the United States of America

To Grant, the most beautiful man in the world. Nobody could ever ask for a more loving and wonderful husband. You accept me for who I am, was and will be. Thank you for never expecting to have married the character, but the real me. The me who doesn't always wear garter belts and stockings, if ever. I promise to toss away some of those flannels I wrote in. You kept your promise from twelfth grade after all. I love you so much.

This labor of love, laughter and even a tear here and there is dedicated to:

Clair - You are my anchor in life and my life preserver every day. I don't think you know how much I rely on you. You are the best sister in the entire universe.

Mom - Thank you for having faith in me, and realizing that I had to sink or swim on my own. You taught me the value of a dollar and how to always find humor and the positive in life.

Steve and Vivid Video - I thank my lucky stars you spoon-fed me all those years under contract and never asked me to do anything you knew I wouldn't do anyway.

Victoria Paris - Troop Leader, you kept me in line when I was sick of reading, re-reading, editing, and re-editing for the past year. You are the world's best friend and soul sister. The Billy Goat did one good thing in life; he brought us together forever. Over and out.

Thomas Vito Sinopoli - You are a man who changed my life the day I met you. You helped me become the woman that I am today. You are a true dude's dude who never said 'no' to me.

Lois - If it weren't for you, I think I would be in a looney-bin today. Anybody who doesn't agree with therapy has obviously never met you.

Tatiana - Mother-in-laws are the best. Thank you for all of your editing and honesty. Your encouragement kept me going.

Dave LaRue - You started off as my agent and quickly became a dear friend. Even though you are many miles away, I think of you daily. Whenever I need an answer on something, you send me more answers than I even knew existed. You kept me safe and laughing on the road, unless you made a wrong turn and I was hungry.

Jack Grapes - You are the best writing teacher in the field. The year in your class taught me how to image moment and jump on the Slausen cutoff when need be.

In loving memory of my father - You are still the only person who can make me laugh and cry at the same time. I miss you so much.

Roscoe, Demi and Rogue - My furry four-legged children who kept me company in the office.

Ninja, Applejack and Jasper - I hope you're keeping my father company.

Just when you thought my dedications were finished......

This page is dedicated to almost every F.O.F. past and present, who has enriched my life, hauled my ass around on the road and fought some battles with me.

Cappy - Mere words cannot describe what you mean to me. You are a fan who became my friend. Thanks for all the CD's and my place in life in ninety-five more years.

Suicide Stan - You know more about my sex scenes than I do. Thanks for the research I needed to help me on my book.

Lawman - Whenever I need a legal question answered, you are the man. Even if it's in a different field than yours, as well as a different state.

Texan Tom – You got two for the price of one when you fell in love with Victoria. We're a package deal.

Dr. Bob - That was the best lunch in Manhattan. I've never had such great Swordfish. Sorry if I scared you without make-up.

JoJo Photographer - You took some great photos of me on stage.

Ric - You took some pretty awful photos of me on stage, but always knew where to find chicken at midnight.

Big Red - Gone but not forgotten. Victoria and I still picture you in shorts and hiking boots looking like the yodeler from The Price Is Right.

Chello - You are a dear, sweet man who is my dolphin in life.

Toolman - You were terrific to have in my corner when fighting a club.

Kandimannn - Thanks for the bags and bags of candy along the way. You owe me a year's membership to a gym now.

Lapdog - You were perfect for a quick getaway at two in the morning with three bags of luggage.

Giggles - May you always laugh in life.

JC - It's about time you stepped up to the plate.

Gary - I hope you're out of your bout of depression.

For the one's who didn't make it in this book, I'll catch you in book two.

1

It took me twenty minutes from my apartment in Hollywood to find World Modeling on Van Nuys Blvd. There was the sign, larger than life above the address. If there's a sign outside, how bad could it be? They were advertising it in plain view. It wasn't some back alley operation, trying to hide from the world. Jim had said over the phone that they were licensed and bonded, whatever that meant.

I had been in this area thousands of times, yet I never noticed that this was here. I never once saw that sign and wondered what modeling agency was right here in the valley.

I parked on the street and put two quarters into the meter. I had no idea what to expect, but two hours ought to be enough.

I held onto the rusted handrail, and climbed the two flights of stairs. My heart was pounding. I had no idea what I was getting myself into. Survival and apprehension each took a shoulder with every step I climbed.

Survival won out as I hit the top of the second story landing.

I stood at the top of the stairs and looked at the front door. The glass door was covered in black tint that was peeling away at the corners. Over the black tint, a white decal read, "World Modeling" which was peeling away at the corners as well.

I stood in front of the door and contemplated what doors in my life I was about to open, and what doors I was about to close. A wave of nostalgia washed over me, and four faces stood out. Mom, Dad, Carol and Marv. The very faces that had let me down, and the same faces that had driven me to stand at this door. Our fighting that led to this last ditch effort of my fight for survival. I was on my own, and I had to survive at whatever cost.

I pushed the door open and cool air hit me as I stepped over the threshold. I could hear the hum of an air conditioner and a man's voice in the room to my left. It was the same Southern drawl I had spoken to less than an hour ago. I rounded the corner, and stood in the doorway. Behind the worn out wooden desk, sat a man in his mid-fifties, smoking a cigarette. A black phone was cradled to his left ear, and he was looking through a photo album.

"Stacey Donovan and Misty Reagan are the only two girls available on Friday. Misty will do anything, and I mean anything, for the right price. Stacey on the other hand, is on a prima-donna kick where she will only do one guy per scene, and no facials."

He looked at me, and gestured for me to sit opposite him. "I'll just be a second," he whispered. "Alright Harold, let me know which one you want, and get back to me. A young lady walked into my office and I've got to go."

"Hi, my name is Jim South." He stood and walked around the desk to shake my hand. He wore a plaid shirt in hues of blue and green that matched his shag carpet. His worn out tan leather belt was cinched at the waist, with a shiny bucking bronco on the brass belt buckle. The dark blue Wrangler jeans were perfectly pressed with a crease down each pant leg. At the bottom of each leg, black leather cowboy boots rounded out his urban cowboy ensemble. His hair was styled in a pompadour, with more Dippity-Doo gel in it than I had ever seen in one application. His face, although kind looking, was covered in pot marks. He looked like Howdy Doody on a real bad acid trip.

"Hi. I called you about an hour ago."

"Christy is it?"

"Yes." My heart was beating a mile a minute. I could hear the gold beads on my dress clink together with every move I made.

"Would you like to sit down?"

"Yes." My heels were killing me.

"I want to reiterate to you that this is nude modeling. Do you understand that?"

"Yes." I understood it, feared it and was excited by it.

"You are free to come and go as you please, there is no contract binding you to me or this line of work if you choose to do it. I only ask of you, that if a man by the name of Reb contacts you, that you do not, under any circumstances talk to him."

"I won't, I promise." What's a Reb I thought?

We sat down opposite each other and Jim gave me some paper work to fill out.

"I will need a copy of your current and valid drivers license for age verification."

Without hesitation, I handed it to him.

Nearly licking his chops, a slight smile spread across his face. "You're barely eighteen."

The first page I filled out was the typical questions: Name, age, height, weight, hair and eye color, birthday, social security number and address.

The second page was unlike any other job application I had ever seen. There were ten questions. Ten very odd questions.

1. Will you do anal?
2. Will you do gangbangs?
3. Will you perform same gender sex?

2

4. Will you do interracial sex scenes?
5. Is there any part of your body you don't want to be ejaculated on?
6. Are there any sexual positions you do not feel comfortable in?
7. Will you perform in bisexual/transsexual movies?
8. Do you have any sexually transmitted diseases?
9. Are you over the age of eighteen with a valid identification card?
10. Do you understand that this is figure modeling, and nudity will be required?

I answered "no" on number eight and "yes" on numbers nine and ten. I left one through seven blank.

Jim came back in the room and handed me my driver's license. "Is something wrong with the forms I gave you?"

"I only want to do magazine layouts, so do I still need to fill out numbers one through seven?" I didn't want to be a pain, but there was no way I was going to do any porno movies, so why should I fill it out?

"Of course not darlin'. Go ahead and leave those blank," for now, he refrained from adding.

"With your permission, and only if you feel comfortable taking the next step, I would like to take a couple of nude Polaroid's of you to put in my book."

I turned my back and began to get undressed. The ring from the telephone made me nearly jump out of my skin. I froze in my bra, undies around my ankles.

"I'm going to let the machine pick that up."

With trembling hands, I unhooked my bra, mumbling an incoherent answer back. I covered my breasts with my arms and turned around. Jim had the Polaroid camera up to his right eye, his left eye was squinting and he was hunched over two feet. He straightened up and took the camera away from his face.

"Would you mind uncovering your chest for a few photos?" I let my arms fall to the sides of my body.

Jim took his stance again. "Stand tall, and throw your shoulders back." Snap. The Polaroid photo spit out.

"Will you turn to your right or left side, and put your arms above your head?" I did as I was told. Snap. The second photo spit out.

"One last shot is all I need. Turn around with your fanny facing me, then glance over your shoulder to look at the camera." Snap. The third and final photo spit out. Jim placed all three Polaroid's on his desk and wrote my name on the bottom portion. "If you leave my office and change your mind, I will give you all three Polaroid's back." It all seemed so normal for such an abnormal situation. There I was, standing naked in a stranger's office, while he took nude photographs of me. I glanced at the crotch of his starched jeans. Not even the slightest hint of a hard on could be detected. I began to get dressed, when he asked the question.

"Are your breasts a hundred percent natural?"

Here it was, time for him to make a move on me. How could I be so naive? My body went rigid. "Yes."

"What size are they?"

"36DD"

"That is truly a rarity to have such large, natural breasts, on such a small frame."

I slid my dress over my head and cinched the belt extra tight. Unsure if I would find him sitting with his pants pulled down, touching himself; I spun around to face him. Jim wasn't even looking at me. He was too busy studying the now developed Polaroid shots, a fresh cigarette dangling from his lips.

"I don't know about you, but I'm starving. Would you care to join me for lunch at Hamburger Hamlet down the street?"

For some reason, I felt safe with this stranger. He was nicer to me than my current bosses Arman and Fred. "Sure, I would love to."

When we got back to his office, Jim and I sat down, once again opposite each other.

"Now it's time to talk real business."

I kept waiting for him to make a move, but it never happened. Jim was a perfect gentleman.

"I'm going to make a phone call to my oldest and dearest friend Ron. He shoots all of the ladies and has been doing this for thirty years. If he's available, I would like to set up a single girl layout tomorrow. Are you free?" No I thought. I had to open up the dress store at 10 a.m., work eight hours there, then haul my ass to Hollywood for my hostess job from seven to ten.

Jim interrupted my thoughts "The pay is $500.00"

Thinking I must have not heard him right, I asked "How much?"

He must have thought his fresh meat was slipping away as he stammered "$500.00, but I'll see if I can get you $600.00 which is top pay for a single girl layout. All of the top names get $600.00 like Traci Lords and Ginger Lynn. Let me call Ron I'm sure he'll agree to $600.00. I'll tell him how special you are." He began fumbling with the telephone buttons.

I couldn't believe what I was hearing. That much money in one day. "I'll do it, I'm free tomorrow." Fuck the two jobs, I'd call in sick later. It would take me over two weeks at both jobs to even come close to that amount. I felt a surge of excitement ignite my entire body, not just because of the hefty one-day pay, but he said I was special. I was special. I was pretty. I was worth something. He liked me, accepted me, and approved of me. I couldn't remember feeling that way, feeling worth anything.

4

I could hear the hum from the air conditioner perched in the window behind Jim and wondered why my dad never told me I was special.

The silence in the room was broken. "Ron, Jimmy here. How was the basketball game last night? Are you going to make it to our card game Thursday?"

Jim pulled the receiver away from his mouth and half whispered to me, "Ron and I go way back, a long way" and put the receiver back to his mouth. "Uh huh, sure." Jim replied to something Ron said. Jim reached for the three developed Polaroid's he took of me and studied my naked image.

I cringed at the thought of Jim looking at my naked body on film. Now he would see my imperfections. My Armenian thighs could stand to lose a few pounds, but I didn't have time or money to join a gym. My boobs, that were once my asset in getting all the boy's attention, were now just an embarrassment to me. Was it my boobs that embarrassed me or was it just an overall shame since my parents had disowned me?

Holding the small photos at the corners between his fingers, he rocked back in his chair and stuck a cowboy boot on the edge of his desk. "Listen my friend, are you busy tomorrow? An angel just walked into my office."

5

2

The year was 1977, we were in an era of self-help with groups like: The Forum, Life Spring, and TA for Tots. These groups helped cleanse one's mind and soul. The last group was me. I was an eleven year old tot.

Clair and I climbed into Mom's orange VW Bus. "Oh girls, you're going to love Star. He's such a great guy. I've learned so much from his group therapy classes."

"What is TA for Tots?" I didn't like the sound of it. It made me sound so young. I yanked on my undies that were lodged in my rear. "I'm not a tot anymore mommy."

Mom turned around and pinched my leg. "You'll always be my baby! Even when you're one hundred years old."

I smiled. I loved being a momma's girl. "I love you Mommy, I better always be your baby." Translation: Don't even think about having another child.

Mom fluffed her hair. "TA stands for Trans Analysis."

"What does that mean?" I asked.

Our mom was into the latest wowie stuff, long before it hit the mainstream. By seven, I had had my astrological chart read and found out I was a triple Gemini. The earth momma who informed me had a twitch in her right eye. "Trouble" was all she said to me. My date of birth added up to eight, which she said spelled money. She moved some charts around, shook her head, and added "Bad money."

"Why do Clair and I have to go mommy?"

"Oh, you'll learn so much about yourselves. You can tell him anything you want and he'll help you through any problems you may have. Therapy is the greatest thing out there, girls, I just love it!"

When I was eight, mom came home with a big plastic tent like contraption. "It's called a pyramid." She placed it in the middle of our living room and stood back to admire it. "I'm going to sit under it every morning and meditate. It's supposed to have great energy underneath."

Try explaining that to your friends when they came over.

"But Clair and I are okay. We have you."

Clair was playing her new game up front. "Look! I finally got all of the balls in the center!"

I hated that game. I had no patience for the toy.

At nine years old, mom got us into hiking every morning before school started. "Wake up girls!" It was pitch black out. "We're going to Dante's Peak today." That was the tallest point of the hiking trail at Griffith Park. "I've got some nuts in my pocket so we can feed the squirrels."

Mom would stride through the trails like she owned the mountain. Clair and I, still half asleep, dragged behind her a few feet. Mom stopped. "Did you see that owl girls?"

"No. It's too dark out here." Who cared about a stupid owl, I had been in the middle of a dream about John Travolta before mom woke me.

Clair and I got to school ten minutes late every morning with twigs stuck in our hair and mud caked all over our tennies.

"Well honey, just enjoy TA for Tots."

"I'm not even a tot. It makes me sound like a baby." I kicked the back of the passenger seat. "I'M NOT A BABY" I hollered.

Clair jetted forward, and her puzzle fell on the floor. "Hey, stop kicking me." She picked it up. "Now look what you did." She began trying to maneuver those silly little silver balls back in the center of the maze under the plastic top.

Mom looked at me through the rear view mirror. "I'm sure you'll find something to talk about." Mom exited the freeway. "Have you talked to your dad lately?"

I looked out the window. "Where are we? It's so ugly and hot out here." I was hot and sticky and not in the mood for some new-fangled group therapy. "No, we called Daddy a few nights ago, but he hasn't called back."

When I turned ten, mom started to see a Vietnamese nutritionist named Tet. In place of Fruit Loops and pancakes in the shape of animals, Clair and I got a big hot plate of brown rice and tofu. "The tofu tastes just like scrambled eggs," Mom raved.

"If it tastes like eggs, why can't we just have eggs?"

Tet called it a macrobiotic diet.

"Oh because this is so much healthier for you. It gives you so much protein."

I took one look at Tet and his home office and called him a quack.

When we got home, mom sent me to my room.

We pulled into a driveway and mom had to stop for a chicken that was in her way.

"Does he have any dogs?" I perked up a bit. I loved dogs. One day I would have a house full of them and a couple of cats too.

"No, just these chickens." Mom found a spot in his dusty lot and parked.

I got out of the car and nearly choked on the dirt swirling around from mom's tires. "Hasn't he heard of concrete?" I coughed for effect only. "Why chickens?"

"Well, he believes in pure food without any hormones."

I stretched my legs. "But if they're pets, what does that have to do with pure food Mommy?" I knelt down. "Come here chickie-chick." The chicken ran away from me.

"Well." I could tell I had finally gotten on mom's nerves. "I think he said he raises them for food."

Just then, a rickety screen door opened on one hinge and a tall, thin, balding man held his arms open. "Jane, how lovely of you and your girls to make it."

And then it hit me. This bad man killed and ate his pets.

Clair got out of the car holding the puzzle in the palm of her hand. "Look! I got the balls back in the center!"

Mom ran over to Star, knocking Clair's arm. The puzzle fell to the dirt. "Fudgesicles." Clair bent down to pick it up.

"Girls! Come over here, I want you to meet Star."

My mommy was hugging the murderer. I saw a chicken pecking at the dirt. Poor little fellow, I wondered when it was his turn to be dinner. I stood up. No wonder the chicken ran away from me.

Clair had reached Star. What kind of a name was that for a man? It was a stupid name for a stupid guy.

"Come over here Christy." Mom wasn't smiling at me, which was a bad sign, so I high-tailed it over to her. I never wanted her mad at me. I was after all her baby. "I'm coming mommy." And she was, after all, the world to me.

"I was just looking at the nice chickens." I shot Star a look and mom shot me a look in return. "They're so cute." I didn't dare look at Mom when I said that, but I just had to say it.

Star reached out to touch my shoulder, which I let drop a few inches to avoid him touching me. "Are you two girls ready to learn something about your inner soul this afternoon?"

Clair touched the puzzle in her pocket. "Uh huh, I guess so."

I stayed silent. If for no other reason than I didn't know what he meant.

"Good. Let's get started and tap into your inner guidance system." My who-a-what-a system? Suddenly a hike at 6 a.m. didn't sound so bad.

"Jane, why don't you pick the girls up in two hours." He kissed her cheek.

Don't get any funny ideas about my mommy Buster. She's mine, not yours. "Bye mommy, I love you."

Clair and I gave her a big hug and I didn't want to let go.

"Have fun, and just let it all out girls." Mom bent down and said out of Star's earshot. "Be nice and behave."

I just stared at her.

Mom got back in the bus and left us in a cloud of dirt. "Alright girls, let's get inside, the others have been waiting."

The others? Who else was here?

We stepped inside his guesthouse, which he called his "healing hands home". "Only warm fuzzies are allowed in here. All cold prickleys must be left on the door step."

I giggled and he stopped. "Would you like to share with us what's so funny?" He wasn't smiling at me like he did around mommy.

"Just that word."

He adjusted his wire glasses and I wanted to step on them. "What word?"

"Prickly."

"What do you find so enchanting about that word?"

"A guy in school Bart told me what that means."

"And what does it mean."

I directed my bad breath one inch from his face. "I call him Bart the Fart."

"I can see that your inner child has some issues that we need to attend to. A wounded inner child will prevail into a critical parent in your later years."

Oh for Pete's sake, why couldn't he just speak English?

Two other kids were already sitting on the gray couch. Two beanbag chairs sat on the ground empty. Clair sat in the bright green one and I sat in it with her.

"Christy, why don't you take the red one on the right."

"No, I'm going to sit with my sissy." I put my arm through Clair's to show that I wasn't going to budge.

Star looked at his clipboard and began jotting some notes. No doubt they were by my name. "Alright, be that way."

"Okay." I reached in my shorts and tugged my undies again. I think the elastic had worn out.

Star sat down across from us and crossed his legs. "We will begin today's session with introductions." He consulted his clipboard and looked around at his room of tots. "Peggy, why don't we start with you." I knew he would save me for last.

"Everybody, when it is your turn, I want you to stand up and tell the group who you are." He made eye contact with everybody but me. "Then, I want you to open up your souls and fill us in on any ailments that you may have." He finally looked at me. "We are all love and will not judge one another. Free yourselves of any fears instilled in you. Let us embrace you and heal you."

"Peggy, it's time to share."

Peggy informed the class about her silly little problem. "My name is Peggy, as you already know." She paused like we would clap for her. "And I am really angry because I have allergies to cats, so my parents

9

won't get me one."

Sit down and shut up.

"Well, would you like to get your aggression out?" Star was grinning. "Yes Peggy, I will put that offer out to you, right here, right now." He stood up and pulled out a large, bright yellow padded club from the closet. "You can't hurt a thing. Just hit it against the wall right here." He pointed to a spot on the wall that was padded as well. "Each time you hit it, tell us why you're mad. Let it out Peggy. Free yourself, heal yourself."

Peggy took the padded object and tapped the wall with it. "I'm mad because I want a cat."

"No, no Peggy really let it out. Hit it hard; scream it out of your throat. 'I WANT A CAT'." Star demonstrated hitting the wall with a matching club, only padded in bright pink. We all jumped when his club hit the wall. Even I was becoming interested, not in her stupid story, but in the force Star gave the wall. He hit it so hard, yet not a scratch or dent was seen.

Peggy stepped back up to the plate. "I wish I didn't have allergies so I could pet a kitty cat." She hit the wall with some good muscle, and I actually felt sorry for her. How sad to not be able to pet a furry kitten and kiss it's face. "I want to be able to play with cats and not break out in a rash." Peggy swung at the wall again. Then she just kept on swinging at that wall, not even talking anymore. "I hate you God for making me allergic." One final swing and the club broke in half.

Star watched the feathers fly around the room. "That's never happened before."

Peggy had crumbled into a heap on the floor. Her floral dress scrunched above her waist exposing a pair of clean white Mickey Mouse underwear. I gave my own pair another good yank out of the crack of my ass. This was getting good.

"Peggy, are you feeling better?"

Peggy pulled it together and sat up, re-buckling one of her Mary Jane's. "Yes, as a matter of fact, I am." She looked out the window and saw a chicken in the yard. "Maybe I'll ask my parents for a chicken instead."

"Try it at home Peggy. Free your fears and reach out to a cat." Star looked at the ceiling. "It's amazing what your mind can do."

Dunkin was next. "I've had asthma for my whole life, and I'm so sick of having to carry an inhaler everywhere." His sweet brown eyes looked so sad. "My mom and dad said I'd probably have to carry this stuff around for the rest of my life." He held up the small canister and shot a spray in his mouth while he was at it.

"Dunkin, I want to ask you to lay down on the carpet. Class, I want all of you to touch his body and fill him up with good, positive warm fuzzies."

Wee Dunkin lay down, and the three of us touched a body part. I placed my hands on his stomach and willed this boy to feel better. Nobody should feel pain. I asked God to help make this problem go away. I didn't know what asthma was, but I knew that it made Dunkin sad, and I suddenly felt sad for him. I bent down and whispered in his ear. "Feel better and be happy that you have a mom and dad who love you."

"Don't you have a mom and dad who love you?"

"I know my mommy does."

"Alright kids. How do you feel Dunkin?"

"I feel peaceful." We smiled at each other. "I'm thankful that I have my mom and dad to help me through this too."

"And don't forget the tot's. You have them as well Dunkin."

"Clair, you're next."

"Well, I seem to have a problem telling my friend Tammy that I don't want to be her best friend anymore. She wants to spend every weekend with me and I want to be with my other friends too, but I don't want to hurt Tammy's feelings."

Star was about to say something when I said. "Tell her that I'm your best friend. You're my best friend forever. Too bad for her, it's her loss, not mine." Damn those undies, they kept crawling back up and somehow it was Tammy's fault now.

Clair held my hand and Star waited to make sure I was finished. "Do you have a problem telling people how you feel Clair?"

"Yeah, I guess sometimes I do."

"I'll tell her for you Clair, I'll tell her you're my best friend, not hers." How dare Tammy try and take her away from me just like mommy's boyfriends thinking they can take her away from me.

Star held up his hand and grinned at me. "Your sister needs to learn how to do it on her own Christy, but we appreciate your input and will process it."

I looked at the clock and couldn't believe we only had forty-five minutes left. Where did the time go?

"I'm going to role play here with you Clair. Pretend I'm Tammy, and tell me how you feel. Be honest and the truth will set you free."

He was such a geek, but I was beginning to think he meant well.

"Hi Clair, it's Tammy. What time are you going to come over this weekend?"

Clair hesitated.

"Clair, what time? My mom will pick you up right after school on Friday and then she can take you home late Sunday night. Just think, we can be together all weekend, just the two of us. Best friends forever."

I shot Clair and Star a look.

"Well Tammy, I kinda want to go out Saturday with Karen."

"Oh, well you only kinda want to go out with Karen, so that means you also want to kinda go out with me. So, what time should my mom pick you up?"

Clair sat up in the beanbag chair. "No Tammy, I do want to go out with Karen."

"What about me?"

"Well, I spent the last four weekends with just you. I want to be with my other friends too."

"Some best friend you are."

"Actually, my sister is my best friend." Clair squeezed my hand. "Forever."

"Fine, be that way. Goodbye."

The room was silent. "How did that feel to tell her the truth Clair?"

Clair stared at her earth shoes. "It felt kinda good."

"Only kinda good? What does kinda mean? Isn't that what you want to tell Tammy?"

"Well, yeah, it felt great."

"Was it so hard?"

"Not really."

"Was it so hard? A yes or a no Clair, take a stand and get off the fence in life."

"No. It wasn't hard."

I would have interjected Star with a nasty comment to lay off my sister, but I let him go on. The sooner Tammy knew I was her best friend, the better.

"Do some role playing at home with your sister or your mom." He shook his head. "You're mom's real good at that role playing, she really let her ex-husband have it but good the other night." He stuck a finger in his ear. "I wasn't able to hear anything the next morning. That lady can really let out her aggressions." He looked at the carpet, "She's a real special lady that Jane."

Was mommy yelling at Dad or Joel? Somehow I knew it was Daddy.

"Alright Christy. Tell us what's on your mind today."

"Nothing really." Suddenly I felt shy around the other kids.

"Come on, dig deep inside and share your feelings with us. What are you thinking about at this moment?"

"Nothing really."

"Then why are you crying?"

I looked up at Star and suddenly I felt safe with him. This kooky man cared about me and was paying attention to me. "Because I don't think my daddy loves me very much."

12

Star got up and brought me a box of tissues. "Why don't you tell me about the first memory you have of your daddy."

* * * *

July 1970
Four years old

My parents got a divorce when I was one. The earliest memory of my father was soon after my forth birthday. The deal was that he got us one weekend a month, and on that hot summer day in July of 1970, my sister Clair and I cramped his style. Shelly, the stewardess he was seeing, had her layover in LA on the weekend that he was to see us. She was a tall blonde with blue eyes and filled out her uniform like a brick shithouse. She had met my father a few weeks earlier on a flight he was taking from LA to Las Vegas. He impressed her with stories about what a high roller he was. Every casino on the strip begged for his business.

"They comp me all the way," he boasted. "Suites, food, massages, you name it." This coupled with his trump card story of how he survived a plane crash in the mountains with his very own Cessna had Shelly seeing stars.

"I walked away with a few, mere scratches." He bragged, pulling out the newspaper article on the crash to show her. Shelly had given our father her phone number long before the 55-minute flight came to a landing.

Our father would light up a room with his dark, tanned skin, almond shaped light brown eyes, thick, rich chocolate colored hair and a set of big, straight pearly whites. He was gorgeous, and his resemblance to Elvis Presley had women swooning all over him. Shelly thought she had landed the big one. She never counted on her new big fish bringing along his two guppies on what was to be their romantic weekend together. Her visions of love and lust were soon shattered when he informed her that today was going to be spent at Disneyland with his four and six year old daughters. Daddy tried with all of his might to get our mom to change weekends for the third month in a row, but she said no, she had made other plans. So off Clair and I went for a fun day at Disneyland in 100 degree weather. Fun for us kids that was.

Shelly, looking quite pale after her third time on the spinning teacups, sat the next few out with our father. Clair and I were to stay in the perimeters of Fantasyland and meet Dad and Shelly back at the bench under the tree in one hour sharp. Clair and I walked from ride to ride. The vision of them necking on the bench was fading with each new ride we went on. We reached a ride that we were too young to go on. We fell below the required height line.

13

"But we're in Fantasyland," Clair told the man at the entrance gate.

"No you ain't," he replied, smiling, and crammed a stick of gum between his yellowing teeth.

"But I thought kids could go on every ride in Fantasyland," Clair said.

"Yea, but like I said, you ain't." His smile disappeared. Sensing danger, he asked, "Where are your mommy and daddy?"

"On the bench under the tree." I answered, peeking out from behind Clair.

"Which bench, which tree?" he asked stooping to our height. The three of us did a 360-degree turn and realized there were trees with benches underneath every three feet of the theme park. Not one of the benches in sight supported my father's ass.

"Do you know how long you've been walking around on your own?" he asked, reaching for the large, black walkie-talkie attached to the belt loop of his black polyester uniform. I immediately began crying while Clair, all of six, tried to remember her school lessons on the big hand and the little hand. Looking at his black plastic wristwatch with a colorful Mickey Mouse in the middle, she shook her head no. Static crackled, buttons were pushed, knobs were adjusted, and numbered codes were read back and forth through the black mouthpiece on the walkie-talkie. Within a few moments, a woman in a matching black outfit brought Clair and me caramel apples dipped in peanuts. I had never seen apples so large. She took our small hands in hers and walked us over to an office. We sat inside the air-conditioned room and ate our dipped apples in peace without our dad grabbing them out of our hands. "Can Daddy try that?" This was never a question, because before we could answer, the goodies in our hands that he was eyeballing were snatched from us. He would take a bite bigger than any mouth had a right to, leaving us with an empty cone, cup or stick.

I was enjoying the final bite of my caramel apple when I heard honking and saw bright red flags attached to the sides of the emergency golf cart heading our way. Daddy looked so small at first sitting in the passenger seat. All I could see of Shelly was a huge mass of bleached blonde hair as she was sitting in the rear seat of the cart facing backwards. As Daddy got closer, his facial features became clearer to me through the glass window of the office. His face was pinched, tense and agitated as hell. Wait 'til Jane, our mother, found out that he lost her babies at the theme park. He jumped off the cart before it even came to a full stop and ran towards the office. Shelly remained frozen in place. Barreling through the office door, daddy glanced at our empty sticks for just a second then embraced Clair and me in his bear-like hug. He was all sweaty and stunk a little but his arms felt good. Safe and secure.

He never heard from Shelly again.

14

"How could he have left us? All of the other daddies at the park went on the rides with their kids, but he just left us alone."

"You my sweet Christy, have some abandonment issues that we will be working on in our sessions. Never forget that you are loved." He handed me another tissue. "Your father needs to own up to his actions."

On the drive home, I was quiet for a change and Clair was working on that puzzle again.

"How did it go girls?"

"It was pretty fun. I did some role-playing in class. Star played Tammy. Will you do some with me this week mom? I want to learn how to say no to her."

"Of course honey. I just love to role-play. I got some aggressions out on your dad last time."

I knew it had to be Daddy.

"What about you sweetheart. What did you talk about today?"

"Daddy." I was so tired. "Mommy, can we stop and get me some new underwear? Mine are so old."

"Sure baby, how many pairs do you have now?"

"None. I threw my last pair away in Star's trashcan after class. They were hurting me down there."

Momma took us to the May Company on Laurel Canyon and I picked out a few pairs.

Next stop Der Weinerschnitzel. I ate two chili cheese dogs, a large basket of fries and drank a strawberry milkshake.

I fell asleep on the long black bench in the back of Mom's bus driving home.

Why was my dad so exhausting?

One week later, I was dressed and ready to go to TA for Tots. "Hurry up mommy, or we're going to be late."

"Hold on Christy, I've got to take out this last hot roller."

I could hear Clair in the den playing with her new game Simon Says. The electronic game buzzed which meant Clair had not followed the sequence of colors correctly. "Shoot!" Clair said, and I could hear her restart the game.

I sat down on my bed and looked at the clock. TA started in forty minutes. "Mom, how long does it take to get to Star's?" I held one of my teddy bears close to me. "Hi Panda."

"I'm ready girls." Mom came out looking beautiful in a patchwork print skirt and matching vest.

"Can I brush my teeth first?" I didn't want Star to think I always stunk.

"Yes, but hurry up. Clair, where are you?"

I heard the game buzz again. "Dang it. Coming mom."

We climbed in the bus and headed out to the hot end of the valley. "What are we doing for dinner Mommy?"

"Going out with Stephen."

Stephen was a nerdy friend of Mom's. I didn't mind him around because I knew there was no way mommy could like him more than a friend. In fact, I couldn't imagine anybody kissing him. His forehead was so sloped it reminded me of a steep cliff. Maybe his mom dropped him on his head when he was a baby. "Momma, why is Stephen so funny looking?"

"That's not a nice thing to say."

"I was just asking."

Mom began to laugh. "I'm not sure why he's so funny looking, he just is."

"Where is he taking us to dinner?"

"Well, we haven't decided. Is there any special place you want to go?"

"Vitellos is always good." Plus I knew that if I ordered the dinner-size plate of spaghetti and meatballs, I would have some left over to take to school the next day.

"Clair, how do you like it there?"

"Sounds good to me."

"Vitellos it is then." Mom blew a kiss to a guy in the car next to us. "Oh, why is life so much fun girls?" She did a little shimmy in the front seat.

And life was so much fun. I loved my sister and my mommy. These were the happiest days I remembered, just the three of us girls.

We pulled up to Star's place and I slid the back door open. "We'll see you in two hours mommy."

"Okay, I'll be in the main house meditating."

Star greeted us on the front step. "Good afternoon girls."

"Hi Star," Clair and I said in unison.

"Do you remember what to leave on this front step?" He pointed down to the broken up chunk of concrete.

"Cold prickleys." Clair answered and we both started to giggle.

"Only warm fuzzies are allowed in," I said.

We stepped into the room, the last to arrive again.

"Today, we are going to learn about a very important phrase in life that we need to always remember." He pointed to a chalkboard and read out loud what he had already printed. "I'm okay, you're okay." He went silent to let it sink in before repeating it. "I'm okay, you're okay." He bowed his head for a moment. "Let's all say it together now."

The four of us tots repeated it back to Star.

"Excellent. Today, let's start with you Dunkin. How did you feel all week?"

He shot some spray in his mouth. "I guess I felt better."

"Ah ha!" Star yelled and jumped to his feet. "You see, it's the power of healing hands. Dunkin, get back on the floor. Class, well, you know what to do, gather around." Star clapped his hands three times. "Come on tots, you can't take time back."

This time I placed my hands on Dunkin's heart. "I want you to feel perfect Dunkin." I could feel his heart beating through his shirt. "I will make you feel better." I heard his voice whisper back to me. "I wish I could share my daddy with you Christy." His eyes didn't look so sad this week.

"That would make you my brother." We smiled at each other.

"I always wanted a sister."

I wished his asthma would go away, and he wanted to share his daddy with me. We all had problems, not one of us tots had the perfect life. I wondered if anybody did, but somehow I knew the answer was no. To one degree or another, everybody had a problem.

"This is wonderful class." Star wiped his glasses off on his robe. That's funny; I don't remember him in a peach robe last week. I thought he was just wearing jeans and a t-shirt. "Class, tell me our phrase of the week just one more time."

We all looked over to the chalkboard and said. "I'm okay, you're okay."

Star beamed from ear to ear. "Peggy, let's go to you next. Did you pet any cats last week?"

For some reason she stood. "Yes, I played with my aunt's orange cat for an hour."

Star sat back and relaxed. "Excellent." He crossed his arms behind his back. "And share with us what happened?"

"I broke out in a horrible rash and had to be rushed to the emergency room."

Star sat up. "What? How can that be after last week with our healing powers at work?"

"The doctors said that tots can't cure it. I'm stuck with my allergies for life."

Star put his face in his hands. "Oh, this is awful Peggy. I was sure the tot's healing powers would work on you. Look at how well they worked on Dunkin."

Dunkin was busy shaking his canister of asthma spray trying his best to get the last few drops out before he went into a full asthma attack.

"Oh, it's okay Star. The next day when I was released from the hospital, my mom and dad took me to the pet store and I got a hamster."

"Oh, Well that's good I suppose." Star looked beat. "What did you name it?"

"It's a she, and I named her Rosie."

"Well, enjoy him I guess." He gave a nervous laugh. "Okay class." Star got up and erased the chalkboard. "Now, recite for me again our phrase of the week."

I thought of my dad. "I'm okay you're not okay."

Clair looked at me.

"Good, good class. Christy, would you like to be next?" Star seemed a bit out of it. "Why don't you open up about your mom for us again."

"I love my mommy and she loves us so much. She said we're her life."

"But that's not what you said last week." He shuffled through his notes. "Oh, sorry, I meant tell us more about your father." Star got up from his seat. "Hang onto that thought Tot, I need to feel some chi running in my body first." Star walked to the corner of the room. "This will just take a second." Star squatted down and rolled on his head. He inched his long legs up the wall until he was in a full headstand. "Much better." His face was turning bright red. "Now Christy, do you believe in your father? How are his emotions towards your lovely mother?"

"He's always talking bad about my mommy. He says she never does much for us but it's him that never follows through with any of his promises."

Star climbed down the wall and did a half-roll back onto his feet. "Tell me more about that, give me an incident."

* * * *

1974
Eight years old

Daddy's black Cadillac pulled into the driveway. Clair and I were spending two nights with him.

"Come on Christy, Dad's here."

It was three in the afternoon and Mommy was still at work. I already missed her and my room at home. Dad had moved back into Granny's house so we were spending the weekend there with Dad. Dad had been seeing a new lady, Carol for several months. She lived in a two-bedroom apartment with her daughter Eve, so when Dad had us for the weekend, the three of us stayed at Granny's.

"There's not enough room in my apartment for five people." Carol told Daddy. "But let's all get together for lunch on Sunday before you drop

18

the girls back at their home."

What a phony baloney she was.

Clair opened our front door before Dad had a chance to knock.

"Hi Daddy!" We said in unison.

Daddy hugged us and took our weekend bags. "Hello girls. Hurry up now, get in the car, Daddy has to be at the IRS in an hour."

Clair and I climbed in the front seat, and Dad shoved our bags in the backseat. One of our bags caught on the seatbelt latch and ripped open. Shoes and clothes for the weekend tumbled out of the car and scattered around our driveway.

"FUCK!" Daddy began picking up the items.

"What's wrong Daddy?" Clair asked.

"I'll tell you what's wrong. Your mother packs your Goddamn clothing in a paper shopping bag from the market. Why can't she just buy you a real suitcase for Christ's sake?"

"She said she can't afford one because you don't pay child support." I goaded him, always defending my mommy.

"I do pay child support. Last month was a little tough on Daddy, but the month before I paid God damn it." He shoved my tennis shoe in the backseat.

"Mommy said that the $25.00 checks every few months don't cover very much."

Dad got behind the wheel. "Is that what your mommy told you?"

"Uh-huh"

"Well, I hope you don't believe her." I'll admit, Dad has had some tough times this year, but whenever I can, I pay!"

But of course we believed Mommy over him.

"In fact, I'll buy each of you a brand new suitcase this weekend. That will show your mother."

"Why are we going to the IRS?" Clair asked.

"Because some asshole, pencil-pusher there is questioning some of the deductions on my return."

Dad threw the car in reverse, and backed out of our driveway, taking a portion of our rosebush with him.

In his nervous condition, he didn't make a full stop at the corner sign, and cut another car off. The other driver honked, and flipped the finger at Dad as he swerved to avoid a crash. It was the wrong day to mess with Daddy. He gunned the engine to catch up to the other driver.

"Did you see what he just did girls?" Dad's black Caddie began to gain speed, closing the gap between the two cars. "Who does he think he is?" Dad began honking, inches away from the other car's bumper. Dad's left hand was out the window; I'm sure flipping him the bird.

"Honk the horn for me while I steer." Daddy told me. "Just lay on it, don't ease up."

I put my little hand on the horn and kept it there.

Just then, the car ahead of us made a left-hand turn. Daddy followed the sharp turn causing Clair and I to slide on top of him. I tried to regain my balance, and let go of the horn.

"Keep you hand on the fucking horn!" Daddy yelled, his body half way out the window screaming obscenities. Years of frustration were let loose on the driver.

"Watch out for the…"

Clair was too late. Daddy's car leapt on a lawn and side swiped three trash cans, sending the full bins flying across the car and lawn.

"Clair, turn on the wipers."

Clair reached over my body to turn them on, knocking Daddy's right arm in the process. Daddy and the car jetted into the on-coming traffic. The other driver honked and flipped the finger at Dad as he swerved to avoid a crash.

The car we were tailing was nowhere in sight. The sound of the horn began to fade out. I think it blew a fuse, just like our dad. We never got our promised suitcases that weekend.

* * * *

"In the past two years, did he ever follow through with that promise of the luggage?"

"No, but mom did. I got a bright blue suitcase with Snoopy on it."

"You see? It was the power of positive thinking that willed you to get the suitcase." Star was smiling again.

"I guess so." But it was because Mom took Clair and me to Hawaii the following summer and she said the paper grocery bags wouldn't be good to check on the luggage belt. But I let Star think it was his positive thinking.

"Clair, did you have a talk with Tammy?"

"No, I just avoided the phone all week."

Star was smiling, but he looked more like a sad clown with a fake smile painted on.

"Okay, that's fine. That's another solution." He looked agitated again. "You're okay, I'm okay." He mumbled under his breath.

Star looked at his watch. "Okay class," he did a double take. "We still have an hour to go?" He didn't sound too happy about that. "I'm going to draw a diagram of your PAC." He got up and drew a pyramid with three horizontal lines through it. A "P" at the top, an "A" in the center and a "C" at the bottom. "Can anybody tell me what this means?"

Of course we all stared at him with blank faces.

20

"It represents the parent, adult and child in you."

I tuned Star out for the next half hour and thought about what new book I would buy today. Momma promised to take Clair and me to the bookstore after TA for Tots.

"So class, do not let your critical parent take control of the wheel and always nurture your inner child. Any questions?" Star looked ready for a nap.

Of course we all stared at him with blank faces.

"Anywho," he took a big gulp of water. "Next week we're going to learn about face time. How to deal with somebody one-on-one."

But there was no face time, Star, or TA for Tots ever again. Mom told Clair and me that the FBI shut down his shady operation. He never got his degree in psychology, or anything, and they had reason to believe through an unnamed source that he was trying to start a cult.

The following few years brought new changes in my life. Nothing major, but enough to push me over the edge that much more.

Dad married Carol and we were lucky if she let him loose once a month to see us.

Mom married a guy named Marv who got stuck with two teenage kids in the deal.

Neither stepparent welcomed us with open arms; we were just a package deal.

They knew that, and I knew that.

I had plenty of school friends and could snap my fingers at any guy I wanted to date. They were pleased as punch to be handpicked by the queen bee. But there was something deep inside my teenage mind and body that bothered me; I just didn't know what it was, so I didn't know how to change it.

Clair was the only person in my life that I trusted; she was the only person who never let me down.

Every so often, I would think back to that hot summer day in Star's office and remember something he said. I had abandonment issues. Did I? And if I did, how could I fix it? And what exactly did that mean anyway? I also thought of Dunkin and hoped he was okay.

This round of marriages came with another new set of stepsisters. I wondered what happened to the previous five. No doubt these two twits would become a blur in my memory soon enough. I didn't need them, I had Clair.

With each teenage year, I became a bit more defiant, until I was spinning out of control.

I didn't even have to look for it, I never did. The opportunity came knocking on my door one day. I just opened the door and let it in.

The ultimate form of rebellion welcomed me with open arms.

The world of pornography.

3

It was August 1984 and I was waiting for my friend to pick me up. I was in front of my apartment building on Franklin and Orchid wearing my favorite jean mini skirt, fuchsia pink blouse and a cheap pair of trendy heals. My British green MG Midget wouldn't start up again. One more bill that I couldn't afford. I was so broke. Working two jobs was not enough to pay all of my bills. I could see the red final notice stamped in bold letters through the envelope. Shit, where am I going to cough up $72.43 in three days for the phone bill and another $400.00 for rent? Now my car wouldn't start. I just turned eighteen and I felt so much pressure.

A white Trans Am was turning left on my street. Now that was a car. T-tops, a gold eagle fanned out on the engine hood and a great sounding stereo blaring "1999" by Prince. I bet his car started up every morning.

After he turned left on my street he noticed me and pulled to the curb. Wow, What a hunk. "Why is a pretty lady like you standing out here all alone?" He smiled, flashing a perfect set of white teeth.

I bent down and stuck my head in the open car window. "I'm just waiting for my friend Keri to pick me up." I could feel my feet vibrate from too much bass on his stereo.

"Would you care for a little company while you waited?"

What a hunk. "I would love it." He had blonde hair, blue eyes and a deep dark tan. The bucket seats in his car had cream-colored sheepskin covers that engulfed my body. This was more comfortable than that broken down bed I slept in every night. Cold air was blasting through the vents cooling my hot sticky body more than that stupid MG could ever hope to do; when it worked. I felt so relaxed and at peace waiting for Keri in this strangers car. This was so much more inviting than standing in the muggy hot summer weather with the dregs of Hollywood all around me.

His name was Greg "Rocky" Rome and he was nineteen years old from Seal Beach. I was so envious. I wanted a car like this. He was so young. How did he get such a great car? If only I had money, but I didn't. I was flat broke.

We sat listening to music in his car and just made small talk. "What do you do for a living?" Rocky asked.

"During the day I work in a clothing store and at night I worked as a hostess at a restaurant on Sunset Blvd."

"I bet you would like to make more money." He looked around the seedy street I lived on. "And maybe move into a nicer area."

Now you're talking. "One day I will." Or decade at the rate I was going.

"You are so beautiful. Have you ever thought about modeling?"

Modeling? "Yeah right, me a model. No way could I be a model. I'm too short." I left out that I had too much baby fat and my boobs were too big.

"No." Greg said, "Figure modeling."

I guess that meant body parts. "Like a foot or hand model?" I admired my long slender fingers.

Greg laughed and reached in the back seat. "This is figure modeling." He thrust a Hustler magazine into my hands. He reached over and opened the magazine to a page that had a small paperclip in it as his bookmark. There he was, this cute California surfer boy in the buff with an exotic brunette holding his erect penis. They were on a colorful beach towel with a few potted plants around them. There was a silver boom box in one corner and a multicolored beach ball in the other corner but the backdrop to this odd beach setting was just a cheap white sheet. The next page had her with her mouth open and his cock just inches away from her red glossy lips and inviting mouth. The next few pages became a blur. I had never seen one of these porn magazines so close up. I was beginning to feel very woozy and suddenly felt the need to feel the hot muggy air again and hear the familiar blasting of horns on Franklin. I finally heard Keri's beat up VW bug round the corner and honk three times.

"I have to go, my friends here." As I reached for the door to leave, Greg thrust a business card into my hand with his home number on the back.

"Think about it babe."

It wasn't 'til later on that night that curiosity finally got to me. I pulled the card out of my back pocket and stared at the front of the business card. "FIGURE MODELING" Figure models wanted, no experience necessary. Earn between $500.00-10,000 a day. It was midnight as I reached for my telephone. I listened to the answering machine give its recorded message about how they were licensed and bonded by the state of California before I hung up. No, I couldn't. But instead of throwing that card away, I stuck it deep in a drawer.

4

Four weeks after meeting Greg, I was in my apartment sitting on the dark brown and tan couch looking out of my living room window, which overlooked the dirt parking lot behind my building. There sat my new to me, but very used, gold VW Scirocco at a twenty-one percent interest rate. At eighteen I had no idea what a rip off the twenty-one percent was. I was just thankful that at eighteen with no credit, no co-signer and a $300.00 trade in on my MG, the nice man at the dealership let me drive away with it.

I turned my gaze from the dusty lot to watch my small color TV that sat on top of my round dining room table. "I Love Lucy" was on and I forgot about my loneliness. Lucy could make me forget about anything. For thirty minutes a day, I could tune out any of my troubles. Lucy was in another jam. She had stolen John Wayne's footprints in front of the Hollywood Chinese Theater and now the hunk of cement was shattered in a thousand pieces. Lucy would find a solution, she always did. I knew every scene of this and every other episode by heart, but Lucy still made me laugh.

The shows ending brought me back to a bittersweet reality. Watching Lucy made me think of Clair. This was one of the shows we watched religiously as kids. It reminded me of kids growing up safe and secure with a mom and a dad. Now I was sad, not secure but insecure in the heart of Hollywood. How ironic it was that the "I Love Lucy" episode was shot two blocks from where I now lived. So much has changed in the years since that was shot. The streets that were once lined with movie stars, glamour and wealth were now littered with hookers, pimps and drugs. How did I get here? I wasn't one of them. I came from an upper middle class family. I didn't even know what a kitchenette was until I moved in here. I went from a gourmet kitchen to a closet door that partially opened with a hot plate, a small refrigerator, one drawer and one shelf.

I dragged the phone across the rectangular, water stained, wooden coffee table that came with this joint and set it right in front of me. Dad had moved out again. He was separated from "the Bitch", but hadn't filed for divorce. I knew his number, I knew it by heart, but I had never dialed it. Clair gave me the number as soon as he moved into his new house. I contemplated what I would say to my dad after not talking to him for six months.

I played with the tan fabric on the couch, pulling out the balled up lint one at a time between my fingernails. I dropped a handful into the ashtray and reached for the receiver. I punched in the number and hoped he wouldn't be home so I could just leave a message. I knew he would call me back. Daddy loved me and missed me too; he just had no idea what to do with a daughter that was deposited on his doorstep at seventeen. His life with Carol had him fucked up and now he was faced with his spiraling out of control teenage daughter who was fucked up beyond belief but not beyond repair.

My thoughts were interrupted by his answer before the first ring was complete.

"Hello" he panted into the phone. He always answered like he was across the room and took a nosedive to get at the phone.

"Hi Daddy, it's me." And then the waterworks began and I couldn't control my crying. It had been six months since I spoke to him and almost a year since my mom and I had spoken. "I miss you." My beloved sister was schooling in London, I was working sixty hours a week and flat ass broke. I think I was having an emotional breakdown.

"Is that you honey?" Daddy's voice purred. He smelled my weakness, which turned him into a pussycat.

We talked on the phone for half an hour as I sat in my hot stuffy apartment chain smoking. "Honey, are you smoking?" Damn he was good. He must have heard me inhale or light up a cigarette.

"Yes." I was suddenly weak and he was in charge. Where was my courage? I had survived for six months on my own and now I folded like a house of cards. He smelled the blood and I fell into the trap I set. I needed the love that I so desperately craved. I was deprived of my mom and dad. I fucked up, I thought I could do it on my own. I was wrong. I hated to be wrong. Dad was right. I hated it when dad was right. I hung up with dad and like an obedient soldier; I did as I was told. I went to my closet and gathered as many clothes as I could carry to my car. I would give my notice tomorrow. I had signed a one-year lease and had only been here three months. But because of a flawless fake I.D. I bought on Hollywood Blvd., the manager leased this unit to a minor. I was only seventeen when I moved in. Dad would handle any problems with the management.

I was to be at my dad's house at six sharp, and he would show me my floor. "We won't even see each other. You have two rooms, your own bathroom and entrance. The entire bottom floor will be all for you." I found it hard to imagine not seeing or feeling my father's heavy presence.

Driving through the winding canyons I followed his instructions but somehow got on the wrong street and hit a dead end. I glanced at my dashboard and the green neon numbers let me know that it was eight minutes past six. Shit, I was already late and now I had to backtrack in the hills. I tossed my cigarette butt out of the car window and shoved a stick of gum in my mouth.

Nine minutes later I saw his street. A twist, turn and a shift into third gear brought me to his address twenty-two minutes past the hour.

There was Daddy in a pair of white shorts that should have been tossed out thirty pounds ago coupled with a kelly green La Coste shirt that didn't quite cover the tum-tum. What a sight he was watering the lawn. I pulled into the carport and waved. He smiled and bent down to turn off the hose, stopping mid bend long enough to look at his watch. His point was made in a five-second gesture without one word to me. I was late. I was bad, I was wrong; I was messing up yet again. I wasn't considerate. I didn't think of others. But I wasn't bad and I did think of other people. I just messed up and then got shuffled from one house to another.

I got out of my car and walked over to dad. "Hi Daddy, it's so good to see you." My eyes became blurry with tears forming fast. I felt like such a baby, not the big girl I thought I was. His strong arms encircled my frame.

"I missed you too honey," He pressed his face against my car window. "Is that all you brought with you? I thought you were moving in tonight. Where did you get that car?"

"I bought it from a dealership." I answered proudly.

"Are you financing it?"

"Yes."

"What's your interest rate?"

"I think it's twelve percent" I couldn't remember now. Twelve percent, twenty-one percent who cares, I got the car with nobody's help.

"Twelve percent!" He shouted. "You got ripped off man, this car should run you five maybe six percent tops and I mean tops." No pat on the back, or any acknowledgment that I bought it without asking anyone for help. Somehow that was overlooked. I did it wrong, as usual. I just wanted to please him, make him proud. Dad scooped up my clothes and I followed him like an obedient lost puppy into my new house.

This house was as cold and as empty as I was beginning to feel. It was made of glass and steel beams with no warmth or feeling. "Follow me downstairs to your quarters." His voice echoed in the sparsely furnished house. The bottom of the tri-level house was where I was to live. There were two rooms with a bathroom in between.

The first room I entered had a mattress shoved against one wall. That was it. No headboard, photos, plants, table, chairs or TV. Just a lone mattress. All alone like me, how apt. Dad threw my clothes on the floor and said I could arrange them later. I opened my new closet door and found it crammed with cardboard boxes. Clothing, books, kitchen and other handwritten labels were across each of the boxes in a black marker identifying the contents inside. On the shelf above the rod was a glass jug filled with coins.

"Carol and I will most likely get back together soon, so there's no need for me to unpack these boxes." Great, where did that leave me? Carol

27

would never okay me coming back into her house.

"We've been speaking every night. She really misses the old fart." Dad chuckled. "She didn't realize how good she had it with me." He adverted his eyes to the ceiling and I knew it was time for one of his ego boosting analogies. "I am her pillar, and without a pillar her house is crumbling. A house can not stand up without the foundation." He looked at me. "I am the foundation." He was on a roll about Carol as usual. "And I think," Dad shoved his finger into his head, "that she has finally figured that out."

Nothing had changed in the months since I saw him. Except for me. I had changed. I had a taste of freedom and now I began feeling like a caged animal. I was looking for comfort and a father daughter bonding, not another talk about Carol. What about me? Didn't he care about how I was feeling? Did he wonder what my life was like, or what I did for my eighteenth birthday? No, he was too busy trying to figure out how Carol was paying her bills without him. Dad's body blocked the doorframe and I felt claustrophobic. "I am the donkey always having to pull her cart."

I followed him into the lifeless, windowless bathroom and he flicked on the light switch. I looked in the mirror and saw my pale and ashen face. Where was that sparkle in my eyes? Where did my fierce independent streak go? "So stop pulling her cart." My new bathroom was completely bare. Not even a bar of soap in the dust filled dish. "Just stop being a donkey."

"Carol is the type of woman who needs a donkey." He pronounced it "dunkey".

The sound from the vent above my head became louder with every word out of Daddy's mouth. His lips were moving, but I couldn't hear him anymore. How could he pronounce the word donkey wrong? I stared at my father's image through the bathroom mirror. I tuned his words out and thought about my freedom.

He flipped off the light switch, which automatically cut the sound of the fan. "She hasn't come out directly and told me her moms moved in, but I'm sure she has."

My freedom would be gone.

"Carol could use her mom's Social Security checks like a hungry dog." His loud voice boomed in the total emptiness of the second room. It was bare. Not a stick of furniture. I realized that this was all about him.

Dad was in full bloom about Carol and had a fresh ear to dump on. The loving husband who was kicked out hadn't a clue what he had done to deserve this treatment. It couldn't have been because Carol caught Penny, his secretary, giving him a blowjob in his car one night. Maybe it was because he blew $20,000 a weekend in Las Vegas. Or even because a girl picked up his phone in a Lake Tahoe hotel room when he went away to "think" for a weekend. No, poor Dad had been shit on. He seemed to forget that she was the one who drove me out of her house after a few months of me living there. Did my dad really think I wanted them getting back together?

Looking at his over exaggerated stance in the doorway, I realized that they were perfect for each other. It was a game of cat and mouse they played, interchanging who played which part. "Why wont she just tell you if that old bat moved in?" I couldn't believe how stupid this conversation was. "What's the big secret anyway?" I began to see the light. "Who cares how she's surviving." I hadn't made an extreme decision to move out at seventeen. I had to save my sanity and preserve my innocence from their madness.

"Have you spoken to your mother?"

I shook my head no. "Can we eat Daddy?" I felt my empty stomach grumbling

We climbed the two flights of stairs to the kitchen. Dad had prepared a feast. Food and Carol were Dad's two main obsessions; neither one were good for his health. He laid out my first homemade dinner in months. Roast beef, mashed potatoes loaded with butter and sour cream and a salad topped with plenty of Russian dressing was laid out before me.

During dinner the talk turned to me. "You thought you had the world by the balls, heeing and hawing all of the time." Dad shoved a piece of gristle in his mouth. "You didn't listen to your old man did you? You can dance all night but eventually you've got to pay the fiddler."

I was saved by the bell when the telephone rang behind me. "Grab that will you honey?" Meat juices were running down his fingers.

"Hello." I answered on the second ring. I knew that voice all too well on the other end and I felt the hatred from deep within.

"Is Joe there?" Carol asked. No hello, no how are you, nothing. I handed the phone to my dad without a word.

"Hello" he said into the receiver. I began eating again with the food going down my throat in lumps now. He listened for several minutes before I heard him reply to what I'm sure was the third degree about me being there.

"She's just going to stay for a while, she called me up today."

I just stared at my plate of half-eaten homemade dinner. I knew that I would now be the blame and excuse for them not getting back together. I suddenly missed my round dining room table in Hollywood, even if I had to shove a book of matches under the leg to keep it from rocking.

Dad slammed the phone down, and dinner was finished in silence.

We watched TV in Dad's room while I rubbed his chapped dry feet. "Harder honey." He would say between snores before he finally passed out for the night. I crept down the staircase and crawled into bed. I stared into the dark, empty room and tasted the salt from the tears rolling down my face. This wasn't home. I knew I was out the second Carol allowed him back. Just him. We weren't a package deal. I fell asleep to the smell of musty sheets.

By the time I woke the next morning at ten, Dad had already left for work. His entire note read, "Off to work, you shouldn't be sleeping in so late." My reply was "Thank you for dinner. Now you and Carol can get back together." With that written, I ran downstairs, and scooped up my clothes from the pile on the floor. I ran up the first flight of stairs and then ran back down to my room. I reached up on the shelf and grabbed the jug of coins.

I threw my clothes in the car and placed my new jug of money carefully on the ground. There was no looking back. I was on my own and would make it work. My dad and Carol had to do their thing, whatever that was. I would only get in their way. I couldn't wait to return to my newly restored sanctuary, my apartment in Hollywood. I wanted to hear the man in the unit next to me, screaming with Tourettes, see the new dress the transvestite would be wearing today and hear the junkie falling on the floor above me. I would still avoid the wanna-be magician making eyes at me from across the hall and would just close my eyes when the cockroaches made a mad dash when I turned on the bathroom light. This far surpassed any house in Beverly Hills. This was my home, or somewhere I could call home, at least until I could afford something better and safer.

As I pulled into the dirt parking lot behind my unit, I could see the familiar sight of the dust spraying in the air from my tires hitting the dry dirt. I grabbed my clothes and the jug of money from the back seat and ran to my door. I threw my armload of clothes onto the torn up easy chair and set my jug on the ground. I headed straight for my bureau drawer. It was still there, right where I left it. Tucked between two pairs of underwear was the white business card. "World Modeling - Figure Models Wanted." I grabbed my telephone and called the number that was on the card. I lit a cigarette and noticed my fingers shaking.

A male's voice picked up on the third ring. "World Modeling." He said in a deep southern drawl. I couldn't believe I was calling.

"Hi, is Jim South there please?" My voice sounded ten octaves higher than usual.

"Speaking." He answered.

"Hi, I was given your number by Greg "Rocky" Road."

"Do you mean Rome?"

"Yeah, I think so." Oh God, how could I have messed up already?

Jim went off on some speech about how he was licensed and bonded by the state of California, and models could make up to $10,000 a day.

I couldn't breathe. "Really?" I thought about having that much money.

"When would you like to come in darlin'?"

"I can be there in one hour" I hoped I didn't sound as desperate and excited as I felt.

I hung up after getting directions and rummaged through my pile of clothes, picking out the sexiest outfit I could find. I pulled out my ninth grade graduation dress. It was shocking pink with fringed sleeves and gold beads tied onto the fringe. Next, I wrapped the gold snake like belt around my waist twice and bloused the dress over the belt. I no longer had the gold shoes that matched, but my scuffed black pumps would do. Even in ninth grade I wanted to stand out.

5

I held my breath and prayed that Ron the photographer would want to hire me for the day. It was just Jim and I in his office on that hot September day in 1984 and he told Ron there was an angel in his office.

Angels were good I thought.

"She's wet behind the ears and I want you to be the first one to shoot her. She's a real beauty with naturally large, 36DD breasts."

I hoped this wouldn't be a problem. Didn't models have cute, small perky ones? Oh shit, I could see that $600.00 flying out of the window. The palms of my hands were sweating. If Ron didn't want me, Jim wouldn't want me either.

"I told her the pay was $600.00 for a single girl layout. When you see her tomorrow you'll understand why I bumped her up to Lords and Lynn salary." Jim smiled at me. "I'll tell her to be there tomorrow morning at ten."

He hung up the phone, shook a parliament cigarette from his soft pack and lit it up with his lighter. It was an ordinary Bic lighter but was put in a silver holder with a horse's head embossed on it. In the horses eyes were small ruby like stones. The jewels in the eyes reminded me of a baby blue tank top I wore to school when I was in the sixth grade. A fox draped in a fur coat had been airbrushed on. Below the fox in red glitter it read 'Foxy Lady' and her eyes had the same ruby red jewels. Wearing this tank top coupled with jean shorts led me straight to the principal's office.

* * * *

"That tank top is not appropriate for a young lady in the sixth grade to be wearing. I'm going to call your mother about this." Mr. Varno's short fat fingers began dialing a number from my open file.

"Your shorts are always too short. I've let you slide but this tank top has made me realize that you've pushed the limit little missy." His bulbous nose and face were redder than I had ever seen before. "Hello Jane," he purred into the phone. "We have a problem at school that concerns your daughter. If you're not busy, I urge you to come over." He hung up the phone and glared at me.

"Your mother is on her way over and we'll just see what she has to say about your attire. I'm sure she'll be appalled at your 'Foxy Lady' tank top. This is not something a ten-year-old should be wearing. You wait right here in my office. Your mother will be here in five minutes. She sounded very upset." He looked at me with beady eyes and then began shuffling through a stack of papers on his desk.

I chipped off some red glitter nail polish from my thumb. "My mommy's boyfriend gave it to me." I told him. He obviously didn't know my mom. No rules, no inhibitions, just a free spirit.

His head snapped up with a bead of sweat rolling down his left temple. "Who gave it to you?"

I began picking a hangnail. "My mommy's boyfriend, he's an Indian." I calmly replied. Just then I could see our bright orange VW van pull up to the school. Mom jumped out and marched up to the school's office.

"Where's my baby?" She demanded. Mom was wearing a dress I picked out for her shopping one day. It was a patchwork dress that we called her "peak-a-boo-dress". It was low cut in the front and if she moved a certain way, one of her boobs would start showing. Clair or I would say "peak-a-boo" which was the code that she was starting to show.

"What happened with my daughter?" She demanded.

The troll like principal began to sweat out last night's alcohol. "Uh, well, I just was wondering if that tank top was something you were aware of and her shorts may be a little too short."

"Hi Mommy." Mr. Varno's smile reminded me of our Halloween pumpkin last year. We left it outside too long and the face started to cave in. It looked sad, just like Mr. Varno did right about now.

"My daughter dresses just like every other sixth grader in this school."

"Well that's true but she's..." He was trying to put it delicately that I was the only sixth grader with a very large chest, tan lean long legs, hips and a nice tight butt.

"Well I won't allow my daughter to be singled out from the rest." Mommy told him.

He clasped his sausage like fingers together and rested his chins on them. He was defeated. Nobody argued with my mommy. He signed an excused late pass and told me to go back to class.

As I was leaving his office I could hear my mom turning on her charm. "How have you been?" She really liked him, but nobody messed with one of her cubs.

The following day I went to school in a multi colored tube top and terry cloth shorts to match.

Pumpkin head avoided me the rest of the semester.

* * * *

33

Jim lit his cigarette and let a stream of smoke escape his mouth. "The way I work is that you don't ever pay me a dime. The money you make is all yours. I get paid $50.00 a day from any photographer you work for. I do not take a cut of your pay."

The glass door opened and a small balding man bustled in. "Jim, I need more models, the magazine business is booming." He stopped and took a look at me. "Are you holding out on me Jim?"

"Victor, I want you to meet my brand new girl. Ron's got her tied up for the next week then I promise you can have her, but she doesn't come cheap. Her fee is $600.00 a day." He showed the man my Polaroids and then Victor booked me for two days the following week. At $600.00 a day, I was already at $1,800.00. Jim gave me directions to Ron's house and told me to call him anytime. He said he would have my schedule booked up in no time.

"You may want to think about quitting your two jobs. I see a big future for you here."

I pulled into the parking lot of my hostess job that evening and sat in my car. For once, I was early. Could I really go through with shooting a pornographic layout tomorrow? It was legal, I think, but was it right? Maybe my mom was going to call me and I could just go home.

* * * *

June 17^{th,} 1984

I woke up alone on my eighteenth birthday. The first phone call came in at nine. It had to be my mom wishing me a happy birthday. "Hello." I couldn't remember how many months it had been since I spoke to my mom, but today was my birthday.

"Hi! Happy birthday!" Clair's voice crackled through the phone lines. "I'm so sorry I can't be with you today."

"That's okay. I miss you Clair."

"I miss you too. I owe you a birthday dinner when I come home from London."

"When are you coming home?" I missed my sister so much.

"I don't know. School is out, but Teri is here now and we're just sightseeing for the summer. What are you going to do for your birthday?"

"Well, I have to go to work today but then tonight I'm going out with Keri to a club."

"That will be fun. Are there any new clubs open in Hollywood?"

"No, not really."

"For the first time, you don't have to use your fake I.D."

"I know, I'm finally legal!" Not that being underage ever stopped me. A tight sweater and a mini skirt got me into any club.

"Well, I have to go but I just wanted to be the first one to wish you a happy birthday."

"I love you Clair."

"I love you too Christy."

I hung up the phone wondering if my mom had tried to call and got a busy signal. I pulled the phone into the bathroom and took a shower. Today at the clothing store, we had to do inventory from ten thirty until four thirty. Half way through rinsing out my conditioner, the phone rang. I turned off the water and tried to calm myself. "Hello."

"Happy birthday Christy."

"Thanks Keri." I felt the conditioner sliding down my back. "I'm just getting ready for work but I'll see you tonight at my place at ten."

"Okay have a good day at work but don't work too hard, it's your birthday."

I got dressed and waited until ten-fifteen that morning before I left for work.

Nobody else called.

I pulled into the parking lot behind the store. I couldn't see the front counter from here, but maybe my dad sent me a big bouquet of flowers. Maybe my mom would come by at noon and take me out to lunch.

I rounded the corner and saw Mandy, the store manager outside smoking. "Happy birthday Christy." She gave me a big hug. "Any surprise calls this morning?"

"Just my sister from London." I smiled but I felt like crying.

"I'm sorry baby."

"Well, the day's not over." But as far as my parents were concerned, it was over. My birthday was forgotten, just like me.

* * * *

Fred tapped on my car window. "Time for work." He pointed at his watch. "People are waiting to be seated."

I smiled and thought about what an asshole he was. "I'm ready." Jim was so nice to me and I hadn't even worked for him yet. I locked my door and followed Fred into the restaurant. There wasn't anybody waiting to be seated.

"They must have seated themselves." Fred and I looked around in the empty restaurant. "Well, why don't you start cleaning off the menus, you must have forgotten to last night."

"I was off last night."

But Fred was already gone.

Ten minutes later, my favorite customer walked in. "How's my special lady tonight?" He always brightened up my nights when he came in.

"Doing great Norm." Just pondering the idea of getting naked for work tomorrow. "The usual table outside?"

"If it's available." He was the most handsome black man I had ever seen.

"I think I can squeeze you in."

"That's my girl."

I wished I were his girl. "You're my first customer tonight," and my favorite. He was always so nice to me. "Is your girlfriend Gina going to be here tonight?"

"No, it's just me." He smiled and I felt flush. I had formed a huge crush on Norm. "I told you, Gina is just my business partner, not my girlfriend."

I still had Norm's business card. "That's right, I forgot." But I didn't forget. "Do you want anything to drink?" Gina was so cute with red hair and green eyes.

"I'll have an iced-tea." He never took his eyes off me.

Gina was always smiling and laughing. "One tea coming up."

"Christy!" I could hear Fred yelling my name. "Bring me a coffee."

I rolled my eyes at Norm. "I'll be right back."

"Hey," Norm touched my arm and his hand felt great. "If you ever need anything, call me."

I did need something. Him. "I will."

Why couldn't he just save me and take me away.

6

Driving over to Ron's house the following morning, I felt a mixture of excitement and panic. I had no idea what I was getting myself into but I could sure use the money. I told myself that I would just do some of these magazine layouts, pay off some bills and that would be the end. On my drive into the San Fernando Valley, I talked myself into believing that nobody even looked at these girlie magazines. I was under the impression that they were only viewed by lonely, single older men in trenchcoats. I would just be another naked body for them to look at. The men probably wouldn't even notice my face. This would all be a dark secret and nobody I knew would ever find out about it. By the time I arrived, I had calmed myself down and was ready to get naked, shoot off a few photos and go home to my apartment in Hollywood. I walked through the front door and entered what appeared to be a living room.

This living room was not like any living room that I had ever seen before. The brown and white tweed couch had been shoved against one corner and in its place were some odd pieces of workout equipment. In the middle of the room sat a rusted workout bench, three dumbbells, two of which were fifty-pound weights and the third, was a three-pound weight, a tennis racquet, and a bright pink water bottle. Floodlights that lit up the room surrounded this ridiculous little set that was supposed to emulate a workout facility. I felt myself starting to sweat but it wasn't from the lights giving off heat, it was because I realized that I was going to be in the middle of this set. Naked. I stood there telling myself that I should just run and never look back. The other part of me kept my feet firmly planted on that worn out wooden floor thinking about the money I was going to make. Just then a small gray haired man walked into the living room from the back of the house.

"Hi my name is Ron." He began wiping the lens on a big black camera that was slung around his neck. I just stood there looking at this odd little man dressed in orange polyester dolphin shorts, a matching tank top and dirty worn out tennis shoes. He stopped wiping his lens and looked at me.

"This is your set today and I would like to take a Polaroid of you right now to see how my lighting is against your skin." I sat down on the orange vinyl workout bench, looked over at him and smiled while he took the first Polaroid of the day. It wasn't like the Polaroid camera that my dad used at family get-togethers and special occasions, which spit out the photo immediately. It was a large black professional one, and Ron pulled the photo out from the side.

37

"Can I see how I look?"

"Oh no. This needs five minutes to dry before I can peel the paper off."

"I've never seen one like that."

"While this is drying, let's get you into wardrobe." I had visions of a whole wardrobe department set up in the back somewhere and followed Ron through the door he emerged from. Instead of a wardrobe department, I walked into Ron's dark hovel of a bedroom. On his bed, which was just a mattress on the ground, lay several leotards, leg warmers and belts in various colors and styles.

He turned on a small lamp. "Why don't you try these on."

I began taking my clothes off wondering when my life had made such a drastic turn. I wasn't worried that this man was going to try anything strange on me, yet everything suddenly felt so surreal and time was moving at slow speed.

"What size shoe do you wear?" Ron asked.

With my back to him, I began changing. "Size 8 1/2." I turned around after I got the first leotard on and saw his rear high in the air as he rummaged through his closet. He turned around after a minute and handed me a pair of white worn out high heels.

Ron had to be joking. "Heels and a leotard?" I asked.

"That's nice but try the other one on." Ron said as he dove back into his closet. He pulled out some earrings and clipped them on my ear lobes as I pulled the straps of the next get up over my shoulders. He took a step back to get a good look at my attire. He made a gesture with his hands moving them up and down by his chest in a short but fast motion. I wasn't sure what this meant so I just stared at him knowing that he would eventually fill me in on this hand lingo.

"Uh, do you want to arrange your chest in there?" Ron said. I walked over to the mirror and took a good look at myself. There I stood in an orange and red leotard with my boobs completely lopsided under the fabric. My right boob was high and in place but my left boob fell several inches lower. This was the result when I didn't wear a bra to keep them in place. I reached my hand under the fabric to even them out. I turned to face Ron again and he thrust a pair of light pink leg warmers at me. The unmatched outfit was now complete. Ron stood back to look at me and quickly wrapped a plastic see through belt around my waist to complete this ridiculous look.

In a quiet voice, Ron said, "Oh, that's lovely."

"Lets go take another Polaroid for your skin tone on the set." I followed him back into the living room with my heels clicking on the hardwood floor. I stood on the set and he took another Polaroid.

Ron peeled the paper off the first Polaroid. "This will be nice." He adjusted one of the lights.

"Can I see?"

"No." He guarded the photo with his life. "I would prefer that you wait until I have it perfect." He took one final peek at the photo and then adjusted another light.

Next stop was the small bathroom, which was now the makeup room. Ron introduced me to Jeri. Jeri was the backup makeup artist he used when his daughter Wanda was not available.

"Wanda is the best but it's hard to book her. Everybody wants her on their sets and movies pay more" Ron rambled on. I wasn't sure what movie she was working on, but I thought how much fun that must be to be on a Hollywood movie set.

Little did I know at the time that he meant a porno movie.

Jeri was a tired looking blonde in her mid thirties with dark circles under her eyes. I could tell that in her teens and twenties she had probably been very cute. I felt sorry for her that Ron was telling me in front of her how much better his daughter was, but when I looked over at her, she just gave me a tired smile and started arranging her makeup on the chipped tiled bathroom counter. Before leaving the bathroom, Ron said that he didn't want me sitting for an hour in hair and makeup in the leotard because it would leave marks on my body when I got naked. I got a dizzy head rush at the word naked. He handed me a worn out, terry cloth bathrobe. "Put this on."

I slipped out of the leotard and leg warmers and Ron draped them on a plastic hanger behind the bathroom door. Everything was so worn out in this house, that I found it amusing that such pride and joy was put into this outfit.

After setting my hair in hot rollers, Jeri began working her magic on my face. The foundation makeup stick was that of a professional, not the Cover Girl style I bought from a drugstore. Its consistency was thick, unlike the watery type that came out of my bottle at home. She took a white sponge in the shape of a triangle and spread the theatrical-style foundation evenly over my face, neck and behind my ears. I closed my eyes as she carefully got the corners of my eyes and lids. Next came the powder, which was pressed into my skin. Jeri paused to find an eye shadow color that would match my leotard, and I looked at my face in the mirror. I looked like a stranger. My skin was now flawless with an inch of makeup, yet my eyes were like small pinholes and my lips were non-existent.

Ron yelled from the set, "I need another Polaroid!" Jeri held up some colors of eye shadow before sending me out to her boss for the day.

"Why don't you sit on that workout bench and pull your robe down so I can see your skin tone for the Polaroid." He adjusted his lights a few inches higher. I sat on the bench and noticed a new light had been placed on the set. It was a smaller light fixture beaming out a ray of light that hit my hips as I sat down. Snap. Back into makeup. I sat back into the director's chair ready for my eyes to come alive. It was exciting getting my makeup done by a professional. I suddenly felt more glamorous that I had felt in a long time. I closed my eyes and felt the odd sensations that were taking place on my face. Wetness above my eyelids: Eyeliner. A soft brush wiping my eyelids: Eye shadow. My eyelashes being pulled up: Mascara. A large feathery brush against my cheekbones: Blush. A firm stroke around my lips: Lip-liner. She finished with a swipe of red lipstick. Jeri then bent my head down and started taking out the curlers running her fingers through each piece as it was unrolled. She fluffed my head of hair; told me to cover my face, then sprayed what seemed like a half can of super hold Aqua Net hairspray. Voila, she was done with her masterpiece of the day.

I opened my eyes for the first time in forty-five minutes and stared in the small warped mirror above the sink. I saw a face that I no longer recognized. I looked like a peacock. My eyes were covered in orange, pink and green sparkled shadow with big red glossy lips. My anticipated new hairdo looked more like the cartoon character from "Annie". I felt a lump forming in the back of my throat but I didn't dare let a tear fall for this mess of colors would be everywhere. Jeri sensed my disappointment and assured me that I needed all of this makeup and coloring for the cameras.

"The bright lights will flush out your makeup and when the photos are done, the makeup will look beautiful and natural."

Natural? This mess? I found that hard to believe.

"Now let's get you back in wardrobe and on the set." I slipped into the leotard and leg warmers and headed onto the set for the first day of what would change my life forever.

For the first few seconds, all I could hear was the humming from the lights surrounding me on the set. They seemed to be much louder than any other lights I had heard before and then I realized that I had never been in a house with lighting five times the normal wattage. Ron broke the silence in the house and asked me for one more Polaroid sitting on the workout bench. Snap. He adjusted several more of the lights then peeled the black paper from the Polaroid.

"Ooh that's nice." he whispered to himself. He showed me the final Polaroid before we began shooting. The clown makeup was a bit better than in person, but I sure didn't look like Paulina, the hot model that I fancied myself looking like after all that time in hair and makeup. Ron positioned me on the bench and told me to look natural while he shot off a few frames to get me comfortable in front of the camera. I smiled at the camera while Ron clicked away. The smile got wider and I began to move my body slightly with every snap of his camera. Suddenly Ron put the camera down and told me not to smile.

"Look sexy".

I just stared at him. I didn't know what he meant. I felt a panic spread over me and my underarms began to sweat. Oh shit, this polyester leotard would show the sweat under my arms and then the orange material would have big wet marks. I stayed silent and the buzz from the lights seemed to get even louder.

Ron squatted in front of me to explain the basics of a sexy face. When he squatted in front of me, my eyes fell to his crotch to see if he was wearing undies under his shorts. Yes. Then I looked to see if he was getting a hard on. No. I knew that this was just another job for him, but I was still more comfortable in that house with Jeri in the other room. Ron contorted his mouth in the shape of the vowels and whispered them out of his over exaggerated lips.

"AAAAAHHHHH, EEEEEEE, IIIIIII, OOOOOOO, UUUUUUU." His lips moved slightly with each new vowel.

"Watch me again and then try them out." He repeated the sequence, then watched me mimic him. After several takes, Ron slung the camera over his neck again. I ran through the vowels with each snap of his camera.

Ron whispered, "Stomach."

I didn't know what he meant, so I kept on reciting the sequence of vowels. I pouted my lips and squinted my eyes even more. Again Ron moved the camera from his eye and told me to suck in my stomach. "If I say stomach, that means you need to suck in your belly."

There I was on my hands and knees on this bench, reciting the vowels, squinting my eyes, pouting my lips and sucking in my stomach. Fuck, trying to be sexy was painful.

"Show all of your fingers on the bench, especially the thumbs." Moving and spreading my hands and fingers, nearly made me fall off the bench, but I finally made it. There, my chipped red nails were all on display. Ron kept shooting, and I moved slightly with each snap of his camera. Ron stopped shooting and stood up straight.

Oh no, what was I doing wrong now? I looked down and counted ten fingers. They were all showing.

"Jeri!" Ron yelled.

Maybe it was my tummy. I sucked in air and got light headed. If I sucked in anymore, I would faint from lack of oxygen.

"Where's the belt? You forgot her fucking belt God Damn it."

Jeri came running from the bathroom with panic in her tired eyes and put the plastic belt around my waist.

"Now that first roll is all a waste," Ron screamed. His face was bright red.

"I'm so sorry Ron, I just forgot." Jeri scampered back into the bathroom.

Ron walked over to me and adjusted it about a quarter of an inch. "There that's much better," he whispered. "Let's do it again and don't forget to show all of your fingers and suck in your tummy."

The mild mannered Ron was back, but I had seen his other side. I began getting into the groove of this. The belt was the first piece to come off. Ron had me hold it in the air above my head, place it between my legs while throwing my head back, closing my eyes and say "OOOOO" with my mouth, then bite it between my teeth, which made me snarl into the camera. Once we were through with the belt, Ron strategically placed it on the set so it was out of my way but still in the shot. Then came the leotard. I slowly stripped for the camera. The right shoulder strap came down exposing my right tit for the next few shots. Ron had me look down and fondle my tit as if this tit was a newfound discovery on my body. Then out came the left. I had to squeeze them together, rub my nipples and dangle them for the camera before taking the whole thing off. Ron stopped shooting and draped the leotard over one leg of the bench.

The camera now back to his eye, he whispered, "Don't forget to suck in your stomach." Next, in the buff wearing leg warmers, heels and the plastic flower earrings, Ron had me sit on the bench and do arm curls with the three pound weight while reciting my vowels. As I spread my legs, Ron switched on the smaller light. I now knew the reason for that lower light. My pussy was as bright as a Christmas tree.

From behind the lens, Ron whispered, "Show me the pink." Once again, I had no idea what this funny little man was asking for and froze in mid air with the weight. Ron put down his camera and stood in front of me.

Ron pointed down between my legs so I didn't confuse it with the lips on my face. "Showing me the pink means to spread your lips for the camera." He then demonstrated some poses for me with his own body. Ron thrust his hips out, ran his fingers through his hair with one hand and simulated spreading his crotch open with the other hand while making a contorted sexy look on his face.

The next few rolls he shot had me in all sorts of foreign poses to my body. Poses I would never find appealing in my personal life, as I was sure not many people would. But then again, this was porno and is definitely not real life.

Three hours later, Ron's camera rewound itself again. "Well, I think that should cover it."

I was still bent over the bench. "Okay, what should I do now?"

"Well, it's a wrap actually."

I turned around and felt the blood rush to my head. "What do I do now?" Maybe he didn't hear me when I was bent over with my rear high in the air.

"You just sign a model release and then I pay you." Ron was putting the used rolls of film in a bag.

"You mean it's over?"

"Yes, that's right. That's what a wrap means."

"The whole shoot is over?" I couldn't believe that I was going to get paid $600.00 for four hours of work.

"Once you get used to posing, it shouldn't take us so long." Ron stopped filling out gum labels and asked. "What other photographers has Jim booked you with?"

"Some guy named Victor. How long does a shoot usually take?" This was so easy.

"Jim knows our deal. I get all of the new girls first." Ron's face was reddening. "A single girl normally takes two hours."

That's $300.00 an hour. "Jim mentioned that you get me all week." What did Ron mean a single girl layout? "I think I'm working with Victor next week." What other types of layouts were there?

Ron's face became pale again. "Good, he should give me the first few layouts." Ron ran his fingers through his mass of gray curls. "It's a gentleman's agreement."

"Oh." What was he talking about?

"Sign my release forms and then I'll pay you." He handed me a pen. "It's a standard release."

"Great, where do I sign?"

I signed three forms and Ron signed my check. "Are you hungry?"

Now that he mentioned it. "Yes, I'm starving."

"I ordered some deli sandwiches this morning." He opened his refrigerator door. "Do you want a turkey or a tuna sandwich?"

"Whichever one you don't want." I didn't want to intrude on his lunch but I was starving.

"How about if we split them both?"

He was so nice to me. "Sounds great Ron."

During lunch, Ron asked me about my life. Where I grew up, did I have any brothers or sisters and what I did for a living before today. One hour and one foot-long sandwich later, I was ready to leave.

"Thanks Ron." I hugged him goodbye.

"Oh no, thank you." His hug back felt good. "I'm sure I'll be seeing you soon."

When? How soon? "I hope so."

Ron never asked me about my parents. He must have known the answer to why an eighteen-year-old girl poses naked. Their parents weren't in their life.

On the way home, I would look at my big fat check every time I stopped for a red light.

"Not bad Christy. Not bad for a few hours of work." I turned up the radio and sang along with Phil Collins all the way home.

7

I felt electricity surge through my body when I pulled up to my bank the next morning to deposit my cherished $600.00 check. It was ten o'clock, which meant I would be late opening the store this morning as the assistant manager. Screw them, it would take me three weeks to make what I made in one day of figure modeling. I would be there by ten fifteen.

I sauntered into the bank like I owned the joint, filled out my yellow deposit slip and stood in line. Ten ten: - The round white clock with black numbers read on the wall above teller #6. Ten fourteen: - And I was headed to teller #2, my least favorite of the bunch. She was a short, fat Middle Easterner with dry frizzy hair, scarred acne cheeks and a bad-ass attitude towards me. She acted like the money was coming out of her pocket every time I bounced a check. Such pleasure shone through her unhealthy eyes when she told me I was overdrawn.

"A check bounced in your account for $32.49 this morning." Scarface joyfully informed me. Without any reply or eye contact I slid my deposit over the oak counter.

"I'd like to make a $600.00 deposit into my checking account."

Ten nineteen, Shit, Arman would be furious his shop wasn't open yet. Hughes, the unlucky recipient of my bad check would just have to redeposit. I had bounced checks at this market before and they had just put them through again. Being in the heart of Hollywood, I'm sure this was a common occurrence.

Teller #2 took my deposit, shifted on the stool, which would never accommodate her rear, and began punching her keyboard as if she was beginning a novel. She shifted her eyes from the screen to Ron's check.

"What kind of check is this?" she asked with accusatory eyes. It was ten twenty-four.

"What do you mean what kind of check? I'm late for work, can you just give me my receipt?" I asked with panic taking over my once cocky attitude. It wasn't just the panic over being late for work, I was already in deep trouble there, but what was wrong with my $600.00 check? Was it counterfeit? Were there no funds in his account? Did fatso know he was a nude photographer? I began to feel lightheaded at the thought of losing my newfound financial freedom when her nasal voice in broken English interrupted my thoughts.

"Is this a personal check or a business check?"

I just stared at her.

"A personal check takes seven days to clear and a business check clears the next day." Her clown orange lipstick lips explained to me as if I was a kindergartner.

My head cleared up and the cocky attitude returned. "Of course it's a business check."

"P.O.M. Agency Photography" she read to nobody. Her right eye squinted; showing poorly applied eyeliner, while her left eye looked me up and down. Her fat paw with no visible wrist finally wrote down my account number, amount of deposit and now current balance. She dipped her right thumb in a round plastic, white container to help her rip the top receipt only off and slide it over to me. My balance was now $307.66, in the black for a nice change: - Ten thirty.

"What do you do for this photographer?" she asked, as I was cramming the receipt into my tan LeSports Sack purse.

I slowly lifted my head and locked eyes with this nosey bitch. Full of self-assurance, I replied, "I'm a photographers assistant."

The lie came out so easy. The lie. The first of many lies in the following two decades of my chosen but not bragged about career. The lie would change my job description from time to time depending on whom I was lying to and what company I was in, but it was always a lie. The lie would be my secret, or so I thought.

8

I could hear the phone ringing as I unlocked the heavy glass front doors. I punched in the alarm code, turned the closed sign around to read open, and answered, "Designer Duds"

"Where have you been? Do you know what time it is? Is this the respect I get for making you the assistant manager?" Arman, the owner screamed into the phone running all three questions into one.

"I'm so sorry Arman, there was a huge accident on Highland Ave., then I realized I was out of tampons so I had to stop and get a box." Smooth I thought, how could a man argue with a girl about such a personal thing. Much too embarrassing, plus, I was on such a roll today.

"Bullshit!" Arman screamed. "You know damn well Mandy keeps a large box of, of those things in the bathroom." Arman threatened to demote me from assistant manager at $5.50 an hour, back to a salesgirl at $5.25. A whopping twenty-five cents an hour difference. I apologized up and down before lying to him that a customer had just walked in.

"Alright, go sell something at least. You're behind in sales today, but let there be no mistake, we will finish this conversation later." I was sure his face was as red as a ripe tomato when he slammed the phone down.

It was nearly eleven and it was already a hot, muggy September day. I turned the lights, cash register, stereo and air conditioner on. There were no customers and I knew there wouldn't be any until the office workers started taking their lunch breaks at eleven thirty. I walked to the front door, which was open, and lit a cigarette.

Why was Arman always yelling at me for one thing or another? He was such a hot-tempered Armenian. I knew he was fucking the chubby blonde manager. I would catch him pinching her plump ass, see them giving each other goo-goo eyes and hear them whispering sexual anecdotes. They were both married but what did I care. Mandy was the nicest person to me in my life. I finished my cigarette and flicked the butt into the street.

I walked back in and started looking through the rack of new arrivals that came in yesterday. Arman got us to buy his clothing, at a measly ten percent discount, saying that if we wore the clothes, they would sell better. I didn't mind the new clothes but even at the discounted prices this was hard to fit into my tight budget. Not being on commission, his strategy didn't benefit me one dime.

The phone rang, God, I hope it's not Arman again. "Designer Duds" I could feel the heat rise in the store. The thermostat read seventy-five degrees but the sweat beading up between my breasts told me differently.

It was more like in the mid eighties.

"Hi, can you talk?" My heart sped up at the sound of his southern drawl.

"Yes, I'm all alone here today." The man on the other end of this phone was my ticket to freedom. "Did Ron like me?" Jim was my knight in shining armor who could provide me with a way to make money. Real money.

"Uncle Jimmy has some good news for you. Ron loves you and a magazine called Velvet already bought your layout." Jim purred these magic words into my ear.

"Velvet?" I never heard of that magazine, but it sure sounded glamorous.

"Ron would like to shoot you again. Do you have your date book handy?"

"Yes, let me get it." The second line rang and I ignored it. Jim was my priority, not some woman asking if we had that dress in the window in an extra large. I reached under the counter, below the cash register where we kept our purses and took out my red plastic organizer. I opened the white pages to September.

"Do you need to get the other line?"

I could see the red light flashing with each ring. "No, they'll call back." What if it was Arman? Oh well, on to more important things. "When does Ron want me back?" I looked at the thermostat. It still read seventy-five degrees, but it was getting hotter in the store by the minute. I slid the plastic lever to the left and set it to seventy.

"Ron booked you for this Friday and Saturday, two layouts on both days, that's $2400.00."

The second line stopped ringing and I think my heart stopped beating. I couldn't believe how much money that was.

"Don't forget you promised Victor, the photographer you met here, Tuesday and Wednesday of next week." I could hear some papers shuffle on Jim's end.

I could barley breathe at the thought of all that money.

"One layout a day, comes to $1200.00 for two days of work."

A customer walked in the store and I smiled.

"Are you with me Christy?" He asked.

"Yes, I'm here." I wanted to yell and scream, jump up and down. I found my pot of gold. I found Jim at the end of a rainbow. "Thank you," I whispered.

"What honey?" Jim asked.

"Nothing, a customer was just leaving."

"I've also booked you on a test shoot with Stephen Hicks for Penthouse. They pay between $5,000.00 for a feature layout and $10,000

48

for a centerfold."

Penthouse? Wow, I couldn't believe what I was hearing. The customer tried to get my attention, but I turned my back on her.

"Doug Hume wants to shoot you for Hustler one week from next Monday. If you're accepted, they pay $2500.00 for a pictorial and $5,000.00 for centerfold. Are you writing down all of your dates darlin'?" Not only was I writing them down in my book, but I was also adding it up on the calculator to the right of the cash register.

If all went well, I could stand to make between $10,000.00-$15,000.00 in a week of modeling. Figure modeling that is.

"Yes, I wrote it all down Jim. I can't believe it. Thank you so much."

"They really love you, and this is just the beginning. You're going to be a huge star as long as you stick with me." Jim paused. "Now what about your other jobs? I really do need you full time."

"I gave my one week notice today." I lied. "I'll work out my schedule with the other girls so I have those days off. The owner here is really cool about everything." I lied again. Arman would blow a gasket if I tried to change my days.

"Don't worry Jim, I'll be there. Did any other photographers like my Polaroids?" I held my breath waiting for his answer.

"Like them? They loved them. They all think you're gorgeous. I don't think you understand how special a lady you are. You have a naturally large chest, a thin body and a beautiful, innocent face."

The customer began fanning herself with a folder, "It's too hot in here to shop."

I shrugged my shoulders. It's too hot in here to work for the next few hours also.

"Uncle Jimmy will be giving you more work than you can handle. Stop by my office tomorrow."

I looked at the work schedule for tomorrow.

"I need you to fill out some stat sheets and meet some photographers that will be here at 11a.m."

I was supposed to open the shop at ten.

"Then if you want, we can all go to lunch at the deli across the street."

"That sounds great. I'll be there by eleven."

"If a man by the name of Reb tries to contact you, tell him you're exclusive with me. Stay away from him. Do you understand me honey?"

Yes, I understood. I heard his words loud and clear. They loved me and thought I was beautiful. Somebody wants me.

It never occurred to me on that day, that my face was the last of my three attributes to be mentioned

Hiss! Clunk! Wheeze! Two hours into my uneventful day and I knew that the air conditioner was broken again. Arman's "cousin" Ali was a repairman, but no repairs made by him lasted longer than a week. What was worse, ninety-five degree heat for the next five hours, or having to call Arman back?

"Hi Arman, it's me." I dreaded this call. "I don't think Ali fixed the air right last week, because it's making those weird noises again and nothing's coming out of the vent." I dreaded his response.

Arman screamed, "GODDAMN IT! I'm not made out of money." Like it was my fault it kept breaking.

I dreaded everything about Arman and his shop.

I looked at my date book with all of my modeling jobs. "It's getting real hot in here Arman, like a sauna." I was now egging this hair triggered cheap prick on. "Customers are walking out. This one lady had a armful of clothes to try on, but then she said it was too hot so she just left them." There was no such lady but I knew he'd be livid at the thought of losing a big sale and maybe yell at Ali instead of me for a change.

"Should I call a real repairman from the yellow pages?" I couldn't believe how much money I was going to make from Jim.

"Ali is a real repairman. Shit, this is the last thing I need today. What do you have the thermostat set at?"

Tomorrow I would meet more photographers, which meant more bookings, which meant more money. "I pushed it down to seventy degrees and,"

"To where? Seventy? That's the problem. You froze out the fuckin' unit. I told you to always keep it at seventy-three NOT seventy. This is going to cost me a fortune now. I may have to take some of your pay to help cover the damages you caused. I'll get back to you. Just sell, and if there are no customers, then clean the bathroom, scrub the toilets or something useful. I can't believe you broke the unit." Slam. I was no repairman, but I knew I wasn't the blame for his broken down, second hand, used piece of shit unit. I had had it with the abuse from this little man. I wasn't getting stuck for the bill on this. I quickly added the hours due me on the calculator at $5.50 each hour, and came up with a grand total of $275.00. I then went shopping in the store and picked out that amount of clothing. The grand total, with my employee discount, came to $267.00. I looked around the store to see what was eight dollars. I grabbed a royal blue beaded necklace in the glass display case to reach my total. I didn't want to rip Arman off, but I knew I'd never see a final paycheck. This made it a clean even break. Arman knew I was always struggling for money to pay my bills, so he felt that he could push me around. He never figured Uncle Jimmy was in the picture now and I didn't need his verbal abuse anymore. On a white sheet of paper from the Xerox machine, I composed my letter of resignation.

Dear Arman,
I know you and Mandy are having an affair and it really bothers me because I like your wife so much. Please do not ever call me again. Don't worry about my final paycheck because I exchanged it for clothes in the same amount. I left the tags in a white envelope in the drawer to the left of the cash register. I quit.

I wasn't even sure what his wife's name was. I just met her once at a Christmas party last year. I didn't care who was screwing whom. I just didn't want him calling me ever again. I was through with him.

I set the alarm code, four hours before closing time, locked the front doors and slid the keys through the mail slot. I pulled out of the parking lot of Designer Duds for the last time. Next stop, home for a quick nap and then my hostess job. At ten after seven, I pulled into the parking lot.

Fred, the manager, made a big to-do out of checking his watch when I walked through the front door. His right arm jetted out, then bent at the elbow, inches below his face. He lifted his glasses up one inch and looked at the time on his fake Rolex watch. He shook his right wrist, and let his arm fall to his side.

"You're eight minutes late."

"I know, I'm so sorry." Yeah, sorry I thought for coming in tonight and having to look at your pathetic face for the next five hours.

"There was a traffic jam at Crescent Heights..." But it was too late for my excuses; Fred had already walked away. In truth, I went home and fell asleep until twenty minutes before work started.

Two hours into my shift Fred asked, "How many iced-teas has that been for you tonight?"

"This is my third one, it's so hot out tonight Fred."

Fred looked at his watch. "Well, you've officially hit your limit of freebees tonight. Any drink from here on out, you'll have to pay for."

"But I have three more hours to go."

He stopped sorting through the paid dinner checks and loosened his tie. "Well then," He gave me a tight-lipped smile, "It looks like you'll be drinking water for the rest of the evening." He unbuttoned the top two buttons on his white shirt and dismissed me with a wave of his manicured mitt.

I plastered on a fake smile and seated the next party that came in. Keep your cool, I thought. Tonight is payday. When your shift comes up next week, the check will have cleared and Fred can shove the hibiscus tea up his ass.

I left at midnight sharp, with paycheck in hand. I got in my car and realized that I quit two jobs in one day. Officially and yet so unofficially.

51

Fuck the two-week grace period. Fuck Fred and Arman.

9

By early November, I had been shooting for over two months. I had posed for every men's magazine: Penthouse, Hustler, High Society and every other newspaper stand, drugstore and monthly subscription available. My life felt so free and wonderful. Through figure modeling, I found my strength, self-confidence, and independence again. My bills were paid; I had a car that started up every morning and several thousand dollars in my bank account. I felt safe and secure for the first time in over a year. Nobody could hurt me, tell me what to do, or take anything away from me. Everything I owned was bought and paid for by me.

I was shooting with a new photographer today. I had never heard of him and couldn't recall any of my girlfriends mentioning his name before. My pay today was $1200.00. That amount added up to two magazine layouts, which would be a long but fun day. I knew what the photographers needed now; a sultry look of pouted lips with bedroom eyes while elongating my body. I could glide from one pose into the next, always knowing where and what the camera needed from me. Spread my legs, squeeze my tits together and arch my back. I knew when to close my eyes, oooh and aaah with my lips for visual effect and entice the viewer with my brown come-fuck-me eyes. I would wet my lips, and partially show my tongue. In just a few short months after turning eighteen, my life had taken such a turn for the better with a new set of non-judgmental friends. I now had pieced together a non-blood family, with no Marv around telling me how worthless I was, slowly chipping away at my once soaring self-esteem. This new found "family" accepted me, praised me, and boosted my deflated ego by telling me how beautiful I was. They welcomed me with open arms, no questions asked. Clair, my anchor in life, was the only link to my real family.

I jumped in the shower, realizing I had an hour before I had to be on the new set. The drill was the same. Get to the location, eat some breakfast, sit in hair and makeup for an hour, shoot off a couple of rolls of film, get paid and leave. So simple it was always the same, just a slight variation from the day before. A change of sequence in poses, a change of scenery and intermingling bras, panties, garter belts, and heels with wardrobes to match the day's set.

I'm lying naked on the brass bed, spread-eagled, touching my clit. I raise my legs in the air, cross my ankles, throw my head back, close my eyes and have sheer ecstasy expressed on my face. I roll over and expose my ass to the lens. I drape my tits over the footboard then raise a nipple to my mouth and lick it tenderly.

Cut to: - The auto mechanics garage, where I have grease strategically smeared all over my body. The mechanic is just inches away, with his hard cock and torn white T-shirt. He is holding a wrench up to my inner thigh, two inches away from my inviting pussy. My left foot is perched on a tire.

Next: - Outside at the pool where I spray suntan oil all over my girlfriend's body, then gently rub it in, paying special attention to her tits, ass and inner thighs. We kiss with the very tips of our tongues touching, then we jump in the water to frolic in the pool. The entire time we are aware of the camera clicking away, capturing every moment, move and position on a frame. The soft humming of the camera lets us know that we have come to the end of yet another roll of film, allowing us a four-minute break.

"Oooh Heather, you're getting a good tan out here." I say. I hear the snap of the camera's back closing, and a short, soft hum letting us know the films reloaded and it's time to pose again.

It was all simulated sex. This was soft-core porn, where no real touching and entering took place. Big deal.

My job was to turn on the connoisseurs of these smut magazines, and I knew I was the best.

The early morning call came in yesterday, Clair's voice sounded distant and on a time delay. She stayed in London for another semester of college.

"Mom and Dad found out, they know what you're doing." Clair's voice crackled through the long distance phone lines. Clair sounded sad, once again stuck in the middle of what was once such a happy family and now torn apart. Sad because her baby sister was reduced to posing naked in men's magazines. Sad because she was helpless thousands of miles away. Sad because she felt my pain last year. Sad because we were apart.

I knew by now that word must have spread like wildfire through the small section of the San Fernando Valley that I grew up in.

I wasn't sad for the first time in over a year. In fact, this was music to my ears. This was the ultimate "fuck you" to the parents who cast me aside. This was to me, the highest form of rebellion. Daddy's little girl buck naked for the world to jack off to. Mommy's baby all grown up, exposing every part of my body for money. Love me, tell me how pretty I am, look but don't touch. Accept me, idolize me, but don't get too close.

"I'm okay Clair. I just miss you so much."

I told Clair what I was doing a month after I had started. I knew she wouldn't judge me. She never had and never would. She just worried about my safety.

I rinsed the conditioner out of my hair and grabbed for the orange towel hanging on the chipped, towel rod. A cockroach scampered across the yellow tile counter. Getting out of this dump was the next thing on my list of things to do once I got a free day from modeling. I needed to find a bug and rodent free apartment in a safe section of the valley.

Thump. I could hear the man in the apartment directly above me falling. His one-hundred pound body falling off of his chair after injecting himself with the poisons of heroine. Ben was the junkie in our building. Several times a week, I could hear the weight of his body hitting his floor, causing the lone hanging light bulb fixture above my coffee table to sway from side to side.

The nameless and faceless man, who I had never seen in my six months here, rattled the wall between our units with his Tourette's syndrome. He would scream obscenities at all hours of the day. Walking past his door I would hear him scream from inside his dark, one room apartment, "Fuck you, you shit mother-fucker. Assholes." Before moving to Hollywood, I had only heard of people with this disease, now I had one for my next-door neighbor.

The 6' 2" transvestite Colleen, with big tits and a cock lived across the hall and up two doors from me. She had blonde hair, silver round glasses that covered up her sad eyes, and long, lean legs I would have killed for. She would cook me dinner once a week and put on a fashion show, modeling the new lingerie she just bought for herself at Fredericks of Hollywood.

A wanna-be magician, Butch, lived across the hall from me. His tattoos were inked from the top of his shoulders to the end of his fingertips, displaying the fires of hell, naked females with knifes through their hearts and skulls with worms crawling through the eye sockets. Butch had a wild look in his eyes. His piercing stare went right through my skin and down to my bones. His crazed, erratic behavior made me check my rickety dead bolt several times a night before falling asleep. Nothing was beneath him.

These were my neighbors. A far cry from the comfort and security I had grown up with. This was life on the streets in the heart of Hollywood.

I got dressed, grabbed my wardrobe for the day and headed out for another day of posing.

The location was at a house in the Hollywood Hills. Jim's directions were precise. A sharp left a veer to the right, and go straight at the second three-way intersection. There it was, a large pink compound nestled in the hills directly below Mulholland Drive. I rang the intercom, identified myself, and the pink gates swung open inviting me in.

As I entered the circular courtyard, the first thing I noticed, were two very large trucks. Their rear doors were wide open, and two young men were hauling cameras out. Not the still photography type that I knew so well by now, but very large, movie set type of cameras. Cords, cables, lights and microphones followed. Something was wrong. Why were there movie cameras? With my car door still open, I followed the round stones that led me to the front doors.

A woman in her 40's was sitting at the kitchen table thumbing through a magazine. Her eyes were scanning an ad, while her right index finger, painted cherry red, was already turning to the next page. A half a cup of coffee sat in front of her near an ashtray overflowing with smoked down to the filter cigarettes. Cigarette. I desperately needed a cigarette. My nerves were on full alert.

She turned a page and looked up at me for the first time.

"Hi, my name is Nora-Nora and this is my brother's house. Are you here for the movie today?"

"No. My name is Christy and I am here to do a magazine layout. Do you know where that's being shot today?"

But I already knew the answer to that. There was no photo shoot for me or anybody else today. The man, who I looked to as a father figure in my life, sold me out. My kind, sweet, soft-spoken Jim, who penetrated my wall and gained my trust, sent me out on this beautiful clear Fall morning to shoot a hard-core fuck film. It was just three days ago that I told him I was not ready to make films. It was that same three days ago that he already had me booked on this movie set.

My savior, my enemy, my God, the Devil himself.

"May I please use your telephone to call my agent?" I had no memory of the name she told me seconds before.

"Help yourself."

I punched in the memorized numbers, and lit a cigarette.

"Jim, this is Christy, there's been a mix-up." I paused to inhale. "You sent me to a movie shoot by accident."

The nice lady in the kitchen, Jim the agent, and I knew there was no mix-up. This was a set up.

"No darling, I told you it was a loop I was sending you out on. A loop isn't a porno film per se, it's just one sex scene. Honey, there isn't even dialogue. Do you think Jimmy would do anything to hurt you? Paul is the top director for Caballero's line of 'Swedish Erotica' loops. He'll be in charge today and he is good people."

I had no idea what he was yakking on about, or who this Paul Swedish was, I was trying to remember if he used the word loop or not before, not that I would have known what it meant anyway. I must have thought it was some new type of film or camera lens, certainly not thinking for a second it had anything to do with making a porno film.

"What ever it's called, I can't do it Jim."

"Oh, but you have to, they need you, and they're counting on you. If you back out now, they have grounds for a lawsuit. This is a verbal contract."

My eyes became blurry at the thought of a lawsuit. All of that precious money I had saved over the months would go straight to a lawyer.

"Honey, are you still with me? It will be a piece of cake for you. It's nothing that you haven't done in your personal life. It's one quick sex scene. In fact, now listen to me closely honey, here's what I'm going to do for you. Normally companies need two to three different positions for every sex scene shot, but right after we hang up, I am going to personally call Paul and tell him to keep you in just one position. Doggie, missionary, or spoon, just let me know what your favorite position is, and I'll let Paul know. It's your call. He'll agree to it, he owes me a favor. The only difference in having sex today, is there will be a cameraman in the room with you."

Yes I thought, and a man I've never seen before will be violating my body.

I sat down on the wooden chair at the kitchen table and began twisting my finger into the yellow phone cord. The woman lit another cigarette and passed it over to me. I smiled and mouthed "thanks".

"Alright Jim, I'll do it today, but no more after this. Loop, video, film, 8 Millimeter, nothing. I just want to stick to doing magazine layouts."

Then Jim dropped the second bomb on me that morning.

"Well, since you didn't object on today's shoot, I've already booked you on another movie set in two days. It's an all-star cast with Traci Lords and Ginger Lynn, and you have the lead role in both. Tomorrow you shoot the box covers with Ron, then you shoot the movies the following four days."

Why was he talking in plurals?

Sensing that he was now about to lose me, Jim quickly added in, "The pay is $1,500.00 each day, which adds up to $6,000.00. If you don't like it after these two videos, I promise on my mother's life that I will never book you on another shoot other than magazines again."

After the initial wave of horror and disbelief of what I had gotten myself mixed up in had sunk in, I found my defeated voice and meekly asked him why he was speaking in plurals.

"Well," Jim began slowly replying, "There are two movies being shot in tandem over the four day period. It's the same production company, crew, and location. It will be like one movie. The first one is called 'On Golden Blonde' and the second one is 'Night of Loving Dangerously'."

The silence that followed was deafening. The voice inside my head was screaming so loud. Why the fuck is this happening to me? Was I such a bad teenager and this was my punishment? Where was my knight in shining armor, the man who was supposed to protect me and save me from this hell?

And then I heard his voice; almost a whisper now.

"Please don't let me down."

Let him down. Run, run as fast as you can. Where can I run?

I saw their images inside my head. My father never made time for us. He was always putting his new family before Clair and me, forgetting milestones in my young life. Joel, the stepfather for six years of my pre-teen life who packed up and left one day, never to be seen or heard from again. Marv, the current prick of a stepfather who made me feel worthless. He didn't understand children. He was unemotional, unloving, unattainable, unreachable, concerned and consumed only with himself.

Jim was it. Jim was all I had. I wanted to call my mama, go home to where I had felt so safe not too long ago. I wanted my old bedroom back. My wooden waterbed filled with 85-degree water. I wanted to stare at the white wallpaper with big green ferns on it that was on the wall behind my waterbed. My childhood stuffed animals lining the top shelf. My collection of Nancy Drew books on the bottom shelf. The seashells found on various family holidays in the Virgin Islands. The photo of Toy and me from our 11th grade prom.

* * * *

1982

I sat on the wooden, bench window seat in my room, painting my toe nails with one of mom's new colors by Clinique she had just bought at Bullocks. Cotton balls were stuffed between my toes. I looked out my window to watch the gardeners mowing the lawn. The smell of fresh cut grass would fill my senses as I wondered what outfit I would wear tonight. Tonight I had a date with Nader. I knew Nader had a huge crush on me. I only liked him as a friend, but I wanted to go out with him and drive around in his midnight blue Pantara.

Nader was two years older than I was, and we went to the same school. I had just entered 10th grade; he was a senior in 12th. I think he was Iranian and his family was wealthy beyond belief. He and his family lived in a gigantic octagon shaped house perched on the top of a hill in Mount Olympus with a 360-degree view of Los Angeles and the San Fernando Valley.

Tonight he was taking me to a party thrown by a classmate whose parents were out of town.

I decided on my turquoise Norma Kamali mini skirt, a tight white T-shirt and white boots. I applied some Dippity-Doo gel on my hair, teased and sprayed it, applied some cherry lip-gloss and mascara and waited for my date.

Nader picked me up at eight with lust in his dark brown eyes. He still

58

couldn't believe I had actually said yes when he asked me out on a date for the eighth weekend in a row. He was so use to me saying no that he almost walked away from me when I accepted. Stopping in his tracks, he turned around and smiled, "really?" he asked. "Uh-huh" I answered smiling back. He had no idea that I was mad at Toy, and this was just my way of getting back at him.

"You look so beautiful tonight," he opened the passenger door for me and I sank into the low leather seat.

I thought to myself, I know, but responded "Thank you."

We backed out of my driveway and headed through the hills towards Mulholland Drive.

"Your car is so cool, does it go very fast?" I asked, knowing that it could.

"Yeah, wanna see?" with that Nader made a right hand turn onto Mulholland Drive and shifted into third gear. Duran Duran began belting out "Rio" and Nader shifted into fourth. By the first verse of the song, Nader was firmly in 5th, his mind entering a different zone while whipping around the winding canyon lane, and the speedometer hit 100 MPH.

Time seemed to stop for me at this speed through the hills. The low body of the car hugged every twist and turn the road had in store for us. The large racing tires were inches away from a sheer drop to the bottom of the ravine.

The fear in my head wanted to tell Nader to slow down, but the sexual charge electrifying my body wouldn't allow it.

I felt the car lurch as Nader shifted into fourth gear, then safely into third. The speedometer's needle dipped back to 40 MPH. Nader turned to me and smiled, his brown curly hair framing his face. "Was that fast enough for you?" he asked, with hope in his eyes that he pleased me.

I nodded my head yes and told him to pull over.

His car slithered to the side of the road and sat idling in neutral. He stared at me, unsure of what I wanted.

My body stretched across the console, raising my mini skirt, which exposed my white panties, as I kissed his full lips. My tongue found his, as his right hand touched my inner left thigh. My right hand held the back of his head and my tongue explored every inch of his mouth.

The sound of Joe Jackson's voice singing "Is She Really Going Out With Him" filled the interior of the car, while Nader's hands touched my breasts over my T-shirt.

I pulled back after the song ended, and told Nader I wanted to go to the party now.

We pulled away from the turn out, tires screeching, leaving a cloud of dust behind us.

We kissed the entire night at the party. Nothing more. I knew I wouldn't want him after tonight. I was in charge; I called the shots, like I always did.

* * * *

"Excuse me Miss, camera coming through."

I turned around, unsure of where I was for a moment. I was in the present, with my right hand still holding the phone, which had been hung up for some time. I had replaced it in the cradle after telling Jim that I would make the movies. I wouldn't let him down.

No more Nader, no more Pantera, no more high school parties. No more was I in control of my life; no more was I in charge. I wasn't calling the shots.

In less than two hours, some stranger would be entering my body. Some nameless, faceless man's cock would be penetrating deep into the core of my soul.

I sat down at the table opposite Nora-Nora as she lit up another Virginia Slim. "Are you alright honey?" she asked with genuine concern.

No, I wasn't all right. I was so totally fucked up right now. Had I sunk so low in my self-esteem, courage and youth that I was about to make a fuck film?

Yes, I had and yes, I was going to.

My life had taken a 180-degree turn since I woke up this morning.

I needed to find a bathroom and pull myself together. After all, it was like Jim said, it was only sex, how bad could that be? I was a brave and adventurous sort of a girl. What the hell, I was always up for something new, and after all, I did enjoy sex. Hey, this may not be so bad after all. I'm sure the guy will be cute, and he'll most likely end up with a crush on me as well. This won't be so bad! Don't forget that $1200.00 pay day either. Hell, I had been doing it for free; Jim's voice rang in my head, reminding me. You can do it, I told myself.

It didn't matter how many times I repeated this in my head. I was scared shitless. My hands were shaking and my stomach was doing flip-flops.

I ventured from the safety of the kitchen with knocking knees through a laundry room, and found myself in a large living room. Silence.

To the left, was a long, dark hall with several closed doors lining each side.

To the right, I could hear a TV blaring a ballgame of some sort, voices cheering and laughing it up with the sounds of crewmembers setting up their equipment. What were they so fucking happy about while I felt so miserable.

"Hey Joe, would you hand me that light? We need to light her pussy

60

up in this scene. I wonder if this one's a screamer like Traci Lords. She nearly blew out Mike's eardrums over the audio machine."

Oh God, they were setting up for the loop.

The action was all to the right, so I made a quick exit to the left. Creeping down the hallway, I wondered who owned this house. Photographs hung on the walls. One was a man and his son fishing, the son holding up a trout for the camera, with a toothless smile. A photo of his daughter at her 12th grade graduation, the red tassel on her cap partially covering her blonde hair as she was hugging her proud papa. The son, now a man, was at the altar with his new bride at his side, staring deep into each-others eyes. Fast-forward several years, the still handsome, now balding father on the greens at a golfing event with his buddies. There was another picture of the father again, this time on vacation, with a young blonde at his side. She could easily be mistaken for another daughter if it wasn't for his hand wrapped around her ass. Both were raising a tropical blue drink to the camera with white smiles, and deep dark tans.

This final photograph brought me to the end of my secluded hall. Snap back to the present I thought. Splash some cold water on my face, empty that full bladder and get into hair and makeup. Stop being such a baby. You chose this line of work; there's no turning back now. What are your alternatives here? None, zip, nada. Going home was not an option. I was not welcome there. You must take care of yourself, nobody else will. Just get through the next week, then it's back to the safety and comfort of magazines again, without disappointing Jim.

I opened the heavy wooden door, to what I hoped was a bathroom and gasped at the sight before me. A large platinum blonde was bent over the toilet bowl. She was stark naked with the exception of wearing red, 5" fuck-me-pumps which suited the occasion perfectly. She was being fucked, her head just inches from the open toilet lid. A man in his mid-forties behind her plump ass was doing the deed. He was dressed in a black silk shirt, with only the three bottom buttons opened. His tan gabardine pants were on, but pooled at his feet. His feet, covered in brown penny loafers, were planted firmly on the ground. The man's knees were slightly bent, his hips and ass thrusting his cock deep inside her pussy.

He almost reminded me of a childhood dog that we used to have who would always get loose and screw any other dog he found. Such intensity in what he was doing. We finally had to cut the dog's balls off.

The man had his hands on either side of her hips for better balance. The blonde had to hold onto the toilet bowl for her balance, and the weight of his body.

I stared, he grunted and she moaned and groaned while her large breasts swayed back and forth, nipples just inches from the open bowl.

Sensing somebody had entered the small room, her face turned towards me. Peeking at me from under her right arm, she half smiled, or was it a wince? After all how could she be having fun? It looked awfully uncomfortable.

Curiosity and repulsion at what I was watching kept my feet planted on the tiled floor. I had never seen anybody having sex before. The closest I ever came to this was in the summer of 1983.

* * * *

Crazy Larry lived in Beachwood Canyon. He was a short, wiry man in his 40's, who loved to talk dirty on the phone with young, teenage girls.

Marge and I actually stayed at his house for two nights in the summer of 1983 when we ran away from home. I was 17 and Marge, my stepsister was 16. A bit too old to be running away from home, but we did. We had one full month of freedom. No curfew, no parents and no shortages of places to crash at for the night.

We had a moped, each other, nerve, and the protection of skinheads, drug dealers and ex-cons. We were like their two little sisters that nobody would dare fuck with on the streets of Hollywood.

One day we called Crazy Larry. "Hey Larry, we want to have some fun with you tonight." Marge purred into the pay phone on Hollywood Blvd.

Within ten minutes, Larry pulled up in his cream colored Corvette. "Hey girls, sorry it took me so long." Larry said, all smiles.

"You should be." Marge snapped at him. She opened the passenger door, oblivious to the parking meter.

"Ooooh" Larry uttered, hearing the fiberglass door meet the metal pole.

"Gimme a cigarette Larry. I've had a real shitty morning." Marge demanded. There was no purr in her voice now. "Would you go already? What in the fuck are you waiting for? Christmas?"

"Uh, what about your sister? Isn't she coming with us? He asked, hoping that I would be there to tame this wildcat Marge.

"Duh. She's following us on the moped. What? Did you think we were just going to leave it on the streets? Don't act so stupid."

So off we went to Crazy Larry's castle in the canyon.

It was dark and decorated in a 70's style, but a nice break from the flop house style of living in the apartment above "Seven Seas", a nightclub on Hollywood Blvd. It was a real bed, a real bathroom and real food.

"I'm starving!" Marge half yelled to Larry when we got to his house. "Is this all you've got for us?" She demanded, throwing open his refrigerator and freezer doors.

My eyes couldn't believe how lucky we were. So much food lined each shelf. Frozen pizza, turkey, ham, eggs, bread, soda, and so much more. I hadn't seen so much food to choose from since we left home two weeks ago. I didn't know what Marge was complaining about, but I kept my mouth shut. I knew I would benefit somehow. Marge always had a plan for us.

"There's nothing in here for me to eat. I need to go to the market Larry. No offense, but you don't have anything I like, and I'm hungry!" her voice was nearly a scream by now.

My eyes stayed glued to the jar of Skippy's peanut butter, third shelf down.

"Alright Marge, why don't we all go to the market." Larry suggested.

"No way Larry. You're staying here. My sister and I will go. You obviously don't know a thing about shopping for young ladies." She said, holding out her hand.

Larry reached deep into the pocket of his much too tight jeans, and handed Marge a $20.00 bill.

"LARRY! I'm so sure!" Marge hollered.

Larry dug out two more twenties. "That's all I've got Marge, I swear." He turned his pocket inside out, some lint flakes falling into his multicolored, shag carpet, never to be seen again.

Marge, not letting up said, "What? Do you expect us to walk there?"

"Oh no Marge, not my vet. No way. Never.

Five minutes later, Marge's skinny body was firmly behind the wheel of Larry's prized possession, me in the passenger seat.

"Where to Sis?" Marge asked while putting on Larry's Ray Ban sunglasses that were tucked into his visor.

"Don't you want to go to the market?" I asked.

"What are you nuts? Did you see all of that great food the pervert has? But hey, I just made us a quick $60.00 bucks. Let's just cruise."

One hour later, and the gas tank reading empty, we pulled back into Larry's garage.

"We're home honey." Marge said, breezing past Larry, tucking his sunglasses into her backpack.

"I got a little worried, you've been gone for over an hour."

"Oh, you worry too much." Marge said.

"No groceries? One hour later and no food?"

Marge stopped walking and spun around to look at Larry. A birdcage, perched on a shelf caught her eye. Inside the cage was a bird dressed in prison stripes, and a sign above it read "Jailbird".

A split second later, Larry had the full attention of her venom again. "No Larry. It's no wonder you don't have any good food here. That market stinks. We'll just have to make do with what you've got here."

Marge then turned to Larry and said in her best baby voice, "We're hungry honey. Will you fix us some dinner while we take a bubble bath?"

Bubble bath? Now that perked up Larry's deflated sex drive. "Sure, anything you two want," He was all giddy now at the thought of finally being able to see us naked. "Should I bring it into you?" He nearly panted. A bulge was forming in his ball-hugger jeans, trailing us into the bathroom.

"No." Marge replied, slamming the wooden bathroom door in his face. "We'll meet you in the den when we're done!" She screamed through the keyhole.

"Ewe! What a total geek he is, I'm so sure, like we're really going to like him." Marge whispered. She emptied an entire bottle of bubble bath into the filling tub of hot water.

"Give me your clothes." Marge said. She gathered our dirty socks, undies, pants and shirts. Wrapping a large towel around her body, she opened the bathroom door to scream for Larry. Larry's body came tumbling in, falling to the floor, an empty glass in his hand.

"What are you doing in here?" Marge screeched. "Get out." And with that, she threw our dirty clothes at him. "Wash these!" Slam. "And we want our underwear back!" She hollered through the keyhole.

With the tub water filled to the top, we both stepped in, causing the soapy water to spill over and onto the floor. Marge took no notice and turned the jacuzzi jets on full blast, making the bubbles foam up to the tops of our heads. Water and bubbles were now flowing rapidly over the side of the tub, inching its way across the entire bathroom floor.

"Marge, there's water everywhere. Should you empty the water a little?"

"Nah, we'll clean it up later." She leaned her head back and closed her eyes.

Fifteen minutes later, we emerged from the tub and stepped into four inches of water, covering the floor.

Marge, always as cool as a cucumber, found a clean stack of towels in his cabinet and mopped up the floor, then threw the soaking wet, soapy towels back onto the shelf and closed the cabinet door.

I found a thick terry cloth robe and Marge found a silk print kimono to wrap herself in, and we ventured out for dinner.

Two things caught my eye as I walked into the den. The first was that Marge had already swiped the jailbird sign from its shelf. The second was, "Valley Girls," a Hal Freeman Production, rated XXX, was splashed across the television screen. Larry sat giggling on the couch, patting the cushion beside him to Marge.

"What the fuck is this Larry?" Marge asked. For a change, there was no anger in her voice. Marge and I were speechless, stunned and curious. We had heard of these movies, but had never seen a porno before.

The girls were so young and cute, driving around in a white

convertible Rabbit. People got naked and sex started flowing. They must have been horny, because where ever they were, they just started doing it: a van, a table, a counter top, it didn't seem to matter to them. Shit, this was so erotic. I had never seen, let alone had myself, such animalistic fucking. Girls were bent over, screaming for more and the guys were giving it to them. Hair was being pulled, asses were getting spanked and nasty words like "fuck me harder, deeper" and "cum all over me," were things I had never heard before.

Marge and I sat with our eyes glued to the screen. From the corner of my eye, I could see Larry touching himself down below, thankfully over his jeans.

When the movie was over, Marge and I sat like two scared rabbits on the couch. I knew Marge would get us out of anything Larry was planning.

"I've got a headache." Marge said. "I think my period is coming." She glanced at Larry. "And I'm a heavy bleeder." She threw in for good measure.

Larry flinched; this was not what the pervert wanted to hear after such a sexual movie. It was dawning on him that whatever sexual fantasies he had of seeing two stepsisters getting it on, was never going to happen.

In a last ditch effort, Larry tried to follow us into our bedroom.

"Ewe! Get out of here!" Marge said, her white, oblong face pinched. She slammed the door in Larry's face for the third time that night, then wedged a chair under the doorknob.

Marge and I got ready for bed in silence, each wrapped up in our own thoughts on what we just saw, but I could see Marge stuffing the silk kimono into her ever-growing backpack.

"Marge, did that movie turn you on?" I whispered in the darkness.

"Yeah, it did, but I wasn't going to let that pervert know."

After two more nights of Marge's verbal abuse, and not even a glimpse of a naked shoulder blade, Larry threw us out, mumbling something about his sister coming into town unexpectedly.

Marge's backpack was overflowing with Larry's belongings when we got back on our moped, heading back to the streets of Hollywood.

* * * *

One year later, I was on the set of my own version of "Valley Girls." Only I didn't feel sexy, glamorous or horny.

I felt petrified with a capitol "P".

Looking at the man and woman doing it bent over the toilet, I realized that if I didn't scram, I might be next on his list to conquer. I slowly backed my way out of the bathroom, pulling the door closed. I began to tiptoe down the hallway, then took off at full speed towards the noise at the opposite end of the house.

10

I scurried back down the hallway, not pausing this time to look at family photographs, and stopped in the still peaceful and empty living room.

To my left, from where I had just escaped, I could hear the bathroom door opening, voices trailed by two bodies emerging.

Oh shit, I was on the move, heading for the den.

"Oh man! Did you see that?" A man sitting on the couch asked a crewmember. "That idiot just lost us the game."

The large screen television in one corner, across from the dark brown corduroy L-shaped couch, was blaring a game.

The crew member, bending over with the crack of his ass exposed, looked up and grunted in response while ripping a piece of gaffer's tape from the roll with his teeth.

The man on the couch looked me up and down.

I smiled. "Hi. I'm Christy."

"Rick Cassidy is the name," he replied with a lopsided smile.

What caught my eye next was in the far-left corner. Hovering at the buffet table was the hairiest set of butt-cheeks I had ever seen.

This person, sensing somebody approaching his territory, turned around, as if protecting the table and the food laid out.

"Hi, my name is Ron Jeremy," He licked the cream cheese off his fingers, then extended that same hand out to me. "Looks like we'll be working together today," he threw his head back, and shoved the remaining half of his bagel, in his mouth.

The way he ate that in one fell swoop, reminded me of a goldfish I won at a sixth grade school carnival. I named it "Goldie". Every morning, I would unscrew the lid off the fish food, and pinch as much as I could between my right thumb and index finger.

I would then hover above the glass fishbowl holding the food, still pinched between my fingers, right above the water. Goldie would get so excited at the smell of breakfast and swim as fast as he could to the top. His wee little mouth would suddenly become larger than him, opening and closing with every fish flake I dropped in the bowl.

After teasing him with a few flakes, I would release my fingers, and fish food would be floating everywhere. Goldie was in fish heaven, eating it up like a vacuum cleaner.

Three weeks later, Goldie got the bends and died. Mom flushed him down the toilet.

Cream cheese and lox stuck to Ron's teeth. "So, how many films have you done?" His eyes flickered back and forth between the Danish platter and me.

"None." I hoped I sounded casual. "This is my first." I was debating on whether or not I wanted to eat anything, but the sight of his schlong, inches away from the food made my already queasy stomach churn even more.

Ron's voice raised several octaves. "WHAT!?" He looked at me, and his hand came to a halt above a bear claw.

Ron eyed the claw, then me. "This is your very first one? So I'll be the first guy to play hide the salami with you?" he was all giddy at the thought of fresh meat.

Hide the salami? "I don't know what the scene calls for." Maybe we weren't in the bedroom after all. Did they move the lights into the kitchen?

"How old are you?"

"I just turned eighteen a few months ago."

"This is great. I really owe Jim now. I'm always asking Jim for the new talent. It's about time he threw me a bone."

"I'm a little nervous." I confided to my co-star.

"Nervous about what? It's only sex."

With that said, his paw-like hand swooped down and scooped up the bear claw.

I decided against food and found my way into hair and makeup.

The big blonde, who was getting boffed in the bathroom earlier, was now sitting in the makeup chair.

"I seemed to have messed up my lips," she told J.R.

Her accent sounded German.

J.R. giggled. "Gee, I wonder who's cock you've been sucking."

J.R. was always fun to have around as the makeup artist on magazine shoots. He was as queer as a three-dollar bill, and always made me laugh with his over the top stories of how he would pick up men.

Last week, when he was doing my makeup on a photo shoot, he told me that the night before, he had gone to a gas station. "And there he was, the cutest looking boy in a tight white T-shirt and faded jeans, filling up next to me. Ooh La La!" J.R. said, rolling his eyes. He stepped back to check out my face. "You look simply beautiful darling. So anyway, we started to talk, and the next thing I knew, I was in the men's bathroom, bending over the urinal, with his huge dick crammed up my ass."

And on and on his stories went.

"Christy, have you met Stevie yet?"

Introductions were made and she was actually a nice girl. She told me she was married to some rich old timer who bought her a new Porsche last month. Three nights ago, she and some girlfriends went to party at Voila, a popular nightclub. She got stinking drunk, and crashed her car into a telephone pole.

"How did you get home?" I asked.

"I jumped in a cab."

"What about your car?" I dreamed of owning a Porsche one day.

Stevie checked out her freshly applied red lipstick in the mirror. "My old man took care of it."

Some girls have all the luck I thought to myself.

Lights, camera, action. It was showtime. "Swedish Erotica #57"

Paul stood at the foot of the brass bed rubbing his hands together, big gold pinky rings clinking in the process.

"Alright kids. Now that I've got you all together in the same room, lets go over the scene." He glanced my way. "You Misty."

I corrected him, "Uh, it's Christy." I wished that big earthquake would hit Los Angeles right about now.

"Oh sure, you can pick whatever name you want for your character," he didn't look at me, but snuck a wink in at Stevie.

Up close, with his clothes on, Paul reminded me of a game show host from the 70's. He wasn't bad looking, but no way in hell was he getting me alone in a bathroom.

"Let's pick this up from yesterday's shoot where Ronnie and Stevie have already shot a sex scene."

"The four of you just went out to dinner and now you're back at Misty's house."

Paul paused and looked up to the ceiling, eyes squinting as if he'd conjured up a masterpiece scenario.

"Ronnie, you on the piano," Paul pointed to one corner. "Rick, you go take a leak," Paul pointed to the opposite corner. "Girls and Ronnie fuck around with some bullshit dialogue, then Ronnie, you get up and leave to find out what happened to Rick. Stevie leaves next, then Christy finally follows, and you all end up in the bedroom. On the TV is the film we shot yesterday with Ronnie and Stevie. Watch for a while, ad-lib some more then the four of you jump into bed and start fucking. Badda-Bing, Badda-bang, and it's a wrap."

In her husky voice, Stevie asked, "Who goes with who?"

Definitely a German accent I thought.

Ron jumped up from the bed. "I get Christy!" His mound of potato salad and a ham sandwich fell on the pink, white and green pastel bedspread. "You promised me, Paul."

Unsure of whom Ron was asking for, Paul asked. "Who?"

"Christy, the new girl." Ron sat down on the bed and began trying to salvage his lunch plate. "Is there any more potato salad?"

Paul's eyes focused on me for the first time that day. "Yeah sure, she can end up with you."

69

I stood on the set, under the intense hot lights in my striped dress, focusing my eyes on my white open-toe pumps. "I wore these shoes to my eleventh grade prom," I said. Nobody paid attention.

The clapboard shut, "take one" was hollered from somewhere in the sea of lights, and the camera started rolling.

Ron began pounding the ivories, told a joke, then got up to find Rick.

My cue. I could see the camera focusing on me.

I froze like a doe caught in headlights.

"Go Christy!" a voice whispered.

The palms of my hands began to itch.

Paul yelled, "CUT!" and walked over to me. "This is your first time, isn't it?"

"Uh-huh."

"Just take it easy. Relax and breathe in deep, then let it out slowly. You can do this honey, after all, it's only sex."

I was sure hearing that a lot today.

"When you hear action, just say what comes to mind. Pretend you're with your best friend right now."

With that, Paul crawled back behind the camera. "Action! Take two."

I looked at her plump body and said the first thing that unfortunately came to mind. "It looks like you've lost some weight."

As the words came out of my mouth, I realized what I was saying. Where did that come from? Oh God, what a goof I am.

Stevie sucked in her breath and stomach simultaneously and stared at me with her mouth open. "Yeah, I've been on a new diet," she finally replied.

Paul yelled, "CUT."

Knowing he had to treat Jim's new girl with kid gloves, he said, "Was that line really necessary?" His face was bright red with anger, and he looked like he wanted to explode. There was no rewinding film, unlike video. Film lost meant money lost.

I thought about the time mom forgot to turn the pressure cooker off and our dinner ended up on our kitchen ceiling.

"Why don't you make a wisecrack about Ronnie? Everybody else does," Paul chuckled at his own joke.

Back Paul went, behind the camera.

"Action! Take three!"

"Does he always joke around like that?" Was that my voice?

"Always." Stevie replied.

"How do you take it?" I could feel my right eyelid twitching my lips frozen in a nervous smile.

Stevie, wanting to get as far away from me as possible, got up to search for the boys.

70

Porn time later, about one second, I got up to find all three of them.

Alas! Like any normal set of couples after dinner, they are watching the tape of Ronnie and Stevie going at it.

Ron urges Rick, Stevie and I to re-enact the scene while he tapes us.

"I'm not that drunk!" I answer. It was funny how that piece of dialogue rolled out of my mouth fast and easy.

Paul's voice whispered from behind the camera. "You will be in about two seconds."

And so it began. My white prom shoes found their way to the bed. Stevie and I knelt on the bed and began undressing each other. Oh shit, I have never touched a woman before. Her boobs are so big and soft. They felt nice. Stevie began caressing my boobs, then slid her tongue over my nipples. Under all of my fear, I found it quite erotic until I glanced to my right and caught sight of Rick. Why was he naked so fast? Oh no, because he's walking over here to join us. Gone was the hint of eroticism, full fear was back.

Tongues were flying until Rick decided to enter me. Before I realized it, Rick's rock hard cock found its way into my body.

I lay there like a log. No emotion, no movement and no encouragement for him to continue, so he didn't.

He glared at me and pulled out, his cock not so hard anymore. Rick sought out Stevie and the warmth of her welcoming mouth.

Ron, not quite as enthusiastic about being paired off with me after viewing my pathetic performance with Rick, poised his body between my legs. After prying them apart, he dove in, head first. After what felt like an eternity, Ron looked at me from between my legs. "Oooh, I love it when a girl doesn't shave or douche."

His voice was in slow motion to me, as was everything else.

"Doesn't this feel good?" Ron asked with panic in his voice at the thought of losing his touch with the ladies.

"Act sexy, God damn it." Paul hissed from an unknown direction.

Hoping I wouldn't throw up I robotically answered, "Oh yes, real good."

Ron, realizing his young, fresh meat was a dud, decided to enter me.

"Are you ready?" He spit in the palm of his hand and rubbed it all over his dick.

Thinking no, I answered, "Yes."

"I like using my saliva for lube the best. I don't care for KY Jelly or Abilene; they're too greasy. I lose the friction feeling." He shared his preference with me while sticking the tip of his dick inside me.

A quart of oil wouldn't lube up my dry vagina. But with enough spit and determination, Ron was now inside me.

I turned my head to the right, unable to watch what was happening to my body, and saw Stevie and Rick inches from me.

"Yeah baby, give it to Daddy." Rick said.

Oh no, not very comforting to me. I turned my head to the left. I caught a glimpse of Ron, who was still going at it to no avail. In addition to fucking me, he was now rubbing my clit at the same time.

I couldn't feel a thing down there. My sex drive had gone into shock, closing shop for the first time.

Shifting my head to the left, I came face to face with the camera's lens, five inches away.

"Lick your lips, moan and groan." Paul's voice whispered from behind the camera.

Like a trained monkey, I did as I was told.

"I'm going to cum!" A man's voice said to my right.

Paul and his camera scurried to the other side of the bed. Ron, at the same time, flipped me over. With my belly on the mattress, Ron scooped me under my belly, and hoisted my body on all four's. Ron entered me doggie style for the first time in my life.

"O.K. Rick, when ever you're ready, give me the money shot." Paul whispered.

Rick's face contorted and his body began to have spasms. Stevie withdrew his cock from her mouth and began jerking him off. Several strokes later, white cum began shooting out of his cock and all over his stomach.

I was sick to my stomach.

Pumping back and forth several times, Ron finally gave up. "It's just not going to happen Paul."

Was everybody glaring at me or was it my imagination?

"It's a wrap!" Paul yelled to the set.

"Towel! Will somebody get the talent a towel?" A P.A. yelled from the now darkening set.

"You have a great set of tits." Paul said handing me my check. "You just need to loosen up a bit, and you can be a huge star."

I unlocked my apartment door, took my clothes off, and turned on the shower. I jumped into the scalding hot water, scrubbing myself with a bar of soap, cleansing every inch of my body.

Concentrating with the bar of soap between my legs, I began to cry. Not a soft whimper, but loud sobs that racked my body to the core. Uncontrollable tears streaming down my face.

I sat in the tub, pulling my knees into my chest, hugging them as close as I could to protect my body. I could feel the hot water hitting my neck and back, as I laid my head on my kneecaps.

"Oh God, why me?" I asked the empty bathroom. "Why weren't you there to protect me Daddy?" But in truth, my dad was never there to protect me.

* * * *

1981

Marv and mom had gone through Clair's room one afternoon and found her diary. Inside of these private pages, Clair wrote about a weekend where she had told our parents that she was staying at her girlfriend's house. Clair had actually spent the weekend with the boy she had been seeing for over a year. A few entries about how she experimented with drugs, coupled with mom finding traces of white powder on a makeup mirror, and Clair was off to Colorado for her first year of college.

"It will be good for you," Marv said one night at the dinner table after he dropped the bomb that Clair was not allowed to stay in LA if she wanted them to pay for college. "Staying in LA will only get you into trouble," Marv's nasal voice said.

Marv never stopped to think about the trouble that I would get into.

To take my sister away from me was like ripping my heart out. Clair and I always had each other. Several stepfathers, stepmothers and a slew of stepbrothers and stepsisters came and went, in and out of a revolving door, but Clair and I always had each other.

When Carol and Dad fought so loud that the walls shook between our rooms, it was Clair who would braid my hair and tell me stories. When one of Mom's boyfriends tried to feel up Clair's pre-pubescent body, it was me who took the pleasure in informing my mom what her good for nothing boyfriend just did. We never saw him again.

We were each other's best friends and nobody could break that bond. Now the enemy Marv was trying.

Marv was never on our side. He was a cold, selfish, pompous asshole.

It was January 1980 and Dad was taking Clair and me home. We had to stay the week at his house for our second week of Christmas vacation.

Mom and Marv had gone to the Virgin Islands for that week, but today they were coming home.

Marv was an okay boyfriend for Mom. At least he had a cool house in the hills that we had moved into, a new Jaguar and was the president of a major record label. Not bad, but I was still leery.

Dad's big canary yellow Cadillac inched its way through the winding streets of our hills. I wanted to reach my foot over and step on the gas pedal to hurry him along. I couldn't wait to get back to my room with my own things, not the cold impersonal room Carol set up for Clair and me.

Dad was blabbering on about how Mom was bleeding him dry for our child support, but Clair and I knew he hadn't paid a red cent in over five

73

years. I wouldn't argue back today. I was much too excited to be getting out of jail and going to my sanctuary.

We finally pulled into our gate, and jumped out of his car with big fake smiles telling him how much we loved him. He had big crocodile tears forming in his clouded brown eyes. Oh no! Here comes the speech about how he wanted us to live with him. He missed us so much and something or other was my mom's fault. In truth, Carol would not allow that over her dead body.

Fuck you, fat ass, is what I felt like saying. He had been knocking my beloved mama all week. I was through listening to my mom being bashed.

Instead, we grabbed our bag of clothes and kissed his cheek goodbye.

"I'll call you!" he shouted, already in reverse.

Yeah right, in about a week I thought as I opened the kitchen door.

What was that huge thing sitting in the middle of our kitchen table? I took a step closer and felt my spine tingle. It was bad news. Real bad. Sitting in the center of our round kitchen table, was a huge bouquet of white roses with two white Styrofoam hearts on each side of the clear vase. A white dove was attached in the middle of the two hearts, and a red satin banner with white lettering read "CONGRATULATIONS" in big bold lettering across the whole display.

It took my brain two seconds to realize that Mom and Marv got married in the Virgin Islands without me. Not only was I left out, somebody else seemed to know about this marriage before me, her own flesh and blood.

How could my mom betray me like this? I had just defended her honor all week to my mom-bashing father and now she went behind my back and married that asshole?

I could feel the lump starting to form deep down, in the back of my throat. I turned to look at Clair, but she seemed unfazed. "They must have gotten married." Clair shrugged her shoulders. "I'm going to call Jeff." She turned and went into her room.

Tears began streaming down my face as I ran out of the house, to my best friend Jill's, five doors down.

Her mom answered the door, and took me in her open arms, holding my sobbing body. She didn't know what was wrong, so she just held me close to her, stroking my hair, pulling me in tighter.

It must have been an hour before my mom came to pick me up. Her eyes were red from crying. Mom knew the pain and betrayal her baby was feeling.

My entire body was in pain and my heart was broken. I had never felt such utter betrayal in my life. I thought we were a team. The three girls stuck together. Clair and I came first. Getting married was a family thing; not something you did behind our backs. Why weren't we a part of this?

Mom and I walked in the door and Marv was sitting on the living room couch with Clair. It was family talk time. The enemy was now my stepfather, which technically meant he was family.

"It was a last minute decision," I heard him say. "We'll have a big party to celebrate with friends." he droned on. I wasn't just a friend, and I didn't care how he sugar coated the stupid party they planned on having, or their lame excuse for eloping.

I was hurt and left out and that was all I cared about.

Clair was my one constant in life. Now, one year later, the enemy was taking my sister away from me as well.

"Please Daddy, don't make Clair go away to college. If you pay for her tuition, she can stay in LA." I begged my father at the dinner table one night soon after Marv drove the knife through my heart.

"Daddy would love to, but Carol's shop isn't doing too well, and money is tight right now."

Dad was always talking about himself in the third person.

Carol kept her eyes focused on her plate of food.

"It's okay Dad, I understand. Maybe it won't be so bad leaving."

Clair was so nice all of the time. I didn't understand. I never understood why Carol was always put before us. Her stupid store was always losing money, and Daddy was always there to pour more into it.

"Will you be okay honey? You know, Daddy is always just a phone call away."

Carol looked up and joined in the conversation for the first time.

"Clair will be okay." Her eyes locked into mine. "It's you I'm worried about."

Carol and I both knew something bad was about to happen.

It was the end of summer in 1982. Clair was packing, to head off to Colorado for her first year of college.

11

Soon after Clair left for college, Marv got his walking papers from work. A new team was brought in. Out with the old, and in with the new, hip, young crew. Marv was neither young nor hip. Marv had been best friends with the CEO of the company. When the CEO retired, it gave the company the green light to can his ass. Marv wasn't paying attention to who he was pouncing on, climbing up the ladder. But he saw each and every one of them as he slid back down.

Coming home from school every day, I would see Marv lying on the couch in our living room bellyaching. It had been four months since he was let go, and he wasn't doing anything about finding a new job. All he did, day in and day out, was complain. He was boring and pathetic and reminded me of a wounded animal just sprawled on that couch every day.

Once, on a rare occasion when he wasn't parked on the couch, I got a good look at it. It now had permanent head and ass indentations.

It was a late afternoon in January. The sun was setting, and Marv was lying there in the semi dark taking comfort in his usual loser position on the couch.

Walking through the kitchen door after school, I saw his oblong head turn towards me. His face seemed thinner and his head of curls more gray. The only other part of his body visible, were his bare feet dangling off the other end of the white couch, nearly touching and knocking over the standing lamp.

"You know, you and your sister have been a real problem for your mother. She's had to work so hard and doesn't get much help from you two girls. Do you realize how much she's had to sacrifice for the two of you? At times, you and Clair have really bogged her down in life," he informed me.

What was he talking about? Mom loved us. We were a trio. Clair and I would do anything to help her out. "What do you mean Marv?" Did he know something that we didn't know? Was she mad at us? I guess my grades could be better, but a "C" average isn't failing.

"Don't get me wrong, she loves you, but sometimes life would have been easier for her if she didn't have both of you. She's never had any help from your father either. What's wrong with him? Why doesn't he help her out financially? After all, he is your father. What kind of dad doesn't help out?"

Fuck, where was Clair? My mom was at work, and I was here, all alone with this prick telling me lies. He had no idea what he was talking about. Or did he? Would Mom have been happier with out us? Did Daddy not really love us, and that's why he never paid child support?

I just stood in the doorway with my backpack slung over my right shoulder. The sun was setting fast, casting a darker shadow across Marv's face. I couldn't see his watery eyes anymore, but his voice rang loud and clear in my head.

"Don't tell her I'm telling you any of this, she doesn't need any more pressure right now. I'm just telling you for your own good. I know how much you love your mom and want her to be happy. Help out a little more, maybe give her some time off and stay at your dad's for a few weeks."

A few weeks at my dad's house? Pure torture, no way.

Marv said his piece and then turned his head to stare at the ceiling again.

Unfortunately, it wasn't until years later that I realized that Marv was the reason that Mom had become so uptight. His rapid demise into depression was causing the tension. I had nothing to do with her unhappiness up to that day in my life.

The following few months brought more strained times in our household. While Mom went to work six to seven days a week, Marv took up tennis. All he could do now was talk about his game, and whom he had played with that day. He had given up on looking for a job. At the dinner table, he would dominate the conversation with his stupid stories, cutting us off if we tried to talk about our day. "Jane, you're not listening to me." Marv's need to be the center of attention got worse every day.

I began to hate him more and more. Didn't he realize how hard my mom was working while his fucking ass was out playing all day?

One day Marv came home from his day at the courts limping. He had sprained his toothpick thin leg on the court, and couldn't play tennis for the next month.

Shit, I was stuck with him at home every day again. He was back on the couch, staring at the ceiling.

It was the first week in April, and Mom was even busier with her tax practice. I hadn't seen much of her in the past month. She worked every weekend now, and until nine at night during the week.

Marv and I were eating dinner one night. "Is Marge coming over this weekend?" I liked it when his daughter spent the weekend at our house. She was my ally.

Marge's weekend visits had diminished to one weekend every three to four weeks by now.

"He's such a downer." Marge told me at school one day. "All he does is complain. He never asks me how my life is, or how school is going. I look at Paul as my real father now." I had noticed in the past six months, Marge was referring to her stepfather as her father. Confusing to me at first, but one hundred percent understandable.

"Dad used to always promise me a brand new car for my sixteenth birthday. Now he says he can't afford it because he lost a shit load of money in his Atari stock. Yeah, right, like he can't cough up a few bucks for a car. Of course Paul is going to buy me one. I love him so much. I wish he was my real father."

"I don't think she's coming over this weekend. She's going somewhere with her mom and Paul."

"Where is she going Marv?" I wished I could go with her wherever it was.

"I really don't know."

"But it's our weekend to have her. She hasn't been over in a month."

Marv bit into a chicken leg. "I know." He was clearly more interested in the chicken leg he was eating, than his own daughter.

Marv didn't even realize he was losing her.

"I really love her. She's my flesh and blood. Clair feels like my own daughter too. We have so much in common with music and movies. Clair is really a hip girl. It's funny how you and I have nothing in common."

The pussy couldn't even look me in the eyes with his verbal slap in the face. We both knew this was true, but did he have to say it? His last sentence was the final blow to me. My anger for Marv erupted from deep within and all hell broke loose inside me. I realized how much I hated him.

Snooping through his drawers one day, I ran across his May Company charge card. Hit him where it hurts, in the pocket.

Marv had a business manager. Chances were, he would never even see his bill, so off to the mall I went, Marv's credit card in my wallet.

Thirty days went by, and no mention of a $445.00 charge, so off I went to May Co. again.

After months of stocking up on the newest trends, compliments of Marv, I was the best-dressed girl in school. "I have it in white and red as well..." I would tell my friends.

Every time Marv knocked me down emotionally, I went shopping. Needless to say, my closets were crammed

I never expected Marv to go in for his year-end taxes.

"Have you been going to May Co. with Marv's credit card?" Mom asked me the second I stepped through the kitchen door after school one day.

"What?" I asked, trying to buy a couple of seconds. I could feel the sweat trickling down my armpits in my new angora sweater.

"You heard me. Did you?" Mom's hands were on her hips, which meant business.

"No. Where would I get his credit card from?" I asked. Lying right through my teeth. The gig was up.

"Marv is ordering copies of his credit card receipts. You better pray it isn't your signature on them."

With that, Mom stared at me with piercing, pissed-off eyes for what seemed an eternity, then turned and walked out of the kitchen.

The color drained from my face, matching my new white Nine West boots. I was screwed.

Two nights later, I went out with my best friend Terry. Grant, a cute guy from school, was having a party at his house while his parents were in the Bahamas.

That night I discovered vodka.

"Where do you live Miss?" The cop asked me from the front seat.

"In Woodland Hills." I slurred before throwing up in the back seat.

"Oh shit! Look what she did to our backseat. God Damn kids these days have no respect."

"Oh, come on, just think back to when we were teenagers." The nice cop behind the wheel said, unrolling his window for a breath of fresh air.

"We know you don't live in Woodland Hills." Nice cop said. "We've been in radio contact with your parents, we're just lost in these hills."

Like I was in any shape to help him.

The following morning, I woke up and felt like somebody drove an axe through my head.

Water was all I could think about at the moment. I had to drink a gallon of water. Why was my mouth so dry?

Pieces of the previous night flashed through my head. A party at Grant's, vodka, and oh God, I was arrested. Back to Grant. I think I slept with him last night. I told him I always thought that he was cute, then I got naked. I wondered if he liked me, I liked him, but I was dating his best friend.

That now made me a drunk slut with a police record.

The hole I was digging for myself just got a little bit deeper. Unfortunately, I wasn't finished digging.

Marv opened my bedroom door.

"You're grounded until your eighteen. The only time you're allowed to drive your car, is to school and back."

With those words from the unemployed, decrepit and wise, he slammed my bedroom door. It sounded like an explosion going off in my throbbing head.

Eighteen? That was a year away.

The following few days at home were horrific. Mom, now worked even later into the night, avoiding the tension-filled home. This left me stuck with that sad, sack of a stepfather Marv until bedtime. No goodnight, no hugs or kisses, no words of encouragement that things would get better. Just me closing my door and falling asleep.

Since I had no car, television, stereo or telephone left in my bare room, I read and took long walks in the hills by our house all week after school.

The following Friday, I dutifully came home straight from school and found Marv and mom waiting for me.

"You spent over $3,000.00 on my charge card!" Marv screamed at me. My mom caught in the middle. Her husband on one side, her baby on the other.

I packed up that night and moved to my fathers. I didn't even call him, I just drove.

Daddy was waiting outside for me when I got there fifteen minutes later.

"Did they call you Daddy?"

"Yeah, you really messed up Monkey."

"I know Daddy. I'm so sorry."

12

The morning after the loop, I woke up and looked at a face in the mirror that didn't belong to me. My eyes were puffy and bloodshot from crying myself to sleep. A piece of my innocence had been taken away from me in that thirty-minute loop.

I took out three ice cubes from the white plastic tray in my freezer, and began rubbing them around my eyes. Wanda was going to have to work miracles on my face today.

Today was the day to shoot a box cover for one of my two final films, videos, loops, or whatever other names were attached to pornos. I had told Jim yesterday that this was it. I know what I said, so there was no way I could be tricked into anything else again. From now on, it was just magazine layouts.

I took a shower, got dressed, and headed out to Ron's studio in the San Fernando Valley, with a quick stop at the bank to deposit my twelve hundred dollar loop money. Looking at my new balance was a small consolation.

I made a left hand turn onto Ron's street, and I suddenly felt on edge, uneasy. Were these people, Ron and Wanda, going to betray me somehow? Were they in on the set up with Jim?

I eased my way into the bathroom, and found Wanda spraying a mane of brunette hair. "Hi Christy. I'm almost ready for you. There's a robe for you to change into." Wanda said. "Aren't you excited? Your first box cover! The more boxes you can get on, the better for your career."

Career? I never looked at this as a career. This was just something to do until I found my real calling in life.

"Now flip your head up, and don't mess up your lipstick." Wanda told the head of hair.

The girl in the director's chair flipped her head up, and looked at me through the now familiar warped mirror. "Christy?" She asked, whipping her head around to look directly at me. "Christy, is that really you? Oh my God, we went to junior high school together. It's me, Gina Valentino. Remember, we had Spanish and P.E. together in the ninth grade. I was a stoner, and you were a sosh." Sosh was a slang word used for the popular, social girls in school. Me.

A stoner was used for the group that hung out and smoked pot in the bathrooms, bushes and behind the handball courts. Her.

My brain was in shock. "Of course I remember you." I tried to think back nearly four years ago. Was I nice to her in school, or did I ignore her because she wasn't in our click? The elite girls, who lived in the hills, were very picky about who we allowed in our circle. Yet, right now it felt wonderful to see a piece of my past.

So here we were, a sosh and a stoner, posing together on a hard-core box cover. I wondered where my elite friends were now. How many of them went off to college, compliments of their rich parents. Or who was still living at home, not worrying if their telephone would be cut off.

Gina sipped her soda through a straw. "Where did you go after junior high?" She asked.

"To a small private school."

Gina had enrolled into the local public high school, while I was coddled at a small private school, and yet here we were, together at Ron's studio, shooting a box cover for a triple-X film.

It's funny how life works.

"Christy, why don't you get in my chair, so I can get you started. I can't believe that you two know each other. What a small world." Wanda said.

I sat in her makeup chair. "Gina, do you ever talk to anybody from school?" I suddenly wanted to hear about people I knew from my past.

"No, never. Do you?"

"No, never."

"Do you remember that P.E. teacher we had? I think she was a lesbian." I giggled.

"What about that perverted math teacher with the bad rug?"

And on we went, reminiscing about a thread in life we shared four years ago.

My hair was set in hot rollers, and Wanda began matching my skin tones to her tray of foundation colors. Gina sat on the toilet in the small bathroom and asked, "Don't you just love this business?"

"I love magazine layouts, but Jim tricked me into doing a loop yesterday, and I didn't like it. The one we're doing this weekend will be my last, and then I'm just going to stick to magazines."

Gina rolled her eyes. "Jim sent you on a loop for your first one? I bet it was for that pervert Paul. Did he try and fuck you in the bathroom?"

"No, when I got there, he already had Stevie bent over the toilet."

"Oh, that's perfect. It's not like Paul to pull that on a new girl anyway." Gina lit up a cigarette.

"Why? Is it normal that all of the directors try to fuck the talent?" Oh shit, who was I going to have to ward off tomorrow?

Wanda began sponging on my foundation.

"No." Gina thought a moment. "In fact, I think Paul's the only one with a reputation like that. Who was your scene with?"

"Some really nice guy Ron Jeremy."

"Ron Jeremy?" Gina and Wanda said in unison. Wanda stopped

pressing the powder on my face, and Gina stopped mid-inhale on her cigarette.

"Jim put you with Ronnie for your very first time? Hey Dad!" Wanda screamed from the bathroom.

Ron came running in, different colors of gel were attached to his shorts with wooden clothesline pins. The square, orange color gel caught on the rusty latch of the bathroom door and tore in half. "What? What happened?" He was panting.

"Jim put Christy with Ron Jeremy for her first movie. What's wrong with him? Is he trying to scare her off?" Wanda laughed. "You would think he would have put her with Peter North."

"Well," Ron said, putting down the light stand he came running in with. He looked down and touched the torn orange filter. "What happened?" He mumbled, inspecting the rip.

"DAD! Pay attention."

Ron snapped to attention. "Sometimes Jim doesn't think. That is truly the best answer I can give you at this moment since I was not there." He rubbed his chin, deep in thought. "Ronnie is a very nice man, but you're right Wanda, Jim should have put her with Tom Byron, Peter North or Marc Wallace. If you would like, I can talk to Jim about this Christy. Knowing Jim, I'm sure he has his reasons."

"No Ron, it's fine. I think it was just the shock of everything yesterday. Ron is a nice guy, it wasn't his fault."

"Oh Dad, you are so weird. What are you going to say to Jim now anyway? The damage has been done. Christy is not going to make any films after these two thanks to Jim scaring her away."

"I'm only trying to help Wanda. You don't have to be so mean to me." And with that, Ron picked up his light stand, and stormed out of the bathroom.

"Your dad is so nice Wanda." Gina said, still sitting on the toilet seat. "He reminds me of the absent minded professor."

I found myself giggling for the first time in twenty-four hours.

"Okay girls, I have to work now. This is a box cover, the thing that will sell thousands of your videos, and I want you to look perfect. Gina, watch your lipstick. Christy, close your eyes."

I could feel the comfort of Wanda's touch on my eyelids. She began to erase any traces of sadness.

Driving out to the location in Sand Canyon the following day, I began to laugh in the car about the box cover shoot.

Half way through the shoot, Gina's spiked heel got caught in my black fishnet stockings, and tore a large hole in them. Ron took one look at my left calf, and panicked.

Rushing over to inspect the damage, he asked, "What happened?"

Gina and I stood silent.

"I just got these. The art director didn't ask for torn fishnets. Oh no girls, this is bad, really bad. I don't have another pair."

"Oh Dad, don't have a cow, it's no big deal. In fact," Wanda walked onto the set, a make believe back alley, and tore the other fishnet. She powdered our noses, and then stepped back. "There, that looks better."

Ron winced, but knew better than to argue with Wanda.

"Stand up straight and hold in your tummies." Snap, snap, and several rolls later, it was a wrap.

I had just shot my first box cover for a film named "Night Of Loving Dangerously".

I popped in my Squeeze cassette, and couldn't believe how pretty the scenery was. Twenty minutes outside of Los Angeles, and it looked like a different state. How was it, that after living in Los Angeles for eighteen years, I had never seen this area? A house sat here and there, and not one high-rise apartment complex or office building. I saw lush green hills of untouched land with horses and cows roaming around. I began singing, and felt the warmth of the sun coming through my windshield. The sky was baby blue, and I couldn't see the familiar ring of smog that hovered around the valley.

Two more miles up the road and I saw the exit I needed. I got off the freeway, and stopped at the red light at the end of the ramp. I looked at the directions on my passenger seat and turned right, driving through two major intersections, before I found the street I needed. I made a left hand turn, and marveled at the large ranch style houses. Their front yards, so perfectly manicured, could fit a whole house on them. Large deep green lawns, pruned white and red rosebushes, with natural wooden fences lined this street right out of a fifties-style sitcom. A home like one of these is what I would miss the most next month at Christmas. Red poinsettia plants lined the walkways, white lights were wrapped around the lamp posts, Santa and a few of his reindeer on some of the front lawns, and a large Christmas tree somewhere inside.

I couldn't imagine why people would let porno companies shoot in these beautiful houses, in such a clean-cut neighborhood. I wondered if the neighbors knew. After all, it was legal, wasn't it?

I saw a white mailbox with a piece of pink construction paper taped on it. Black lettering read "Night", with an arrow pointing down a long driveway. I looked at my directions, and made a right hand turn. I didn't know what "Night" meant, but it was the same address on the piece of paper Jim had given me.

The house was well hidden from the street, down a long, flagship driveway.

I parked behind a mid-seventies style black Corvette, and saw a pair of handcuffs dangling from the car's rear view mirror. How odd I thought, and grabbed my wardrobe from the back seat.

I walked up the cobblestone path, and a song by The Clash, "Should I Stay or Should I Go" popped into my head.

I should go I thought, as my right hand turned the brass doorknob. I knew that I would stay. As I began to open the front door, I thought about why I was going through with this. I had nowhere else to go if Jim got mad at me. If I could just finish these two movies, Jim would keep booking me on magazine shoots. If I left, Jim would be mad, and might cut off future magazine layouts.

At least my friends Ron and Wanda would be here. He was in charge of shooting the stills, and Wanda was doing the makeup and hair.

Oh boy.

I opened the front door, and stepped into the foyer, and was met by a pleasantly plump woman. "Hi. My name is Gladys. My husband Earl and I own this house. Are you part of the talent today?"

I instantly felt safe with her around, like a grandmother that wouldn't let anything bad happen to me. "Yes, I am."

"Well then, just follow me to the makeup room." Her large frame led me into the living room first. "All of the meals prepared today by the caterer will be set up right here in the living room."

As much as I loved food, I barely heard a word she said. The living room floor to ceiling windows overlooked the back yard. Ten feet beyond the pool and beautiful landscape, was a large lake that had to be thirty feet long, filled with crystal blue water. "What is that?"

Gladys stopped walking. "Oh! That's a man-made lake Father and I had built with the house when we bought the lot."

"Your father lives here too?"

"Oh no honey." She began laughing. "I'm sorry, I forgot to ask you your name."

"Christy. Christy Canyon."

"You haven't shot before here have you?"

"No, it's only my second movie."

She raised her eyebrows. "Oh! Well, I refer to Earl as Father. It's just a name that stuck with me throughout all of our children and grandchildren."

Wow. What an open-minded granny she must be, allowing people to shoot in her house. She probably wouldn't have flipped out if one of her kids used a credit card or got a ticket for drinking and driving. "How many kids and grandkids do you have?" I wanted to be one of them.

"Four children, and seven grandchildren so far. Here, follow me into the kitchen and I'll show you a photo of all of them."

I followed her through a swinging door into a huge kitchen, also overlooking the back yard. It had pale yellow walls, with white trim and white counter tops.

A huge island, with four barstools, was in the center of this country kitchen. Above the island, hung a rack with shiny brass pots and pans. It reminded me of something Dad and Carol had hung in their cold heartless kitchen. But hung in here, it looked warm.

Three ceramic hooks, shaped and painted like roosters, held red and white checkered hand towels, to the right of the white refrigerator. The towels reminded me of a family picnic we had had so long ago.

A set of keys dangled from a hook above the built in desk. The keychain, with square beads in colors of the rainbow, read "#1 Grandma." It reminded me of something I had made many years ago at summer camp only mine said "#1 Mommy". "Your kitchen is so beautiful." I wondered what ever happened to that key-chain.

The sun was streaming in through all of the windows, and everything felt so safe and normal, until I saw a naked girl sitting on some old geezer's lap.

"Tell Daddy what you want for Christmas." He had his hands real close to her breasts.

"Let's see, I think I want you!!" She squealed with laughter.

"Oh Father! Cut that out now!" Gladys joked.

That's Father? Her husband?

"The old goat likes you young ladies, but don't worry, he never bites! He's just a big old tease."

More like a big ugly pervert.

Why did everything in the world of porno almost feel so normal and then something like this made it seem so bizarre?

"Father, I would like you to meet a new gal in the business, her name is Christy."

"Well hello young lady." He stood up and the girl in his lap slid to the ground.

"Ouch." I heard from below.

"It's so nice to meet you." He shook my hand

I saw Ron walk in the kitchen and felt safe. "Nice to meet you too. Your house is so beautiful." Well, one of those two statements was true. "Hi Ron!" I ran over to him and gave him a big hug.

"Why hello Christy! You're right on time. I'm just setting up the lights for your sex scene with Ginger Lynn and Jamie Gillis."

Ugh, I felt that abnormal feeling again. Two girls at once? I had never even been with one. But for some unknown reason, I liked the sound of working with girls better than working with guys.

"Have you met Chanel Lindsay yet?" Ron asked.

The girl had gotten up off the ground, and was staring at the pool.

86

"No, I haven't."

"Chanel, I would like to be the first one to introduce you to Christy Canyon."

She turned around and looked at me with vacant eyes. "Hi Christy, it's so nice to meet you." Her finger was caught in a piece of hair she had been twirling around it. "Do I get to fuck you today?" She yanked her finger out, taking several strands of her blonde hair along with it.

"I don't know actually. Ron said my first scene is with two other girls Ginger Lynn and Jamie Gillis."

Looking at this beautiful young girl made me think of my father and one of his many adages in life. "The lights are on, but nobody's home."

Chanel began to giggle. "Jamie isn't a she, he's a he!"

"That's correct Christy." Ron broke in. "He's one of the finest actors in the business. He lives with Amber Lynn."

"The girl I'm working with today?"

"No, that's Ginger." Ron put down his half-eaten bagel. "It's kinda confusing, but we have three girls in the business with the last name Lynn." He began ticking off his fingers. "There's Ginger Lynn, who you're with today, there's Amber Lynn, who lives with Jamie, and there's Porscha Lynn who wont be here today."

"Wow, are they all related?"

"No. Not at all. It's just one of those weird coincidences." Ron picked his bagel up again and shoved it in his mouth.

It's weird all right, just like this whole business. But I was also getting curious. Who were these people, and what was their story?

Someone shouted from the other room, "Ron! Where are you? We needed that light in here five minutes ago!"

"Gotta go. You can put your wardrobe down this hallway," he pointed, "the first door to the right."

I heard a splash outside. "Thanks Ron." I looked out the window, and saw Chanel swimming naked in the pool. The sun was beating down on her and the water, and I thought about how free and peaceful she looked doing the backstroke from one end to the other. She could care less who saw her naked. I wanted to be like her, not caring about my body and who saw it. She seemed so easy-going and carefree. I, on the other hand, felt my body was ugly. My legs were too heavy in the thighs and my boobs were too big, unlike her cute perky ones.

Ever since sixth grade, I had had to wear a bra for support.

* * * *

My best friend Greta and I were playing tennis after school. The local high school kept their gates unlocked until six every night during the week.

Sue, Greta's mom, would come by after work and watch us play for fifteen minutes before the schoolyard closed.

I ran from side to side, chasing the fuzzy green ball, missing more than I actually made contact with my racquet. I wasn't a good player, but I always felt so free running, chasing, and if I got lucky, hitting the ball.

My long, thin legs bent at the knees, and I threw the ball high in the air. It came back down, and my racquet met it halfway; it was a decent serve. Greta returned my serve with a backhand. It skimmed the net, and made it back onto my side of the court.

I ran up to the ball, pulled my right arm back, had a mental flash of being Lindsay Wagner from the Bionic Woman, and hauled off as hard as I could, the racquet hitting the ball dead center.

The ball went back over the net, over Greta's head, over the back line and kept on going over the fence and onto the busy street.

Greta and I stared at each other.

"We don't have anymore balls." Greta said. "You lost three of them today."

I giggled. "It's my bionic arm."

Sue got up from the bleachers. "Hi girls."

"Hi Mom."

"Hi Sue."

"Can Christy come over for dinner tonight?"

"I would like that very much, as long as her mom is aware of it."

"Oh, she said it would be okay with her, as long as it's okay with you Sue."

"Good. I've been meaning to talk to you about something Christy."

I panicked. Oh no, what did I do wrong? I don't want Sue upset with me. During Mom's busy season at work, Sue was like a second mom to me.

We started to walk to her olive green station wagon, Greta and I a few steps behind Sue.

"Is your mom mad at me?" Greta shrugged her shoulders.

"I don't think so."

Sue got behind the wheel and lit up a Virginia Slim. I stared at the back of her no-nonsense, Peter Pan hairdo.

While trying not to choke on the thick stream of smoke she exhaled, I asked, "What did you want to talk to me about Sue?" My eyes began to water from the smoke hitting me in the face.

We stopped at a red light, and her eyes looked at me in the back seat from her rear view mirror. "Has your mother spoken to you about wearing a brassiere?"

88

"You mean like a training bra?" I had read about girls wearing them in a Judy Blume book.

The light turned green, and she took her eyes off of me. She began excelerating. "Actually, I think you're much too big for a training bra by now."

I absent-mindedly cupped my boobs. I looked to my right and saw Greta checking out her own chest, still as flat as a board.

Sue continued, "I've been watching you and Greta play tennis for the past two weeks, and you're, well," she flicked her cigarette butt out of the one inch crack in the window, and then rolled it back up, "bouncing all over the court." Sue's voice faded in the back of my head. "I'm quite shocked Jane hasn't noticed."

I wondered myself why my mom hadn't noticed. I folded my arms across my chest; across the thin cotton tank top I was wearing and felt embarrassed.

Greta, clearly bored with a topic that wouldn't include her for years to come asked, "What's for dinner?"

I looked over at Greta. There was nothing there, nothing poking through from under her tank top. Then I thought of the boys at school who all vied with one another to buy me lunch in the cafeteria, allowing me to save my own money. Weren't the boys squabbling among each other, saying it was their turn to marry me in back of the handball courts at recess? Greta was always the minister, never chosen for the bride in our silly little game.

A bra. I was ready for a brassiere. I felt a smile spread across my face. Surely there was nothing to be ashamed of.

The following day, my mom's secretary took me to The May Company, and I purchased my first bra. A bright red, 32B bra in the woman's department.

* * * *

Chanel got out of the water, and flopped her thin body down on a green lounge chair. Her legs fell over the sides, exposing her pussy to anybody that walked by or looked. Her head rolled to the left, her mouth wide open. Her body began to slide down, and I think she passed out.

I wondered if part of the reason for her carefree attitude and easy-going look was attributed to the fact that she seemed to be loaded on some sort of a downer.

Realizing that Chanel was in a deep slumber, I picked up my suitcase and headed to the wardrobe room.

I found the door Ron had pointed at and opened it.

A guy with a tight, toned and tan body was hanging up a black leather garment bag in the buff.

I had never seen such a firm, smooth ass before. Not a tan line in sight.

Hearing me enter, he turned around. "Hi. My name is Peter North." He lit up the room with his thousand-watt smile. "Did I leave you enough room for your clothes?"

I nodded, and stood rooted, with star-struck eyes, like when I was a nine-year-old Camp Fire Girl and got to meet David Cassidy.

"What's your name?"

"Christy Canyon."

"Oh yeah, Jim told me about you. You're the new girl who finally decided to make films. In fact, I think I'm working with you tomorrow." He scanned the first page of his script. "Yeah, with Ginger outside."

"I get to work with you?" I couldn't believe my luck.

"Yeah, I hope you don't mind." With the goofy way I was acting, I don't think he knew what to think of me.

"No! Not at all, it's just that the other day I worked with a guy named Ron, and, well, I just figured the actors in this business weren't so young." And hunky.

"Oh yeah, Ron's a cool guy."

We both let it drop at that.

I wondered if there were more like him out there.

"Can I just tell you one thing Christy," Deep concern set in his brown eyes. "It's really the only thing you have to know about me in a sex scene."

"Of course you can tell me." Maybe he was going to tell me that he easily formed a crush on girls that looked like me.

"Do not touch my hair."

"Your hair?"

"My hair." He glanced in the mirror. "It takes me a long time to get my hair like this, and if anybody touches it in a sex scene, I lose all of my concentration."

I didn't want that on my conscience. "I promise you Peter, I will not touch your hair. Anything above your shoulders actually."

"Thanks!" His smile was back. "I'm going to take a shower and go home. I'll see you tomorrow."

"Are you done for the day?"

"Yeah, I worked this morning with Traci."

"Oh. Who's she?"

"Traci Lords, the set nympho, and the cold as ice bitch."

This was getting more interesting by the minute.

Peter left me in the room, and I thought about how cute he was.

I put my overnight bag on the ground, and thought about what a bizarre morning it had been so far. But certainly not in a bad way, it was almost comical.

I pulled my red terry cloth robe out of my suitcase and undressed. Wanda would kill me if I walked into hair and makeup without a robe on. She was always telling me how unflattering indentation marks on the body from clothes looked on camera.

I hung up my dress, bra and underwear on a wooden hanger to the right of Peter's black garment bag.

I had a better feeling being on this set, than I had on the set of the loop. The cast and crew were younger, nicer and the house had a cozy feel to it, even if Father was a pervert. I would just have to stay away from the grasp of his paws. I had warded off more than him before.

I was just about to slip into my robe when I heard a knock at the door.

"Come in." A good-looking man in his mid thirties walked in.

"Hi you must be Christy. I'm Michael the producer of these two movies that you're in." He stuck his hand out.

"I'm so glad that I was able to get you to be in my movies. Jim told me that this was only the second shoot that you've been on, and I want you to feel comfortable. If there is anything I can do, just let me know."

"Thank you. Has anybody ever told you that you resemble Mel Gibson?"

Michael laughed, "I think I've heard that once or twice. Well, I just wanted to welcome you here. Is there anything I can get for you?"

"No, just tell me where Wanda is set up for makeup."

"Out this door, and two doors down on the left."

"Thanks."

"No problem Christy." He closed the door and left without ever taking his eyes off of my face.

I slipped my robe on, and thought that he was kind of cute too.

Peter and Michael, so far, so good.

I left the solitude of the wardrobe room in search of Wanda. I was also curious about the others on the set today. I walked the short distance to Wanda's room, and opened the door.

The guest bathroom was set up for hair and makeup. Several sets of hot rollers were plugged in, various shades of all types of makeup were lined up on the beige counter tiles and a petite blonde was sitting in Wanda's makeup chair, naked and spread eagle. Each leg was resting on the arms of the director's chair.

She was applying a layer of a white, paste like substance on her pubic hair. She was painting with such passion, as if she were creating the next Mona Lisa.

She looked at me through the reflection in the mirror, after her final stroke with the brush. "Hi! My name is Ginger Lynn. What's your name?"

She had striking big blue eyes.

"Hi. I'm Christy." This girl was so cute. Like a California beach bunny.

She twisted her torso towards me, careful not to move her hips, legs and crotch. "Oh! Jim's told me so much about you. It's so nice to finally meet you." Her pixie face and smile reminded me of a high school cheerleader, not a porn star. "It looks like we'll be working together today and tomorrow." She began fanning her pubic area with her hand, and blowing air through her lips down there.

Maybe this was normal. Happy and naked people running around, and I was just out of it; prude, shy and inexperienced. They were all so excited and full of positive energy. I wanted to be like them, yet I found myself cinching the tie around my robe even tighter. "I've never been with a girl before."

Ginger stopped blowing, and her hand stopped waving. "Never?" Her big blue eyes were round with shock. "Not even in your personal life?"

"No." Was that so unusual for an eighteen-year-old?

"Wow. That's amazing, I'll be your first." She got a far-away look in her eyes.

I guess it was unusual.

"Well, don't worry Christy, I'll be extra gentle with you today." She resumed fanning her crotch. The sparkle was back in her eyes, "Don't worry, this will be dry long before our scene." She giggled, " I've got to have the top match the bottom color."

"What is that stuff anyway?"

"A blonde booster. I just got back from three weeks of shooting on location in Hawaii, and the sun and saltwater made the hair on my head lighter than the hair on my pussy." Concern set in her eyes. "But don't misunderstand me, I am a natural blonde."

"Oh I can tell." Actually, I couldn't tell. "Where's Wanda?"

"She'll be right back, she just had to touch up Janey Robbin's makeup on the set. I think the guy came on her face, and then she had to do some dialogue after the scene."

Came on her face? "Why did he come on her face?"

Ginger looked at me like I was a total idiot. "Didn't anybody tell you?"

"No, what?" I wanted to learn as much as I could. I'm not sure why, since this was going to be my last video. Wasn't it?

"The guy always comes on the girl. Tits, pussy, ass, face, it's called the money shot. Without an external come shot, the sex scene is a total waste." Her voice was very business like.

"Oh, I see." But I really didn't.

"Oh, one more thing, Wanda put the douches in the master bathroom.

You'll find them in a white plastic bag with the Fleet enemas."

Enemas? I remembered my mom putting one of those up my rear when I was five and constipated. Why did they need those awful things on a set? I didn't dare ask, for I knew it would all make sense sooner or later. Actually, I could ask Wanda in private, when I was alone with her.

"Thanks."

"Just to let you know, I like the taste of Summer Rain." Ginger licked her lips, "What flavor do you want to taste on me?"

Was she flirting with me? "Oh, the same." I hadn't a clue as to what she was talking about. Flavors?

"I'm going to wash this off now, then we really should run some dialogue Christy."

"Oh sure Ginger, just come and find me when you're ready."

Ginger jumped off the chair, and into the shower.

I sat in Wanda's chair, and wondered why such an adorable girl got into porno.

A few minutes later, Wanda walked in. "You're here! Your scene is up after this one, so we'd better get started on you."

"I met Peter North and Ginger Lynn already. They are so good looking, I can't figure out why they would be in this business."

"Well you're good looking and you're in it."

"Yeah, right, not like them. Those two are like Ken and Barbi."

"Yes you are, you just don't realize it."

But Wanda already knew the dynamics of this. It didn't matter how good looking you were, if you didn't think so, you were a prime candidate for porn, someone to stroke your bruised ego.

Wanting to get off the subject of my looks I asked, "Wanda, what are the enemas and douches for?"

"Well, when a girl does anal scenes, she need to clean out her rectum first with a enema, or she'll shit all over the guys cock during the scene."

"Oh, I see. Well, I don't do anal."

"And the girls all use the douches before their sex scenes to taste and smell fresh when you go down on each other."

"Oh, I see. I never thought of that." I wondered what a girl smelled and tasted like. Did Summer Rain have a taste? What exactly was Summer Rain anyway?

"Hey, I met that guy Michael, the producer. He's cute."

"He's adorable." Wanda stopped working on my makeup. "You know, you two would be so cute together, and he's single."

"Oh, why would he want to go out with me? He could have anybody he wanted."

"Don't be so hard on yourself kid." Wanda started unrolling my curlers.

Didn't Wanda understand? If my own parents didn't want me, what man would?

A grip poked his head in. "Thirty more minutes Wanda, and we'll need the talent."

After Wanda gave me perfect hair and perfect makeup, I walked down the hallway towards the bright lights set up in the last bedroom on the right. Four more steps and I would be on the second set of a porno film. My second to last as well. I stood in front of the double doors and felt a stream of water gush out of me. It couldn't be my period, I just finished it two weeks ago. I held my knees together and hobbled back to Wanda. "Wanda, something's wrong with me."

"What? What happened?" Wanda put down her ham sandwich and stood up.

My knees were pressed together. "This gallon of water just came out of me." I pointed down below. "Help! What is it?" Wanda could fix any problem.

Wanda licked a piece of mayonnaise from her lip. "Did you douche?"

"Yeah, do you think I was allergic to it?"

"Did you sit on the potty for a minute afterwards?"

"No." I put my hand against the crotch of my cotton panties and rubbed. "I can't work with a problem down there." I could feel tears of frustration. Jim would be pissed with a capital "P" if I backed out at the last minute.

"So you didn't let the liquid drain out then?"

"What?" I looked at my hand. No sign of blood, just clear and, I sniffed the hand. "It smells like baby powder."

"Always sit on the toilet after you douche, so it drains properly." She was eyeballing the thick sandwich.

"Oh." Boy there was a lot to that birds and bees talk I never got. "Thanks Wanda." I turned around to leave and panicked again. "Oh God, I used the baby powder scent, Ginger asked for the Summer Rain."

Wanda had a piece of ham between her lips. "She won't even notice." She sucked in and the ham was gone. So was I.

Two steps away from the door and I heard "ACTION". I crept to the door and ran into Michael.

"After a few minutes of Ginger blowing Jamie, I want you to enter and join them." He put his finger to his mouth. "I'll just whisper your entrance."

I could feel my heart racing. It wasn't from a sexual charge, yet it wasn't from fear either. Nerves, but not dread. I could hear the clock ticking to my right. Several more ticks, and my few minutes would be up. Then what? Then I would join a guy and a girl in a three-way sex scene. A girl, now that peaked my interest. The guy I could do without, at least that

94

one. Peter on the other hand was a different story. At least I got to work with him tomorrow. I felt a smile spread across my face and wondered if that was from excitement. I looked up at Ginger, her mouth taking in every inch of Jamie's dick. Her lips moved up and down, her ass and now blonde pussy were partially in my direction. What would it feel like to be with a girl? Ken, the grip told me to keep my heels on during the scene. "It shapes your legs and really turns the viewer on." The nail on the right heel was showing, what if I stab her with it by accident? I knew I should have gotten a new pair.

"Christy, we're ready for you." Michael was waving me onto the set.

I stood rooted on the green shag carpet.

Michael kept on waiving. "Come on, you're up."

I took two steps forward.

Michael's arm radius got bigger with each wave. "Yeah, you can join them now."

Ginger kept giving Jamie head but averted her eyes in my direction and turned the corners of her lips up in a smile.

That was all I needed. Ginger wanted me.

I climbed on the bed and began kissing Jamie. Somebody put their hands on my boobs. Gingers were still on Jamie, so that left Jamie's hands on me.

Ginger whispered, "Sit on him." She smiled at me again.

Where do I sit? She was still on his dick. Did that mean I sat on her mouth on his dick? My God this was confusing with three people.

"Get on his face." Somebody whispered.

I squatted on his face and felt his wet tongue inside of me. I also felt a charlie-horse in my left leg. Without moving my lips I said, "This is uncomfortable."

Again, a whisper came from the room. "Then let Jamie fuck you."

I didn't care about HIM, I wanted Ginger. I got off Jamie's face and laid down on the bed. Stomach first.

"Oh, so you like doggie-style?" Jamie asked.

I froze and felt Jamie go behind me and pry my legs open. "Dog?" And for some odd reason I thought about a white dog we had when I was in elementary school named Loki. Mom said it meant crazy in Spanish. The dog did go crazy one day and bit three kids on our block. The neighbors circulated a petition and we had to put Loki to sleep.

Jamie hooked his arm under my stomach, and tried to hoist me up.

Having none of that, I stayed flat on my stomach.

Jamie sighed and found his way inside of me, but not very well. I could hear a chuckle in the room and somebody whisper, "Turn her over."

With beads of sweat on his brow, Jamie managed to get me into a new position never taking his dick out of me.

This didn't feel to bad, but what a strange position. I was balancing on my right elbow and ankle. I looked up and saw Ginger playing with herself. She looked at me and winked. I moaned and Jamie, obviously thinking it was for him, moved faster inside of me.

Michael smiled and gave me a thumbs up.

Wanda came in and stood in the corner. She smiled and rubbed her right tit for encouragement.

Jamie pulled out of me and Ginger reached over to kiss me. My lips were sealed shut.

"Open your mouth and let me feel your tongue." She reached down and touched my clit.

My mouth flew open and she slid her tongue deep inside my mouth. I slid my tongue inside her mouth and felt my body explode with sexual excitement. I was French-kissing a girl! I reached up to feel her boobs. So soft and small in my hand, unlike anything I had ever experienced. I could feel the onset of an orgasm when I was so rudely interrupted. "Ginger, sit on my cock."

Ginger slowly took her tongue out of my mouth, and with her eyes never leaving mine, she lowered herself on his cock.

I sat and watched her gliding up and down on his cock, feeling like a third wheel.

The whisper was back. "Sit on his face."

I positioned myself this time so some of my weight was distributed to my hands. I was poised over his face but didn't feel a thing.

Jamie whispered, "Move down a couple of inches Christy."

I looked down and saw that I was about a foot away from his mouth. I lowered my body and felt him. Target reached.

Ginger looked at me and whispered, "I want Christy."

I jumped off of Jamie as fast as I could, nearly scratching his cheek with my bad heel.

"I'm going to lay down, and I want you to '69' me."

I recalled doing that once in eleventh grade with a boy, and climbed over her body. I felt her hands open me up, and then I felt electricity. Her tongue was moving in and around my clit.

I stuck the tip of my tongue against her clit, and wiggled it back and forth. She began making small circles against my clit, so I did the same to hers. I felt her finger slip inside me, and I did the same to her. If what she was doing to me felt so good, then it must feel good on her too. And then I felt a tsunami of an orgasm explode and pulsate on her finger. My body racked with aftershocks. I had just come from a girl eating me out.

Jamie's face came into view and I remembered that I was on a movie set.

"I'm going to fuck Ginger's ass now."

96

I felt a tinge of jealousy until I realized that I got to do this again with her tomorrow. And that cute Peter too.

Jamie began screwing Ginger's ass. This was something else new to me. I had never seen a guy go into a girl's rear. I wasn't even aware that people did this. It looked like it would hurt like hell, but Ginger was moaning away.

Ginger was on her stomach and I looked at her small back and shoulder blades. Her smooth tan skin was flawless with her blonde hair cascading down her back. She was beautiful.

I looked over at Wanda who was air clapping for me.

I glanced at Michael. He was giving me the okay sign.

The grips looked like they wanted a nap.

Maybe this wasn't so bad after all. Jamie pulled out and gave us the money shot, all over my left cheek and Ginger's back.

Ewe! I bent my head down and wiped it on the bedspread. His cum stank, just like he did right now.

But not Ginger, she smelled like a rose garden. I wondered what perfume she was wearing when Michael yelled, "It's a wrap!"

The cameraman yelled, "Lunchtime!" And the crew ran out like rats.

"You were great Christy." Ginger said. "I'm going to tell Jim to book you on my next movie."

I didn't mention that this was my last. Was it?

Never one to pass up a free meal, I ate lunch with the cast and crew outside.

"So, what did you think?" Michael asked.

"It was fun. I had never been with a girl before."

His eyebrows shot up. "Never?"

Why did people always react like that?

"So, are you going to switch to girls after being with Ginger?"

Boy he was good looking. "Never."

The P.A. broke the moment. "Your call time is ten tomorrow Christy. We're going to do all of your dialogue so read and memorize the script."

I smiled at Michael. "Okay. No sex tomorrow?"

"Naw, we'll do both of your sex scenes the last day. Peter can only work a half day. He forgot he had a scene in the morning somewhere else." The grip flipped through some pages on his clipboard. "Cool. See you at ten."

"Doesn't that ruin your schedule Michael?"

He put his face into the sun. "No, it's just porn."

"You know, I'm not a great actress." I felt the sun on my face. "In fact, I'm not even a good actress." I opened one eye to see if he was mad. His eyes were still closed against the rays. "Actually, I can't act at all."

"Who cares, It's just porn."

97

Driving home, I thought about all of my new experiences today and all at once I wasn't dreading the next two days. Actually, I couldn't wait for my call time tomorrow.

I fell asleep with out reading my script.

Nine forty-five and I was pulling into the driveway for day two.

"You're early." The P.A. looked at his watch and scratched his head. "That's a first."

I helped myself to the stack of pancakes. "Will you pass the syrup Wanda?" Ten of us sat around the kitchen table, talking like we were old friends. Ginger was telling us about how she was going to cross over into mainstream acting. "So I have this agent who said I would be perfect for a new show coming out next Spring on ABC."

"You wont leave the adult business will you?" I found myself missing her already.

"Well Christy, I'm a real actress and I need to move on."

"Ginger." The P.A. came in with the clipboard, "You're first up, so when you're done with breakfast, get into hair and makeup." He studied the page. "Looks like you're getting fucked by two guys in this scene."

I was sure ABC wouldn't be too pleased about that.

"Okay, thanks Bill."

I finally knew the P.A.'s name.

I finished my breakfast talking to my fellow actors. Everybody seemed so at ease here, waiting for their turn in Wanda's makeup chair, and then, their sex scene or two for the day.

I on the other hand only had to do dialogue today.

Michael pulled up to the set around eleven, just as I was shoving the last piece of pancake into my mouth. "So, did you learn your lines?"

I froze and felt the syrup drip down my chin. I knew I forgot to do something important last night. "Oh sure, got it memorized." I swallowed the last of my breakfast down in one lump. Michael would be so pissed at me and then he would tell Jim who would also be pissed at me. I smiled at Michael. "I'm going to get ready." I made a mad dash for Wanda's room.

"My agent told me that I had to stop making adult films and enroll in a top acting school." Ginger shut her trap so Wanda could apply a lip-liner. "He said with my looks and talent, I would make it big in Hollywood."

I wasn't sure how long she would ramble on about herself so I broke into their one sided conversation. "Do either of you have a copy of the script?"

Ginger smiled, "I have one in my black leather bag you may borrow." She pointed to her bag on the ground to her right. Wanda was applying something on her, so Ginger just pointed to the left.

"Thanks Ginger." I grabbed the script and tried to remember my character's name.

I went back into the kitchen and saw a guy and a girl laying out by the pool naked. I envied them and their ability to feel so free with their bodies. I took two steps closer when a voice interrupted me. "Why don't you join them?"

I turned around and saw Peter North. He was even cuter today than yesterday. "I thought you were off today."

"I was, but the girl I was going to work with cancelled, so here I am."

I thought of two things. "Why did she cancel?"

"The director said her husband found out what she was doing everyday, so her career came to an abrupt halt."

"Her husband didn't know?" And then I thought about my parents. They knew what their baby girl was doing, why didn't they make me stop?

"Yeah I guess she told him she was a Sears catalogue model."

The thought of my parents put a damper on my excitement of seeing Peter, so I went to my second thought. "Does that mean we get to have our sex scene today?"

"Yeah, as long as Michael can arrange it. He didn't think I was going to be here."

I felt panic and excitement. "We were just going to shoot my dialogue stuff today." I took a good look at Peter's face and body and excitement won out. I thought of the script and panicked.

"I'm going to find Michael and tell him I'm here. I'll see you by the pool Christy."

"Okay." But was it okay for me to be naked out there? I stepped onto the patio and felt the warm sunshine on my body. Just like yesterday talking to Michael. I walked over to an empty lounge chair, sat down on it and looked around. Nobody was watching me, so I took my dress off and laid back on the lounge chair and began looking at Gingers script. She had highlighted all of her parts with a pink highlighter, and wrote out the cast of characters with who played whom on the front page. I said a silent thanks to Ginger for being so organized and found my name written by the character Louise.

"You're going to get funny tan lines if you keep your bra and underwear on." Michael was standing above me smiling. "Listen, Peter's here, so we're going to do your dialogue scene in the boat on the lake and then go into your three-way sex scene with him and Ginger. How does that sound?"

"It sounds fine."

"I'll come and get you in thirty minutes so Wanda can start on your hair and makeup."

"I think Wanda has a crush on you." I loved starting trouble.

"I think I have a crush on you." He turned and walked away.

My heart was racing. I knew I had a crush on him, but he had one on me? He had to be kidding. I looked down at my large white cotton panties and sturdy bra. Now there was no way I could take these off and lay out here naked. What kind of girl would he think I was?

Thirty minutes later, Bill woke me up. "Miss Canyon, Wanda is ready for you."

Somewhere in the last thirty minutes, Gingers perfect script had blown into the pool, face down, and I didn't know what the boat scene was or one word of dialogue.

I sat in Wanda's chair, and Bill scrounged up another script for me.

Wanda began working on my face. "Christy, I need your full attention."

The only thing I saw of the script, was my name at the top. So there was a script for me after all, I thought as I chucked it on the floor.

Peter sat across from me in the boat on the man-made lake.

"Do you know your lines?" Michael asked.

I looked into the water and shook my head no.

"Do you know any of it?"

I kept shaking my head no.

"The opening line at least?"

I kept on shaking.

"Bill, go grab a pad of paper, a pen and some tape." Michael said.

"Okay boss."

I looked up at Michael for the first time and he was still smiling at me. "J.D., I want you to shoot this in close-ups only. No wide angles for this scene."

The cameraman looked up from his camera perplexed. "What? You don't want one double shot of the two of them?"

"Not unless you want to catch Christy's dialogue taped on Peters forehead." He smiled and said. "Let's shoot this thing."

So, there I sat in a boat, the camera inches away from my face and my dialogue taped all over Peters face on baby blue paper.

Nine tries later and it was a wrap.

I walked back to the house, my heels sinking into the grass with each step.

Michael caught up to me. "You did great."

I stopped walking and sunk four inches. "Are you crazy? I can't act my way out of a paper bag." I pulled a heel out of the grass and tried to regain an inch or two.

"Only crazy about you." That killer smile was back again.

I held my hand up to my forehead to block out the sun. I opened my mouth to say something. What, I didn't know, when J.D. broke in.

"Hey Michael, we're going to light the next scene."

Never taking his green eyes off of me he answered, "I'll help you."

J.D. and Michael walked back to the house and I stood rooted into the soil unsure of why he liked me.

"Okay." J.D. said. "Ginger and Peter start off on the lounge chair." J.D. looked around and found Ginger looking at herself in the reflection of a sliding door. "Ginger, let's start with you going down on Peter. Christy, we'll give you a cue, then you join in the fun."

Fun? I took a look at Peter and Ginger. Yeah, I think fun would cover it. I could see Michael watching me from the corner of my eye. I looked down and saw clumps of dirt and a few blades of grass stuck on my heels. I sat down on a chair and took my shoes off. I heard Ginger's sweet voice say something to Peter, but by the time I looked up, she already had her mouth wrapped around his cock sliding up and down. I focused in on her pretty pink g-string undies and looked between my legs at my ugly large cotton ones. I made a mental note to buy some new ones. Making sure nobody, Michael in particular, was looking at me, I slid out of my undies and cleaned the heels of my pumps with them.

"We're ready for you Christy." J.D. whispered.

I chucked the mud-stained undies under the chair and walked up to the lounge chair. Ginger was stroking his cock and licking his balls at the same time. "Come and join us." Ginger's voice cooed. God she was so cute. Ginger moved his rock hard cock in my direction. I bent down on the lounge chair and began giving Peter a blow-job. His cock filled my mouth and I felt myself get wet. My lips didn't go down as far as Ginger's had and I wondered if he realized that compared to her, I was very inexperienced. I reached down and felt his balls which were hard and moist from Ginger's saliva. I had never touched this part of a man before. I tried to go deeper on his cock. I wanted to be like Ginger, and take all of him in my mouth. I felt the hot sun beating down on my bare ass sticking up towards the sky, as I took another inch of him. I felt my eyes begin to water and my throat begin to constrict. Oh God, Wanda would kill me if my mascara began to run. I gagged and eased up a few inches on his now not so hard cock. I kept my lips moving up and down on the top three inches of his cock. Ginger, the pro that she was, came to my rescue. "I want to feel Peter's cock with you." She whispered and began stroking him back to his full attention. Her hand glided up and down on his shaft and I backed up a few inches. I guess it was her turn to take over. I could see Michael laughing to himself in a chair to my right and I felt out of place. Why was it that my co-stars kept losing their erections with me?

J.D.'s voice whispered, "Why don't you start fucking her now."

I didn't know which "her" he meant until Peter guided me onto my back and spread my legs open. I laid back and felt the tip of his cock enter me, and I pushed my hips up several inches wanting to feel all of him inside me. As I wrapped my arms around his bare back, I could feel the heat of the sun on his skin. I held his body in close to me and wrapped my legs around him as well. Just as I was about to have a major orgasm, Peter whispered in my ear, "The camera can't see anything with our bodies so close to each other."

Cameras? For a few minutes, I forgot people were all around us. Peter tried to lift his body up several inches but I was determined to come first. I looked over his shoulder at his tight ass pushing his cock deep into me, and held it down so I could grind my clit against him for a second. Then I felt it begin. My body began to convulse and I let out a moan as I came all over his beautiful cock buried inside me. Before I had time to bask in the afterglow of a great orgasm, Peter had flipped me over on the chair and began doing me from behind. Since I was sixteen and lost my virginity, I had never had sex in this position. Now, I have been screwed like this three times in twenty-four hours.

Maybe there were things I could learn about sex from making these films. But then again, after tomorrow, I told Jim under no circumstances was I going to do another one.

I thought of my three-day paycheck, the major orgasm I just had and the idea of having sex with Ginger again.

Maybe I would tell Jim just one more film.

I was bent over the chair, barely aware that Peter was still pounding away, when I felt something hot and wet spraying all over my lower back. I looked back and saw Gingers petite hand jerking the last drops of cum out of his cock. She bent down, stuck her tongue out as far as she could, and began licking his semen off me.

Her eyes were on me, but her tongue was for the camera.

I straightened up and Peter began kissing me with the tip of his tongue, no lip lock involved. My eyes were on Ginger, but my kissing was for the camera.

I was beginning to understand how this worked.

My tongue still connecting with Peters tongue, Ginger began kissing my boobs.

I would definitely tell Jim just one or two more films.

"It's a wrap." Michael yelled and made a beeline for me. "Are you going to stay for lunch?"

"Depends on what you're serving." I tried to be so cute, but actually, I would have stayed no matter what was served.

"I think today is lasagna, but tell me what you want tomorrow and I'll make sure it's served."

We were interrupted by a voice to our left. "What the fuck is this?" Bill had my dirt stained undies hanging from the tip of his pen. He was inspecting them a few inches from his face.

"I happen to love lasagna." I hooked Michael's arm in mine, wanting to get him away from Bill and my undies. "Let's eat."

I could see a grip join Bill and I steered Michael into the house.

After lunch, I packed up and headed to my car.

"Hey wait!" Michael came out of the house. "You didn't tell me what you wanted for lunch tomorrow."

I got in my car and unrolled the window. "I want lasagna again."

"You're easy."

I started my car. "Only when it comes to food." I shifted into reverse and backed out of the driveway.

Next stop was Bullocks for some cute underwear.

My call time was eleven but I didn't want to miss breakfast on the set so I arrived at ten. I pulled into the driveway and was disappointed that Michael's car wasn't there yet. Scrambled eggs, bacon and bagels were on the menu today. I couldn't believe how well they fed us on sets.

By ten thirty, I was out by the pool soaking up the sun. I kept my new undies on, but braved it topless. I laid back, closed my eyes and thought about work. Good sex, good money and good food. Maybe this job wasn't so bad after all.

Bill woke me up. "I hate to wake you up, but it's eleven fifteen and Wanda's ready for you."

I wiped the drool from my cheek and looked down. Forty-five minutes of sun, and for the first time, I no longer had tan lines on my boobs.

"We're going to start with your girl-girl scene with Ginger."

"What guy is with us today?" Maybe there were more cute ones like Peter.

"Nobody, it's just you and Ginger."

Oh my God, I finally get her all to myself.

"Then we'll shoot your sex scene with Mark right after that." He looked at his paperwork. "And then you're done."

I felt a little sad that it was coming to an end.

I formed an instant bond with the people on this set. I had become one of them.

After hair and makeup, I went into the bathroom to find the box of douches. I made sure I found Gingers favorite flavor 'Summer Rain' and took two. I was just about to sit on the toilet when I heard a familiar noise from junior high school. The flick of a Bic lighter and then water bubbling. I looked to my right and saw a figure hunched over behind the frosted glass shower door.

I walked over to the shower door. "Who's in there?"

The door opened from the inside. Sitting in the tub was a thin white naked body. He smiled at me with red, glassy eyes. A trail of smoke escaped his thin lips. He released one hand from around his red bong and held it out.

"Hi, I'm," he coughed and sputtered for the next minute. I held on to my box of douches fascinated at the odd sight in front of me. He withdrew his hand and held it up to his mouth. He finally managed to eek out through bouts of coughing, "I'm Marc Wallace." He gave me a stoned smile and bent his head back over the bong. His right hand fired up a lighter and he wrapped his lips around the top of the bong and sucked in deep. Water began bubbling in the bong, and a trail of smoke began to rise. His back hunched over further as the smoke filled his lungs. I began to count the vertebrae on his spine when he looked at me and held the bong in my direction.

"No thanks."

The smile never left his face as he began to slide the shower door closed again.

As stoned as he looked, I didn't think he would mind if I sat on the toilet and douched. I sat long enough for the water to drip out of me and wondered if that was the same Mark I had a scene with later in the day.

I left the smoke filled bathroom and felt hungry. I think I had a slight case of contact high.

I was smearing the last bit of cream cheese on my bagel when Ron walked in. "Hey Ron, I just met a guy named Mark Wallace, do you know if that's who I'm working with today?"

Ron put down his light stand. "Yes, he's a very nice boy. All of the ladies enjoy working with him."

"He seems very nice." Should I tell Ron what I saw?

"He's stoned twenty four hours a day."

It was the end of the day and Michael was writing my check. "Can I give you some advice?"

"Sure." I was going to miss seeing him everyday.

"Don't spend every dime you make. Save it."

"I will." And I was saving a large portion of each paycheck I got. "I'm pretty good about saving my money." I had seen my mom struggle raising two kids with no money from my dad. I had learned the value of money and what it represented. Freedom.

"You want to have fuck you money."

"What's that?"

"It's where you have so much money you can tell everybody to fuck off." He handed me my check. "One more thing."

I was still trying to understand what fuck you money was. "Yeah?"

"Do you want to go to dinner sometime?"

I felt an adrenaline rush through my body. "I would love to."

Driving home from my shoot for Paradise Visuals, I began to think about the last three days.

I had never come so much and felt so free doing it. Nobody seemed to care, or notice how loud I moaned and groaned, or how hard my body shook with each orgasm I released. In my personal life, with the hand full of men I had been with, I was always embarrassed to let loose when I climaxed. I never wanted the guy to think I was some sex-crazed maniac, so I stifled my orgasms. But over the last three days, I realized how much fun it was to just enjoy sex. I thought of my girl-girl sex scene with Ginger and I felt a bolt of electricity between my legs. She had positioned our bodies at the end, so our pussies were touching and rubbing against each other's. She had called it the scissors position. Our legs were spread apart and our bodies were close together, our pussies were touching, clit to clit. Ginger was grinding hers deep and hard into mine, I pushed back, feeling my clit, lips and pubic hair mixing with hers. The feel of her body connecting with mine, and the thought of having lesbian sex was the most erotic feeling in the world. I climaxed all over her as she held my body and kissed my lips.

Three more miles on the freeway and I would be at the Van Nuys Blvd. exit. The exit for World Modeling. I looked at my paycheck and moved over one lane to the right.

I thought of my sex scene with Marc Wallace and moved over one more lane.

My scene with him was for another movie we were shooting, "On Golden Blond." His lithe body joined me in bed, his mouth, which reeked of weed began kissing my neck and boobs. As stoned as he was, and as glazed as his eyes were, there was something so sexy about Marc. His mouth began making its way between my legs, stopping long enough to linger on my stomach. I raised my hips, just wanting to feel his tongue between my legs. Fuck the foreplay, I was about to come without him even touching my clit. I felt so free and turned on. A basic stranger was about to have wild, passionate sex with me. His tongue finally found its way and I instantly climaxed.

I looked at the clock on my dashboard and moved over one more lane. I was at the off ramp for World Modeling.

I pulled into the parking lot and sat in my car. I would tell Jim just one more movie but only for a fun company like Paradise not for Caballero.

I began taking the stairs two at a time.

Jim was positioned behind his desk, surrounded by open photo books filled with Polaroids of naked ladies. "Well Hello darlin'" A balding man sitting opposite Jim turned around.

His hairless face, adorned with liverspots checked me out from head to toe. "I want her in my film." He smiled, showing me a set of small, brown chipped teeth.

105

"This here, my friend Harold, is Christy Canyon." Jim lit up a cigarette. "But, I'm sorry to say that she no longer makes films, my good man."

"But I want her." He stood up and walked around me. "uh-huh." I heard from behind me. "Yep, she'll be perfect for the sex scene in 'Flesh and Ecstasy'." He folded his arms and rested them on his tummy. "Name your price for one scene. A three way with Nicole West and Nick Niter."

"Harold, you weren't listening, Christy quit making films."

"Twelve hundred dollars." I told this funny little creature.

Jim dropped his smoke. "What? I thought you told me that under no circumstances would you ever do films again."

"Well," I wondered if Nicole was as cute as Ginger. "Can I see Nicole's photo?"

Jim whipped the book around, his eyes never leaving mine. "What made you change your mind?"

"Well," I saw her photo. Not as cute as Ginger, but nothing to sneeze at either. "When are you shooting this film?"

The creature answered, "In two days." He took a strand of my hair between his yellow stained fingers. "Oh yes, you're perfect."

Jim broke in, "Are you sure you want to do this?"

"Yeah, lets take it one film at a time for now."

I left Jim's office with directions to a location in the hills of Encino. I got in my car and headed to the bank to deposit my fuck you money.

I had found my new home in life. I found people just like me. Misfits.

13

I came home from my two-hour day of shooting "Flesh and Ecstasy" and took a good look at the dump I was living in. The very place that had once been my sanctuary, while earning minimum wage, was now well below my standards, while earning thousands of dollars a week.

Walking into the bathroom, I turned on the lights and saw my roommates scamper into the cracks in the wall. I was sick of seeing those filthy cockroaches.

I walked into my bedroom and pulled up the blinds, all half of what was left on them, and saw a bum passed out under my window. I was tired of not being able to open my window during the heat wave we were having. Would it have killed the owner to install air conditioning units?

I opened my front door, which led into the hallway, and saw the tail of a rat slide under the door into a utility closet across the hall.

I turned on my TV, and sat on the complimentary couch that came with the apartment. I had finally had enough of that familiar coil climbing up my ass.

I reached for the telephone.

"Hi Jim, it's me."

"What's wrong?"

"What do you mean?" I heard the junkie take a tumble to the floor above me.

"The shoot today?" Panic was now in his voice. "Did you make it there?"

"Yeah, my sex scene was the first shot of the day." I heard gunfire not too far from the alley in back. "I was in and out." I chuckled at the pun.

"Well," Jim paused. "Was it okay?"

"Yeah, I actually had fun." I could hear police sirens in the distance.

"And."

"I think I'm ready to do another one." The sirens were a block away, getting closer.

"Well," I heard Jim suck in his breath. "I went ahead and booked you on another shoot in two days."

I looked out my living room window and saw the bum taking a leak against the wall. "How many days is it?"

"Two and a half days. The partial day is for half your rate because it's just some quick dialogue."

I did a quick calculation in my head and heard a cop over a loud speaker. "Put your hands behind your head and get on the ground." Two and a half days equaled three thousand dollars. "I'll take it."

Jim finally let out his breath. "You're an angel."

I locked my window and closed the drapes. "Who am I working with?"

"The diva herself requested you. Miss Traci Lords."

I hoped she was as cute as Ginger Lynn. "I'll be by tomorrow to get the directions." I heard the choppers flying above. "I gotta go."

I grabbed my car keys and went in search of a new home.

It was time to move.

Two days later, I got off the freeway in Woodland Hills and found the location. A Tudor mansion was alive with crewmen hustling about. "I have to bring in that other chair. Lords said the one she's using hurts her ass."

"She's an ass if you ask me." A grip said under his breath.

"Are you kidding Jake?" He put down the large red padded chair he was carrying. "I would bark like a dog if she asked me too."

"You're just a kiss ass Luke." Jake muttered.

Luke had a dreamy look in his eyes. "I would if she asked me too."

A man yelled from the doorway. "Where's the fucking chair? Traci said if it's not under her ass in thirty seconds she's walking!"

Luke picked up the chair, "Coming Boss."

The man walked over to me and smiled. "You must be Christy."

"Hi, nice to meet you."

"I'm Boyle, the director. Follow me and I'll show you where hair and makeup is." He wiped his nose. "Do you want any blow?"

What I wanted was breakfast. "No thanks, maybe later." The breakfast buffet had bacon, eggs and a fruit platter.

"Suit yourself, but if you change your mind." He patted his shirt pocket.

"I'll let you know."

He led me down a hallway nearly tripping over his own feet, which couldn't keep up with his mouth. "These three days will be a blast. I've got a great crew here and the crew really..." Blah, blah blah, he went on about nothing until we finally reached the last door. "Here we are, I'll come and check on you later." He opened the door. "We'll be having deli sandwiches for lunch, so let Jake know what you want in the next two hours, he's got a menu and will take your order."

Boyle's coke induced ten-minute talk about lunch was interrupted. "Shut the fucking door and get out of here!"

The girl in the red chair looked at Boyle with cold green eyes. "I hate deli food Boyle. I want Thai food for lunch or you can call it a day."

"Thai it is." Boyle said backing out as fast as he could.

Rachel, the makeup girl asked, "I thought you loved that deli." She sprayed and teased a piece of hair. "Let me know if this hurts."

"I don't feel a thing." Her eyes shifted over to me. "I do like that deli,

108

I just love to make Boyle jump through hoops." Her upper lip rose with each word on the left side. "And he always does." Her lips stopped moving and I noticed they formed a perfect pout.

"I love Thai food." Like she cared. "My name is Chri…"

She cut me off mid-name. "I know exactly who you are." Her eyes watched every move I made. "Tom Byron gets to fuck me today." Her eyes reminded me of a TV show I watched as a kid called The Six Million Dollar Man. His bionic eye could scan and read anything.

Standing in the same spot Boyle left me in, I felt naked in my jeans and T-shirt. Her eyes seemed to read my private thoughts.

With her upper lip curling at each syllable, she continued. "I made a bet with Tom Byron that he couldn't make me come more than three times in our scene today."

I had no idea what to say to that so I just stood still.

"I let Tommy fuck me at home sometimes."

I didn't know who Tom Byron was, but I sure knew who she was. Miss Traci Lords.

Luke popped his head in, "Traci, we'll be ready for you on the set in five minutes." '

Rachel sprayed the last of Traci's hair. "You're ready kiddo." Traci just kept sitting. "Before I started making films, I was a virgin."

"Really?" And I thought I was inexperienced when I started in this business. "Where did you grow up?"

She took a sip of soda through her straw. "Las Vegas."

"Oh, I love Vegas." But I really hated Vegas. It reminded me of horrible trips with my father, driving there in his big black Cadillac.

I said to Traci. "It's always nice and hot there."

Carol, Eve, Clair and I would pile in his car for the long hot drive through the desert while he chain smoked listening to a ball game.

"My sister and I grew up in Los Angeles. Does your family still live there?" I asked Traci.

Dad always locked the windows so there was no escaping his smoke. Driving there, Dad was always in a jovial mood at the thought of gambling, his favorite hobby. His eyes would light up like one of those slot machines. "I can feel it in my bones girls. Daddy's going to win big this time." He said that every time.

"Yes, my family still lives there and I support them."

"You do? That must be tough."

Driving home from those hellish trips, were worse than the drive there.

"How old are you Traci?"

Dad always lost at the tables, slots and even Keno in the coffee shop. "I'll get those assholes next time!" He would scream, pounding the black

109

steering wheel.

"I'm twenty-three. How old are you Christy?"

There was always a next time for these family trips to Vegas. And of course he lost every time.

"I turned eighteen in June."

Dad complained that the blackjack dealer threw his game off. "Did you see that stone cold look that son of a bitch gave me?" He lit up his fifth Benson and Hedges as we got on the freeway to go home; home to Mommy and my pink room. "That fucker knew he was throwing me off."

"Why didn't you change tables Daddy?" I asked through a cloud of smoke.

Dad adjusted his rear view mirror and looked at me in the back seat. "They don't know who they're fucking with." His finger hit the window lock button extra hard.

Yes they did. One of the many gamblers who thought that their next trip was going to pay off that big win. It never came.

Luke popped his head back in. "Uh Traci, I hate to bother you, but we've been waiting for twenty minutes on the set."

Traci stood up and her floral robe slid to the ground. "I'll get there when I'm ready."

Luke stood in the doorway about to say something then closed his mouth.

"Wanna suck my titty?" She held one out to him and pouted her lips.

He looked at his watch and smiled at her. "When ever you're ready, we'll see you on the set." His eyes were glued to her large areolas, just like my eyes were. "Take your time." He backed out of the room and slammed his right shoulder blade against the doorframe.

Traci began putting on a bra and underwear. "Don't you love to fuck with people like that?" She slipped a sundress over her head. "Did you see the look on his face? I bet he'll have a big black bruise by tonight." She began laughing at the way she made him so nervous. "Guys are so pussy whipped. Show them some beaver and titties and they'll do anything for you." She took one last look at herself in the full-length mirror. "I guess I've made them wait long enough."

She stopped at the door and turned around. Her face became angelic, her eyes now soft and warm. "Christy." Her voice was a whisper now. "I can't wait to fuck you after lunch." My heart skipped a few beats at her sultry voice and bedroom eyes. She had to be the sexiest woman I had ever seen, and she wanted me!

I opened my mouth to say something but she was already gone.

Rachel interrupted the trance Traci left me in. "I better get started on you."

I floated into the red chair. "Traci is so sexy."

Rachel began setting my hair in hot rollers. "She's also a chameleon."

Wasn't that a flower? "I like her."

Rachel was working on my makeup, when I heard Traci in the next room. "Is she all right?" It sounded like a child was screaming and crying.

"That's just Traci having one of her famous orgasms.'"

Sitting at the lunch table over a Thai food buffet, the boys were fawning over Traci.

Tom Byron sat on her right. "Traci is the horniest woman alive."

Traci smiled. The left side of her mouth went up much higher than the right side.

Dan T. Man on her left said, "Traci can't get enough, can she?"

Traci stopped eating and pouted her lips. "Dan, will you rub my shoulders? They're sore."

Dan put his fork down, got behind her and began rubbing. "Is this the right spot?"

I had never seen anybody move so fast.

My co-stars Rikki Blake, Candi and I were ignored.

"No." Traci looked at me and winked. "Move to the left."

Like a faithful pup, he did as he was told. "How's this?"

Her eyes were smiling at me. "Fine I guess." Dan's plate of food going cold, Traci began eating again.

Boyle came in wiping his coke filled nose. "Hey Traci, I got a woody just watching your scene."

She ignored him.

With wild eyes, he continued. "I heard about your film last month "Sorority Sisters". He shook his head from right to left. "Did you really fuck all of the extras on the diving board?"

This caught my attention.

Traci was back to spitting nails. "What's it to you?"

"They must have been the talk on campus those lucky bastards."

Her eyes were back to icicles. "You'll never know."

Rikki asked what I wanted to ask. "What happened?"

Tom answered. "We were shooting a college scene, so the director hired twelve extras from U.C.L.A. When I got through with Traci, she still needed more, so she took them on one at a time outside."

"Was it part of the script?" Rikki asked.

"No. I had them for lunch." Traci answered.

She fucked twelve guys for the fun of it? I stared in disbelief, Rikki thought of another question to ask her, Candi kept eating and Dan kept rubbing. Boyle, in the corner snorted another line of coke.

"That's nothing." Traci continued. "When I was in High School at Redondo High,"

Wait a minute. That was in California, not Las Vegas.

"I snuck into the boys locker room after a game and fucked the whole football team." She boasted. "It was how I lost my virginity."

Wait a second. She told me she was a virgin when she got in the adult business.

"Traci, didn't you tell me in the makeup room that you grew up in Las Vegas?"

"I never said that." Her eyes were as cold as ice now.

"Oh," was all I could say. I know what I heard and I knew she was a liar. I just had no idea how deep and dark her web of lies went.

In an instant, her eyes softened. "Are you ready to make me come?" Her baby voice asked me.

I just shook my head up and down and remembered what a chameleon was. It was something like Traci that could completely change in seconds flat.

After lunch, Boyle explained how the scene would go. "So, we'll start off on this loveseat with,"

"No we wont." Traci broke in. "I want it in front of the stone fireplace on the divan." Traci sat down on it, once again, pissing on her territory.

Boyle touched his pocket of cocaine. "Okay." He looked around at the lighting that had already been set up the loveseat. "Guys, lets move the lighting around to the fireplace."

A few grunts and groans and thirty minutes later, the lighting was switched to Traci's request. Boyle emerged from the bathroom with sweat running down his face. "Are we set now?"

Traci looked at him with an over-exaggerated pout.

Boyle pleaded with his eyes that she would be satisfied. "Traci?"

"Lets get going Boyle." Traci snapped. "I don't have all day to wait for you." She scowled which made the upper left portion of her lip curl to an all time high, nearly touching her nostril.

Boyle smiled, regardless of her screaming at him. The queen was happy. "Let's shoot this thing."

Candi and I sat on the divan making idle chitchat until we decide to compare our boobs; normal, every day type of things that girlfriends do. In a porn film that is. I touched Candi and found myself becoming more comfortable with a woman. I took her breasts in my hands, touching, feeling and squeezing. No more was I nervous about being with another woman, now I found myself curious. I wasn't going through the motions with shaky hands like I did with my past lesbian scenes, I found myself enjoying the sensation of touching and being touched by a female. I lowered my mouth to suck on Candi's nipple and saw Traci watching me from the hall off camera. Her lips were pouted, and slightly open. The cameraman moved to the left and I saw that Traci was naked from the waist down, her finger sliding in and out of her pussy.

My lips were almost around Candi's nipple but I didn't want to take my eyes off Traci. With her eyes barely open, her whole body began moving up and down on her finger. I stuck my tongue out as far as I could, hoping it would connect to Candi's skin, not that I really cared. Watching Traci was much more erotic.

Candi began touching me, but I kept my eyes on Traci. Watching her watching me was turning me on. Traci stopped gyrating on her finger and opened her eyes. Without taking her alert eyes off of me, she took her finger out of herself and brought it up to her mouth.

I wasn't sure what part of my body Candi was occupying herself with; I was under Traci's spell. And Traci knew it. Candi asked me something. What, I don't even know. Traci had opened her mouth and slid her finger inside. She began licking and sucking her come, never taking her green eyes off my face.

"Tom, Traci, time to enter." Boyle whispered.

Traci smiled at me and walked onto the set with Tom.

I couldn't believe Traci had just tasted her own come. I had never dreamed of tasting myself. I wondered what I tasted like without the aid of douches. I wondered what any girl tasted like without douching first.

Traci shooed Tom and Candi off the set. It was just she and I. Traci whispered, "I can't wait to make you come." In her right hand she held a dildo. I felt my pussy get wet and I hoped it didn't make a big wet spot on my maroon teddy. Traci would think I was such a beginner. I said a mental thank you to myself for investing in this sexy teddy two nights ago and hoped Traci found it sexy on me. Traci took control of me, spreading my legs wide open.

I had no idea what a dildo felt like. I had seen them, heard about them, but had never used one of them. Yes, I was actually that naive. Traci opened my lips down below, exposing my clit, which was already beginning to throb. She lowered her head and touched my clit with the tip of her tongue making small, delicate circles around it. I pushed my hips up wanting to feel more of her. Traci just moved her head back, keeping the same amount of pressure on my clit. She slid her tongue into my pussy and tongue fucked me while her right index finger took over where her tongue had been.

My head felt light, and I saw colorful dots dancing in front of my eyes. Oh God, was I about to faint? And then I felt the orgasm begin in the tips of my toes. Had I ever felt an orgasm begin that far down in my body before? No. My legs began to shake and I held onto the divan for dear life. Traci put the tip of the dildo in her mouth and then slid it into my pussy. As soon as the tip entered me, I felt my body explode. With each wave of my orgasm, Traci pushed the dildo deeper inside my body.

It was the most orgasmic feeling in the world. Never before had I felt such pleasure, exhaustion and euphoria. Traci took the dildo out of my pussy and began giving it head. My pussy actually hurt from throbbing so hard.

"Now I want you to fuck me with this." She handed it to me and whispered, "Not too hard, my pussy is sore from fucking so much last night." And in some odd way, that turned me on. I had never met somebody who fucked so much. I slowly put the dildo inside of her and began moving it in and out. I wondered whom she fucked last night. Did she have a boyfriend? "Is this too hard?" I whispered. Was she married? Wanting to do what she did to me, I bent down to lick her clit. Instead of being erotic, I managed to jab her in the stomach with my fingernail while breaking my fall over the divan. "Sorry." I mumbled. I was in a semi upside down position, which reminded me of a childhood game I use to play called "Twister". I didn't feel very erotic at the moment. In fact, I felt down right ridiculous, like a baby hippo trying to look and act sexy. I looked down, or was it up from where I was, and realized that the dildo was now sliding in the general vicinity of her thigh and hip. Upside down.

"Kiss me." She demanded.

Grateful to release both of us out of the mess I created, I bent down to kiss her but she whispered in my ear instead. "Just rub your tits on my pussy. That makes me come so fast."

Unsure of how she could still be aroused, I re-grouped my body and rubbed my nipple on her clit.

"Go lower." Traci whispered.

I looked down at my boobs and realized that my nipple was caressing her bellybutton. I inched my body down, found her clit, and resumed my rubbing.

I wasn't sure if I was doing it right until she began moaning. Her hips began moving up and down on my nipple, her voice becoming louder with each thrust until she screamed at the top of her lungs, "I'm coming."

From this?

Out of the corner of my eye, I saw the soundman Chuck throw his head set down, and stick a beefy finger in his ear, jiggling it up and down. He opened his mouth as wide as he could several times before sticking a piece of gum in his mouth and chewing on it. I remembered doing this once when an airplane was landing and my ears popped.

Traci pulled my face into hers and began kissing me. I felt her tongue slide around in my mouth, around my gums and on my teeth. I soon forgot about the soundman and his popped eardrum. I let her explore my mouth and felt myself becoming turned on again. I hoped Traci would use that dildo on me again and this time, I didn't want to come so fast. I wanted to build it up inside of me even longer. The thought of a man's body part inside me and Traci's gorgeous face above me was such a...

114

"Rikki," Boyle had the audacity to interrupt my next orgasm, "get in the scene now."

The nerve of her intruding in on us.

Traci sat us side by side and began eating out Rikki. Instead of feeling like I was about to come, I felt jealous. As a consolation, Rikki stuck her finger inside of me. No match for Traci's.

The script calls for Traci and Rikki leave for a meeting, and I end up alone on the set.

"Just play with yourself for a few minutes." Boyle whispered.

I picked up the dildo and begin putting it inside me. Somehow, it wasn't as much fun as when Traci was using it. I thought of her and eked out a mini orgasm.

Suddenly, I just wanted to take a nap. Traci had worn me out.

At the end of my last day, I went in search of Boyle to get paid. The last three days were so much fun. Thinking back on my first loop, I realized that that was just a bad experience. I felt at home with these people. Where was that crazy Boyle? I walked outside by the pool to a cabana where I heard noises from inside. Not caring that I was going to interrupt Boyle snorting coke, I pushed the door open. On her knees, with red lips around a guys cock, was Traci. Her hands were around his hips, pushing him deeper into her mouth. I stopped in the doorway and Traci averted her cat like eyes to me. She took him out of her mouth, but kept licking the tip. "Do you want to taste Daddy's cock Christy?"

I backed up one step. Clearly he wasn't her dad, he looked to be in his mid-thirties. "No, that's okay, I was just looking for Boyle." In fact, I think she told me her dad died when she was a kid. "Have you seen Boyle?" Or did she say her dad still lived in Nevada? "I'll go look for him in the house." Actually, over the last three days, Traci told me that her Dad was dead and alive. I backed out and began closing the door when Traci said, "Fine, be that way. There's just more for me." I peeked through the crack in the door, and Traci began giving him head again. I was already forgotten.

I walked back in the house and saw Luke. "Hey, do you know where Boyle is?"

"Yeah, I just saw him go into the laundry room with Heather."

"Who?" I asked, but Luke was already gone. It was lunchtime and I was no match for Sloppy Joes.

I walked through the kitchen, found the laundry room and heard a big snort from behind the door.

I opened the door and saw Boyle and a tall thin girl bent over the washer snorting lines of coke off a makeup mirror with a rolled up bill. The girl finished her line, wiped her nose and extended that same hand to me. "Hi! I'm Heather Wayne." So chipper from the coke, she kept on talking. "You must be Christy Canyon. Everybody has told me so much about you. I already told Jim to book you in my next movie. Want a line?" She held out the rolled up bill to me and I noticed it was a fifty.

Boyle poured more coke out of his vial. "Let's all do one together." His razor blade began making three perfect lines. "This one's out of my stash Heather."

Heather shoved her two vials into her pocket. "Excellent!"

I thought back to my high school prom. My best friend Jenny and I had shared some coke in the bathroom that night.

Boyle rolled up two more fifties, and handed me one. "Ready? On your marks, get set, go."

I bent my head over the line and watched it disappear from the mirror, up my left nostril. I instantly felt a rush in my body. I felt alive.

I wondered what happened to Jenny. My prom had been six months ago, yet it seemed like a lifetime.

"Now it's my turn to treat." Heather reached back in her pocket and pulled out one of her vials. She tapped some white powder out, took the razor from Boyle, and made three more perfect lines.

My life had taken such a radical turn since prom night.

The three of us bent over and snorted it up simultaneously. I felt wonderful. "So Heather, how long have you been in the business?" I tasted a bitter sensation in my throat. "Did you grow up in this area? I did. I just love this business so much, don't you?" Suddenly I loved everything.

"Yes, it's the best, and I think Jim is the best too! He always keeps me busy and gets me my day rate." She poured another two lines out, which we snorted up in two seconds. "Do you live around here Christy?"

"No, right now I live in Hollywood, but I started looking for a place in the valley. Hollywood has gotten so creepy. Do you live around here?"

I wondered what happened to my prom date.

"Actually, I live with the director Bruce Seven in Canyon Country."

Another two lines went up our noses. "Oh, I shot around there for two movies I did for Paradise Visuals. Have you worked for them?" Where was Boyle? I didn't want to use up all of Heather's coke.

"No, I haven't yet, but I hear that it's a great company. Maybe you can put in a good word for me."

I wondered whom I would work with in my next video.

"Yeah, of course I will. The guy who owns it said he's going to call me to go out to dinner and I'll tell him how great you are."

"God Christy, would you do that for me? You're such a great friend."

I had known her all of fifteen minutes. "Hey, that's what friends are for." Maybe I could buy some of this from Boyle. I didn't want Heather to think I was going to use up all of hers. "Are you going to get your own place?" I was getting hot and stuffy in this laundry room.

116

I wondered what Grant from high school was doing right now.

"Yeah, I want my own pad." We emptied her vial and snorted the last of her coke. "Hey! I just had a great idea. Let's become roommates Christy! Wouldn't that be great?" Heather stuck her rolled up fifty in her vial and snorted any remaining traces of white powder. "Look how we became such great friends so fast. We have so much in common."

Yeah, we both made porno films, and could snort a vial of cocaine in thirty minutes.

"Does Boyle have more of this?" My hands were shaking. "I'll get the next gram." Suddenly that lunch buffet that I was so looking forward to didn't sound good at all. "Where is Boyle?" In fact, food sounded repulsive.

"Let's go find him." Heather wiped the mirror with her finger, and then wiped it on her gums. "Take the rest, it numbs your gums."

My entire body felt numb and heavenly.

It didn't matter what my friends from high school were doing. "Let's go Heather." I locked my arm in hers.

We emerged from the laundry room and found Boyle talking to the man Traci had been blowing in the cabana. "Hi girls, I'd like you to meet Spencer. He owns this house."

I had my new set of friends.

Heather and I both said hi and how much we loved his house. "It's so pretty. One day I'm going to own one just like it! Then we can be neighbors!" Heather prattled.

Spencer looked at me. "You should have joined us Christy."

Sex right now sounded as bad as food. Luckily Heather broke in, "What do you do?"

I wondered why Traci would have sex with this creep.

Not taking his eyes off me he answered. "I'm in the import, export business."

That always covered a lot of territory I thought. Translation; I was sure he was a drug dealer. "Cool." He gave me the creeps. "Hey Boyle, I'm about to take off." Spencer and his shaved eyebrows were ruining my perfect high.

"Yeah Boyle, Christy and I are going to find a place to live together!" She put her arm around me. "We're best friends."

Boyle got up. "I'll be right back Spence. Follow me Christy. I'll pay you and have you sign a model release."

I followed Boyle into the study and he pulled out two release forms, which I never bothered to read. "Hey Boyle, can I get two grams from you?"

He pulled them out of his pocket. "No problem. They're one hundred dollars each. The best stuff around."

117

A hundred each? "Great, I'll take two."

I wondered where he got this great stuff.'

Boyle counted out my pay less two hundred dollars for the coke.

Happy and as high as can be, I signed away all of my rights on the dotted line.

"Thanks Boyle, I had such a great time." I needed another line and a cigarette.

"You were great Christy. Here's my card if you need anything."

I looked at his business card. "Hey, I live in Hollywood too!" I was amazed at how much I had in common with these people.

"Call me anytime and we'll party together." He traced my right nipple through my T-shirt and I felt like barfing.

I wondered who would actually fuck this guy.

I stepped back. "Sure will." Sure won't. I didn't need him fondling me, or anybody. I could afford anything I wanted. "Thanks again."

He pulled his un-wanted hand back. "I definitely want you in my next production in two weeks with Ginger Lynn." He put my model release away.

"Just tell Jim when it is!"

"You're really terrific."

And I did feel terrific. I felt on top of the world. Heather and I partied for the next twenty-four hours. I wondered about everything on several grams of coke. I found my new niche in life and my new best friend. I just never bothered to wonder what was happening to me.

14

It was my first full day off in a week, and I had to trek over to Jim's office to pick up a script for a movie that I was shooting in January. JANUARY!! It was late November, but Jim insisted that I pick it up today.

The movie, being shot in San Francisco in two months, was by a director named Alex de Renzy. Jim told me that Alex only shoots every few months, and it was an honor to be picked for one of his films. I didn't feel so honored in having to interrupt my precious time to pick up a script on my day off.

"It's real important that you come by my office by eleven this morning. I don't ask much from you, so I would appreciate it if you did Uncle Jimmy this one little favor."

"Okay, I'll be there by eleven." It was true. Jim never asked me to do much, besides my job, so I figured I'd humor the man and actually be there on time. I was so conditioned to work, that I didn't know what to do with my time off, although a trip to the mall and a pit stop at Boyle's for another few grams of coke was always a good place to start. Throw in a movie and dinner and it was time to work the next day.

I walked up the familiar flight of stairs, swung the glass door open and shouted, "Alright, where's the stupid script?" as I rounded the corner into Jim's office.

A man with jet-black hair was sitting in the chair opposite him. The back of his head was huge, like a large boulder. I stopped in the doorway and cringed at the way I asked Jim for the script, so bratty and demanding. I had no idea he had company. The large head swung around and looked at me. His face looked strangely familiar. He smiled a big white, toothy type of smile. A real dental creation. His skin was a deep, dark tan, which went well with his white Puma jogging outfit.

I kept staring at him, trying to place his face. I knew I should have known him, but I didn't know from where.

His tongue probed in the back of his mouth, like he was fishing for a piece of food lodged in a back molar. He finally stood up, well over six feet, and stuck his hand out to me. I reached out with my own hand, a natural reflex. I felt drawn to this stranger with such charisma. Our hands connected, and I felt electricity surge through my body.

"Hi, my name is Max Baer." Our hands stayed connected, as well as our eyes. His large paw-like hand felt warm and safe wrapped around mine. "Hi, I'm Christy. It's nice to meet you, I think, that is, unless I've met you before. You look so familiar."

Jim's cowboy southern drawl broke our spell. "That's Max, he played

Jethro on 'The Beverly Hillbillies'."

Max swiped a sideways glance at Jim, still holding onto my hand, "Thanks Jim, what a character to be remembered as," but Max didn't seem embarrassed. I suddenly felt like a star-struck teenager. I wasn't a huge fan of the show, but I vaguely remembered watching reruns late at night before I fell asleep when nothing else was on. The last episode I saw was several months ago. Jethro was on his hands and knees, crawling around on the ground, barking like a dog.

"That's why you look so familiar to me." I was suddenly all goo-goo eyed. A real star was one foot in front of me, touching me.

Our hands released, and my eyes focused in on a large gold medallion that was around his neck. "That's pretty." I heard myself say.

"What, this?" Max touched the gold hunk and began spouting off a long-winded story about where it came from. I on the other hand, didn't hear one word he said. I was too busy kicking myself for acting stupid. By the end of the history lesson on his necklace, Max stuck a toothpick in his mouth. He swirled it around with his tongue and folded his arms across his chest. The toothpick found a resting spot, and Max said, "I've done a lot since those days, I sure hope I'm not always known for just being Jethro. I do a lot of writing and directing and I'm also in the middle of pitching an idea to HBO. Did you see the movie 'Ode to Billy Joe'?"

The title sounded familiar, but I think I was only about five when it came out. "No, I didn't see that one, but I've been meaning to rent it." Not that I even owned a VCR.

"Maxie Baby has been dying to meet you Christy."

Why me? I turned to look at Jim, forgetting that he was even in the room with us. "What?"

"Maxie just broke up with his girlfriend Misty Reagan."

"You were with Misty?" She had to be one of the nastiest chicks in the business. "Misty was your girlfriend?" Why would this handsome, successful man want her?

His hands were now grasping the chair back, and he got a far away look in his big brown eyes. "Yeah, until she chased me around the house with a butchers knife."

"Why would she do that?"

"Because she's fucking nuts!" Max yelled. "That's why." His eyes focused in on me. "Jesus H. Christ you're beautiful.'"

Max didn't seem to be grieving much for Misty.

"Maxie here is a big fan of yours."

I looked from Jim to Max. How did he know who I was? I had only a handful of magazines hit the stands so far, three or four at the most. My first few videos hadn't even been released yet.

"Of mine?" I asked Max.

"Do you like sushi?"

"I love it."

"Would you like to go to dinner one night this week?"

I stared at him with my mouth open, unable to compute why he was asking me out.

"With me of course," he threw in.

"Yes! I'd love to." I couldn't believe this famous movie star was asking me out on a date. I opened up my red date book, and told him Wednesday would be best for me. "I'm shooting a box cover in the morning, but I'll be done by two."

Max sat down and asked what movie the box cover was for.

I suddenly felt a twinge of embarrassment that he knew I made pornos for a living. How could he respect that? He made real movies, like Billy Joe.

"'You Make Me Wet' is the movie title." Now I was really humiliated. The name alone sounded so porno. I hoped that he still wanted to go out with me.

Max leaned back in the chair and crossed his right leg over his left knee. Swinging his right foot, he asked, "Who fucked you in that film?"

I froze for a moment. Did he just ask what I think he asked? A little shocked by the blunt question, I answered, "Ron Jeremy."

He smiled, "Ronnie huh? He's got a big cock. Do you like it?"

Although these are normal questions people are curious about, I didn't know why this movie star had to ask them in such a vulgar manner. Maybe I was just over worked and touchy. He seemed like a nice guy, and after all, he was Jethro. "Yes, I always like to work with Ron, he makes me laugh." The word work sounded so strange coming out of my mouth, but it was after all just that, work.

"He only makes you laugh, not come?" Max opened his black leather date book. "Well, what time and where should I pick you up on Wednesday?" His silver Mont Blanc pen in hand.

"Seven is perfect for me." I reached across Jim's desk to grab a piece of paper so I could write down my address and directions for Max. My right arm brushed against Max's left arm in the process. Through the material of his shirt, I could feel his heat. Body heat. Pure sexual heat. His crudeness from moments before suddenly vanished from my mind. In two nights, I was going out with a movie star!

I left Jim's office and headed straight to the mall. I deserved a new outfit for my date. Visions of love and even marriage filled my head. I pushed them away. "Don't be ridiculous." I said in my empty car, as I pulled into a parking spot near Bullocks.

Opening the heavy glass door landed me in the cosmetic department, and I found the thought drift back into my head. Can you imagine if I married Max Baer? What would my parents say then? Maybe I wouldn't be so bad in their eyes after all. If I married him, I could quit making films. No man who really loved me would want me having sex with other men.

I was just about to walk down the bridal path when a woman sprayed some vile smelling perfume under my nose. My grandmother's face now filled my head. "Isn't that a lovely scent?" She asked.

The fairy tale daydream came to an abrupt halt, and my eyes focused in on my surroundings at Bullocks; Jars of creams, bottles of perfumes, and tubes of lotions and lipsticks. "No." I replied and sneezed on her.

I found my way to the escalator and headed up. I could find my favorite designer section in this store with my eyes blindfolded. This date was so special; who knew what it would lead to. Suddenly, the handful of men I was seeing seemed like such small potatoes, a waste of my time. With the exception of Michael, I wasn't sexually attracted to anybody in the past few months, until I met Max today.

I took my time looking through the two T-racks of suede and leather outfits. I pulled out a pair of black leather pants and a jacket. Too hard looking, not feminine enough for a first date. My eyes zeroed in on a coral blue suede dress. I put the black leather back and pulled out the blue dress. It was cut low in the back, with a scoop neck in front. I held it against my body and looked at myself in the full-length mirror. The hemline stopped four inches above my knees. Sexy, yet not sleazy. I found my size and glanced at the price tag. $245.00. It was a bit pricey, but worth the potential payoff; a husband.

I took the dress into the dressing room and hung it up behind the door. I quickly took off my white Jag dress and chucked it in the corner. I carefully slipped the suede dress off its hanger and slid the soft fabric over my head. I stared at my reflection in the three-way mirror. This was the most beautiful dress that I had ever seen. Sold.

Next stop, Sacha Shoes of London, five doors down in the mall. I found a pair of white four-inch pumps with blue jewels clustered at the toes. What a perfect match, a good sign. Sold.

I got home and hung my new dress, still in the garment bag, in my closet. The shoes, still in the box went below.

The following day, I went to shoot a movie called "Doctor Desire". Although I was only going to do one sex scene, it was a doozie. This was going to be my very first ménage a trois with two guys. Driving over to the location, a house in Brentwood, I began to panic at the thought of having to please two guys at once. I had been with two girls at once, and even a guy and a girl together, but never two guys. It seemed like so much work for one girl.

I found the address, parked on the residential street, turned off the ignition and sat in my car. I closed my eyes and tried to imagine how I could keep two guys excited at once. My concentration drifted, and I saw Max's big handsome face grinning. I wondered what he looked like naked, and how he felt in bed. The light tap on my window jolted me into reality, erasing the image of a buck naked Max Baer. It was Jerry, the tall, skinny blonde production assistant. "Is everything okay in there?"

"Yes, just thinking." I opened my car door, grabbed my wardrobe bag from the backseat, and handed it to him.

While we walked up the driveway, I asked Jerry whom I was going to work with in my scene.

Jerry took a folded piece of paper from his back pocket and found my name on his call sheet. "Steve Drake and Billy Dee."

I tried to picture their faces, but couldn't. "Are they cute?"

"Oh Christy, I'm a guy. I can't judge that. I think you and Traci Lords are cute." His usually white face was now lobster red.

I smiled at his embarrassment and his compliment. "I guess you're right." I paused. I needed to know something about two men who I was about to have sex with one hour from now. "Are they nice?"

"Yeah, they're really great guys. You've never worked with them before?"

"No. Don't forget, I've only been making films for about a month."

"Still," he opened the wooden front door, "It's a pretty small group of talent. I'm surprised you haven't run into them on a set."

"You're right. I always seem to work with the same handful of guys, Peter North, Ron Jeremy and Tom Byron."

Neither Jerry nor I thought it was odd that I was about to have sex with two faceless strangers.

Jerry led me into makeup. Which was set up in a guestroom located behind the laundry room. The smell of fresh, clean sheets reminded me of the comfort of home for a second, until I heard J.R. screech, "Hey girl, are you ready for some of that black cock today?"

I parked my ass in his makeup chair. "What? Who's black?"

"Billy Dee, dummy. Well, he's half black, half something, but the half between his legs that really matters, is all black." J.R. puckered up his lips, and looked at himself in the mirror. "I wouldn't mind wrapping these lips around his chocolate bar. Have you ever been with a black man before?"

"No, and I've never been with two guys at once either."

"Girl, where have you been? Oh well, let's get started." J.R. began his routine of foundation, powder, and heavy-handed eye makeup, using plenty of blue eye shadow with black eye liner. J.R. looked through his drawer of lipsticks and asked, "Are you nervous?"

I thought about it for a minute. Did I still get nervous before I performed sex scenes in front of a camera for the world to see? "No. Not really. I'm over the nervous stage by now." The thought of somebody renting or buying my videos never bothered me. I was just one of the many girls they chose from in the video store behind the red curtain. I was sure nobody really looked at my face anyway, just my body, and what was being done to it.

"Everything that I've done on film are things that I've always wanted to try and experience in my personal life, but never knew how to go about it. I remember when I was seventeen, I went to a club in Hollywood, and there was this really pretty girl at the bar who was flirting with me, I think. I thought about how I would love to see what sex with a girl was like. What it felt like, how it would be different than being with a guy."

J.R. pushed up his glasses with the tip of the blush brush, "Well, don't look at me. I've never been with a girl either."

"There was no way that I would have initiated it, and she never did, so it never happened."

"Why didn't you just go up to her and stick your tongue down her throat? I always do if I see a cute guy, and it always works for me." J.R. found the tube of lipstick he was searching for.

"Because that's not my style J.R. I'm actually shy."

"Not from what I see you doing on film. Driving those cute boys so crazy."

"That's what makes making films so much fun. I get to live out my fantasies, learn about sex, and get paid for it at the same time. I get into this business, and who would de-virginize my female cherry? Ginger Lynn. It doesn't get any better than that. I can do anything I want on film, and everybody accepts it with out question. Tom Byron couldn't care less how loud I scream when I come. I could ask Ron Jeremy to screw me in any position, and he would with out hesitation. I could talk as dirty as I want to Paul Thomas, and it would only turn him on even more. Peter North wouldn't care where I grabbed him to pull his body closer to me."

J.R. interrupted. "That's where you're wrong. Touch Peter's hair, and he may deck you. That man is obsessed with his hair."

"In my personal life, I'm much more reserved, but on film, I become somebody else.

"Why do you think that is?"

"Partially because it's so much fun to become a different person, to be this character who can do anything with out being critiqued."

"What's the other part?"

"To save the real me. I can show my body doing all sorts of nasty things, but my mind is mine. They can't have that. They can't have all of me. The fans just get to see the part I want them to see. If I give them everything, I won't have anything left."

The director Harold Lime walked in. "Are you almost finished with our star?" He winked at me, and I realized he had no eyelashes, reminding me of an amphibian I dissected in seventh grade.

"Just a touch of cock-sucker red lipstick, and she's all yours." J.R. swiped the tube of lipstick from side to side. "Now rub, then blot." He handed me a white Kleenex.

It was time for my first three-way with two guys. Two guys whom I had never even met. Just another adventure, I kept telling myself.

I followed Harold up the spiral staircase, and knew immediately where my scene was about to take place. The bedroom on the left had four movie-set lights, shining down on the bed.

I asked Harold if there was a script.

"No. This scene is real simple and should go fast. I want you to climb on the bed, and begin masturbating. In a few minutes, Steve and Billy will walk in, find you playing with yourself, get turned on and join in."

How porno I thought as I crawled on the bed. I leaned my back against the headboard, in the center of the mattress. Lights began turning on, and bodies started to fill the room. The director got behind the camera and told me to start whenever I felt like it. I spread my legs open, shut out the world, and began touching my clit. I let my mind wander into another place, a place where I felt safe and secure. I went to a place where I had only one lover touching me, one person bringing me to an orgasm. That person became Max Baer in my mind. His fingers were touching me. He was telling me that I didn't have to make films anymore. His voice was saying that he loved me. Loved me. How long had it been since somebody told me that? Was it my boyfriend in eleventh grade? It was okay, Max was telling me now.

Somebody in the room shifted his weight, and I remembered that I was on a movie set, and automatically switched into character for the cameras. I brought my right middle finger up to my mouth and slowly licked it, then put it in my mouth and sucked on it, like it was the best piece of candy I had even tasted. I took it out of my mouth, and traced it down my body to my left boob and let it linger there, making small circles around my nipple. I wet it with my mouth one more time, then spread my pussy for the camera with my left hand, while I put my right finger deep inside me. Stay in character I thought, and I let a moan escape my lips as I thrust my hips up two inches towards the camera.

Jack, the director, whispered, "The guys are going to come in soon so bring yourself to a climax." I kept fingering myself, thrusting my body even faster into the camera, holding myself open even wider. I let out a moan, and wondered how I ended up here. I began thrashing around on the bed, pulling at the sheets, thinking about how thirsty I was. I started gyrating on that lone finger, gripped by excitement and fear at what was coming next; two men with me. I began to climax for the cameras, and it occurred to me that I had forgotten to put deodorant on this morning.

The door opened, and two men in construction gear walked in. Why they were wearing hard hats was a mystery to me. It must have been from an earlier scene, prior to them finding me in bed, playing with myself. I remembered that the cameras were still rolling and sat up in bed to look at the two men.

I was amazed at how good-looking the two guys were. Billy Dee was a light skinned black man with beautiful light green eyes. Steve was a handsome, All-American looking guy who also had light green eyes. They took one look at me in bed, naked with a finger partially inserted in myself, and gave each other a high-five.

The hats came off first.

My heart began beating faster as each piece of their clothing was removed. Billy's hard body was chiseled, showing off every muscle. Steve looked like a guy I would have dated in high school. In fact, I think Clair dated a guy who could pass for his brother. Now I was about to get both, at once, for the first time. I made a mental note to tell Jim to book me with either of these two on a future shoot. I felt a surge of sexual energy for these two guys and wished that they would hurry up and get nude.

I began touching myself again and heard my own voice in the silent room. "Would you hurry it up?"

"Eager little one, aren't you?" One of the boys said. I just smiled. Since this was film, and anything goes, I of course wasn't embarrassed.

Shirts and socks flew in all directions until they were finally in their birthday suits.

Their naked bodies climbed onto the king-size bed, hard-ons first. I automatically grabbed each of their members, one for each hand. My fears and nerves flew out the window, and I instinctively knew what to do. My mouth wrapped around Billy, making it the first time I had a black one in my mouth, in my hand and soon, in my pussy. I could feel myself getting wet. Really wet. I kept stroking Steve with my left hand. Taking Billy as deep in my mouth as I could, I looked up at him. His beautiful eyes were watching every move I made.

"Your mouth feels so great Baby Girl." Since no script was involved, he must have meant it. He loved the way I felt licking every inch of him. This fueled my hunger for him even more, as I slid his cock even deeper into my mouth, touching the back of my throat with it. For the moment, I forgot about Steve, concentrating on what was in my mouth. Then I felt Steve, and I remembered he was there too. He entered me from behind, doggie style.

With one in my mouth, and one in my pussy, my head began spinning from the sexual excitement; two guys filling me up at once. One was pleasing me, while I was pleasing the other. The camera, lights and people vanished from my mind. It was just the three of us naked, alone on the bed. One pulled out, and another one entered me. I lost track of who was where in my body. Who I was sucking, or who was fucking me didn't matter, I didn't care. I just didn't want it to stop. A set of hands pulled me at my waist, and I was on my back.

I grabbed his hips between my legs and pulled them in closer, deeper inside me. I wrapped my legs around his lower back, holding him in as tight as I could. I reached up, above my head, and pulled another set of hips down further, filling my mouth up even more, holding on tight, not wanting to let go.

Someone's words broke the rhythmic motions; "Oh God, I'm going to come," came from somewhere on the bed. "Me too," said the second voice.

"No, not yet." I heard my own voice say, or was I just thinking about saying it. My mind and body were in another galaxy. This was the best sex I had ever experienced. The first shot sprayed all over my chest. I looked above me, and saw Steve's face. His hand was stroking the last drops of come out of his cock, touching his balls with his other hand. His mouth looked lopsided, but maybe it was just the angle I was at.

Then I felt the second shot. It was Billy. His left hand was grasping my inner right thigh. His right hand was holding his cock several inches away from my stomach. Semen began covering the lower half of my stomach, as well as the top of my pubic hair. Billy's piercing eyes never left my face. "Rub it in Baby. Rub my hot cum into your body."

My right hand reacted to his command, and did as it was told. I began to rub Billy's cum into my skin. With my left hand I began to rub Steve's cum around my boobs.

"Cut!" Was yelled from inside the room, and I was brought back to reality. Reality was a room full of people. Somebody asked what was for lunch. I felt the semen begin to dry on my skin.

Billy bent down and kissed me on the cheek. "Great scene, sexy girl." He turned to Jerry, "Man, you got any water for me? I lost a lot of body fluids just now." He looked over his shoulder and winked at me.

Steve handed me a cup of water. "That was great Christy. I hope we get to work together more." He tilted his head back, and drank his cup of water in one gulp.

I sipped at my glass. "Oh we will Steve. I'm going to tell Jim that I want you in my next movie." And I would. Both of them actually.

"Great." He smiled, but his eyes were already somewhere else. "Hey Christy, can I jump in the shower real quick? I'll be out in five minutes. I've got to run and pick up my girlfriend."

His girlfriend? "Sure." Just then, Jerry brought me a damp towel.

"Thanks sweetie." Steve said, already half way to the bathroom.

Where was Billy?

I found him in the far right corner of the room talking to the director, with a towel wrapped around his body. "So, are we still on for the game tonight?"

"You bet." The director replied. "Third row center."

"Cool man, I'll see you when you wrap. Just come by my pad." Billy turned to leave, then stopped and looked at me still naked, still in bed. He took four steps over and was standing above me. He reached down and stroked the left side of my neck. "You felt real nice kitten." He smiled, tightened the towel around his waist, and left the room. He left me right where he found me one hour ago, naked in bed.

The sheets were messy, torn from the corners exposing a powder blue mattress. The satin comforter was heaped in a pile on the floor. A large wet stain covered one of the pillowcases. Was it water, semen or just body perspiration?

The lights were being turned off, and equipment was being wheeled and carried out of the now dark room, and into the library for the second scene of the day. Cords were yanked out of the sockets, and laughter drifted in from downstairs. The front door slammed. Somebody was leaving, or maybe new talent was showing up.

Water stopped running from somewhere to my left. "It's all yours Christy." Steve was standing in the doorway, dripping water onto the forest green tiles on the bathroom floor. "I don't see any more towels, but I'll leave you mine." He smiled, "It's not too wet."

"Thanks." I pulled the corner of the damp sheet over my body.

Steve shook his head from side to side. Drops of water from his hair landed on the mirror and began to roll down. He ran his fingers through his hair, looking at himself in the full-length mirror. "I forgot a comb." He ducked back into the bathroom, emerging minutes later fully clothed. "I hung the towel up over the shower door to dry." He bent down and scooped up his boots. "That was really fun. I'll see you."

I was alone in the room. The room that was so full of energy fifteen minutes ago. Fifteen minutes ago, my body was in ecstasy, now my body felt empty. I propped myself up in the bed, and thought about what had happened in the past hour. It was sexual, it was exciting and it was a turn on. And then it hit me. It was my job, and it was their job. It was just fucking. No romance, no attachments, no deep emotions. It was just another day of work. Just pure, raw, uninhibited sex.

Max was buzzing my intercom at seven sharp. I pressed the security button, and took one last look in the hallway mirror. Perfect. My doorbell rang, nearly as loud as my heart was pounding.

I opened the door. "Hi Max." I had moved into my new place just in time. "Come in." I couldn't imagine what he would have thought about me if I still lived in that fleabag apartment in Hollywood.

He stood in the doorway and checked me out from head to toe. "You are so gorgeous.'"

So far, my nearly $400.00 investment for my outfit was paying off. "Do you want anything to drink?"

"What do you have?" He was looking around my living room. "Cute place."

"Thanks." I hadn't been to the market in a while. "Water or orange juice."

"No, we should get going. I made reservations for seven-thirty. Have you been to the sushi place at the Beverly Glen mall?"

Stay calm I had to keep telling myself. "No, but I heard it was great." Actually, I didn't even know one existed there.

Max turned around and gave me a hug; a huge, safe embrace. His large arms and hands engulfed my frame. He squeezed my body tighter and buried his face in my neck. "You smell great." I wrapped my arms around his neck, and let my right hand touch his back. It felt so solid and protective, like a brick wall.

"We better get going or we'll never make it to dinner." His voice was suddenly soft and sexual.

I didn't want to let go. I wanted to feel his body close to mine, and I knew that after dinner I would have him. Since getting into the adult business, it was the first time that I wanted somebody, without a camera shoved in my face, pussy or focusing in on my tits bouncing up and down. I locked my front door and followed Max to his car.

He opened the car door for me, something that had been neglected by the boys I had been dating, and I slid into his car. I felt the black leather seats of his silver Audi embrace my body. Safe and warm, just like Max's arms. I was beginning to like every part of Max. I loved the feeling of being taken care of by him; a real man who knew how to treat a lady. Max closed my door and walked around to his side. In the past few months, I had begun to get the old me back. The me that got what ever I wanted, and I decided that I wanted Max. The innocence from high school was no longer there, instead, I found a more powerful me. A bit more calculated which was necessary for survival, but I knew how to get what I wanted again. No more Marv or Carol around to knock me down.

Max zipped over the canyon telling me about himself during the thirty-minute drive.

"I leased out my house in the canyon to a guy who owns a chain of fitness clubs for ten thousand a month. The asshole didn't water the lawn, and now the entire yard, front and back is dead."

"Ten thousand a month? Why didn't he just buy his own place?"

Max plowed on, "This house is gorgeous. I stole it years ago, and was

129

able to hang onto it during my divorce. My ex, in return, got my royalties for life from "The Beverly Hillbillies".

"You were married before?"

"Yes, but she wasn't into swinging and after we got married it soon started to fall apart."

Swinging? Maybe in the 70's he was into that sort of thing. "Do you ever want to get married again?" I asked casually.

"Oh sure. One of these days." His hand found its way to my inner left thigh. I spread my legs open two inches. "So, tell me about the movie you shot yesterday?"

"Well." How much should I tell him without turning him off? I wasn't sure how he felt about me making pornos. "It was just one quick scene." With two gorgeous guys. "No big deal."

"With who?" His hand was inching up my dress.

"Billy Dee and Steve Drake."

"Did they both get to fuck you?" His hand was touching my undies.

"Yes." Oh I hope he didn't think I was sleazy.

"Who's cock did you like better?" Max turned right into the parking lot, and an over eager valet appeared at my door. Max withdrew his hand; I closed my legs, unsure of why Max was so curious about my sex scene with two guys.

"This is the best sushi in town." Max put his arm around my waist, and led the way to the front door.

The chefs behind the counter all shouted something in a foreign tongue, and the hostess led the way to our reserved, romantic table.

I didn't want to talk about my job so I began asking Max questions about himself. I had no desire to talk about my day at work, and was quite relieved when Max yacked on and on about what he was pitching to HBO.

As Max was talking, I kept looking at his handsome face. He was so animated and had such zest for the projects that he was working on. Max was so full of self-assurance and confidence, that I felt safe and secure with him. He just seemed to take charge of a situation, something that at eighteen, I was already so tired of doing for myself. On the heels of one story, I began asking him about another story. The last thing I wanted to do was bring up my job. With a real man like Max, I was shy about how I was supporting myself. It was so abnormal in the real world. His were tales of real actors and real scripts. Mine were of hushed locations and three-page scripts in a business that was bordering the legal laws.

Max was right; this was the best sushi I had ever tasted. I could have eaten more, but didn't want him to think I was a complete pig, so I quit ordering California rolls and yellowtail long before my belly was full. One final slice of orange and we were done.

Back in the car, Max's hand immediately found it's way between my legs again. "How about going to my house for a jacuzzi?"

I spread my legs open one-inch for his hand to explore. "I didn't bring a bathing suit."

Max roared with laughter, at what he thought was a joke. I let out a nervous laugh as well. Nervous at saying something so ridiculous. Why would I need my swimsuit? I was planning on having sex with him tonight. I quickly changed the subject. Let him think I said a funny. "If you rent out your house, where do you live?"

Max's left hand held onto the black leather steering wheel. He looked in his rearview mirror and switched lanes. "I have a ranch in Van Nuys. Once his lease is up, I'm going to move back into my mansion."

Wow, two houses.

"I also have a chalet in Lake Tahoe." He averted his bedroom eyes to me for just a moment, and I felt my heart skip several beats. "You should come up with me this winter. It's so romantic right on the lake." His fingers were caressing my underwear. I'll go I thought, just tell me when.

"You wake up in the morning, and the ground is covered in a blanket of snow." He began a long-winded story of how he acquired the chalet, and my mind began to wander. I started to fantasize about a life with Max; a mansion in the canyon, a ranch in the valley and a chalet in the mountains.

Max interrupted my thoughts; "We're here." He turned onto a side street one block away from the San Diego freeway, in the heart of Van Nuys.

I guess it could be considered a ranch style house, but not what I had conjured up on the drive over. I had pictured a real ranch, with real farm animals and my very own chestnut brown horse. Max took me on a tour of his home. It was very stylishly decorated; masculine, yet not cold, feminine, yet not frilly. Just right. "Did Misty decorate for you?" I felt a bit of jealously creeping in. How did she get so lucky with Max? The idiot was living with him, being taken care of, and she pulls a knife?

"Misty? She couldn't match up her own socks if the housekeeper didn't ball them together. No, I hired an interior decorator." Wow, a housekeeper and an interior decorator.

Max grabbed me around the waist and began kissing the back of my neck and shoulders. "God, I've been wanting to do this since I first laid eyes on you."

I hoped he could still smell my Georgio perfume. "In Jim's office?"

Max let out another hearty laugh, reached through the opening at the back of my dress and cupped my boobs. He whispered in my ear from behind, "I've been wondering what these would feel like." Then he squeezed, hard, like one would to inspect a ripe melon.

I had to bite my lip to stop a yelp from escaping. He must not have realized how sensitive I was there. My silence gave Max a green light. He began squeezing even harder, pulling my body into his. I had to grab onto the kitchen counter with all of my might so I didn't tumble over in my heels. "Really?" I asked, not even sure what he said ten seconds ago.

He panted, "Uh huh." Then began dry humping my right leg. "I love big titties." With both hands, he began exploring my chest. I began to see the back of his hands stretching and pulling at my costly suede fabric, leaving stretch marks. The harder he squeezed, the harder he humped, and the harder I thought about what was wrong with this picture as I grasped on for dear life to his farm animal designer tiles. A rooster was under my right hand, a cow under my left, and a horn dog on top of me. I wondered what was wrong with the bedroom and a nice king-size mattress. "Max, should we go to your room?"

His left hand found it's way down to my full bottom undies, and settled on my left cheek. He began trying to wedge his middle finger through the tight elastic near my crotch. "How did you like both cocks in you at once yesterday?" I could feel his spit in my earlobe.

More erotic than this shit I thought. "It went well."

His clumsy finger finally got through, and he began stroking what he thought was my clit, but was really the excess fabric on my large cotton undies. "Tell me about it."

In my odd position, bent over the counter, with his body pressed against mine, I found it hard to breathe, let alone narrate a story. With both hands on the counter top, I tried to push my body up several inches. As hard as I pushed, it was to no avail. I had a 220-pound monkey on my back. I turned my face, lavender by now from lack of oxygen, and whispered "up." He eased up several inches, taking a lock of my hair, which had entangled itself in the clasp of his gold medallion. "Ouch!"

Max released his intrusive hands from my chest, which I was sure was black and blue by now, and said, "Let me get that." I heard him rip my hair free and saw the ends of my hair flutter in front of my eyes, looking singed.

I turned around to face Max, feeling the air fill my lungs again. He was ever so gently pulling strands of my hair from his clasp. I automatically looked down at his crotch to see the outline of his raging hard on. After that foreplay, he must have been about to explode, unless he already soiled himself. But he was as flat as a pancake down there, not even the slightest trace of an erection had come to life. My hand had a mind of its own, and touched the crotch of his black jeans. Surely that ten minutes of torture hadn't been for nothing. But nothing was all I felt. I tried to think of the romantic chalet in Lake Tahoe and suddenly I remembered how much I hated the snow and cold climate. Now a condo on the beaches of Maui...My right nipple began throbbing between his thumb and index finger and then the pain shot through my entire body. I made a noise with a sharp intake of breath.

Max smiled, "Oh, you like that huh?" and eased up. "Now, tell me all about Billy Dee and Steve Drake both fucking you." He thankfully backed up and began rubbing his crotch.

I felt the onset of a migraine.

I straightened my dress and caught my reflection in his Sub Zero refrigerator doors, which reminded me that I was getting hungry again. I looked like somebody who was just run over. My mascara was sliding down my cheeks, my perfectly applied lipstick was now hovering near my eyes, and my hair looked like it had been through a wind tunnel. My once figure fitting dress was now hanging on my frame, one size bigger, lumpy in the vicinity of my chest. I touched my nipple for reassurance that it was still intact. I straightened my dress, as best as I could and glared at Max. "You want to hear about me getting fucked by two guys in a fuck film?"

Max smiled and bounced up and down on the balls of his feet. "Yeah, yeah, tell me!" A small outline in his crotch began to wake up. Now I was speaking his language.

Against my better judgment and my naiveté, I began to tell him about my scene from "Doctor Desire". "So, the scene began with me playing with my pussy, inserting a finger inside, and rubbing my clit with my thumb at the same time."

Max made a disapproving face, and shook his head from side to side. "No! No! Get to the boys. What happened when they came in?"

What a sick fuck. I began "They both got naked." There were no horses in his back yard. It was barely big enough to fit a lap pool. Ranch my ass.

All giddy like a kid on Christmas morning. Max begged, "Go on, go on!"

I reached under my dress, and adjusted my underwear. The crotch of the panties had been shoved up deep inside me. "Well, they walked up to the bed,"

"Cocks first." He tossed into my own story.

I eyed the refrigerator. "Okay, cocks first." It sounded right. "And I grabbed Billy first." Max let out a moan, and began rubbing his hard on. I watched him from the corner of my eye, and continued, "Then I put Steve in my mouth."

"Steve's what?"

"Steve's cock." Max wasn't even looking at me anymore. He was now in his own world, sitting on a chair in the corner of the kitchen, with his jeans pooled around his ankles, and a hard on in his right hand.

I continued my story, throwing in as many nasty words for body parts as I could think of, rotating the four that I came up with. Between the words cock, dick, prick and cunt fucking, I opened the refrigerator door. I popped open a chocolate snack-pack pudding, and began eating it, making an "Mmm!" sound with each large bite from the small tin, pretending it was part of my story.

Max was really going to town on himself by now.

Next, my eyes zeroed in on a new hunk of Brie cheese, my absolute favorite. I reached for it and began to peel back the plastic wrap, raising my voice two levels higher to drown out the noise. I looked at the tip of the Brie, and then back at Max. His head was now thrown back, and I knew the end was near. I sunk my teeth into the cheese, and shoved it back into his fridge, teeth marks and all, sans the wrapping.

I turned to face him, just as he began to ejaculate on his thigh. Gross I thought, and began to chuckle thinking back to only forty-eight hours ago. I was ready to say "I do," and now I couldn't wait to say "Goodbye" for good. The very thing about my work that I was ashamed of, was exactly what turned him on. Go figure.

After his final moan, he looked at me with weary eyes, and asked, "What's so funny?"

I fed him a line of bull-crap, knowing he would buy it. "I always giggle when I cum." I caught my smile in the reflection of his toaster, and quickly wiped off a piece of cheese stuck on my eyetooth.

"Good, good, I'm glad you came too." He smiled, just like Jethro.

Now I would like to go.

Max pulled his jeans back on and walked over to me. Yuck! I wouldn't want to be his maid, washing those pants.

"I know these two good looking guys who would love to fuck you while I watched."

"Oh really?" I bet you do. Now I knew why Misty had been his girlfriend, she was right up his alley. He should have stayed with her. "Who?" I asked purely out of amusement.

"They're Chippendale dancers." Max began rummaging through a kitchen drawer until he found a calendar. "I can show you their photos." He flipped through several months until he found July. He gave them a loving glance, then turned it my direction, which was now a safe distance opposite him at the kitchen counter. "Look at these sexy fuckers. Wouldn't you love to ride them?"

"What about you?" Now I was testing the waters. "I want to see you with them," I flirted. I had to find out if the great Jethro swung both ways.

"Oh no way man, I'm not into that shit. It only comes out my ass, nothing gets in." He looked a tad disgusted at me for even suggesting it.

It was one of those dates with Max that was so insane that it was actually fun. I looked at the full color photo for the month of July.

Johnny was wearing a pair of thong underwear in red, white and blue, with his left foot hoisted up on a white stool. Dougie, his partner, was holding a lit sparkler in each hand, wearing skimpy red Dolphin shorts. I could not see one piece of hair on either body. They were real smooth looking, like a baby seals.

Both dancers looked like they would prefer a firecracker up their ass than pleasure me.

"Yeah, they're real good lookin' guys."

Max got all revved up again, and touched his crotch. "Should I call them?"

"Yeah, sure, but I got to go home now. Early wake up call for a movie, and Jim will kill me if I show up late. Give them a call when you get back after taking me home."

"You're making another movie tomorrow? With who? What guys?"

Oh no, round two was not going to happen, ever. I wanted to get home to that ham sandwich I couldn't stop thinking about. "Oh, it's just a girl-girl scene."

Max scowled. "Alright, let's go."

"I really enjoyed my evening with you." Max said, pulling into my driveway.

I opened the car door before he even came to a full stop. "Me too! Call me next week."

"Next week?" He looked puzzled.

"Perfect! Bye!" With my key already in hand, I ran up the stairs to the front door, and never looked back.

I crawled into bed thirty minutes later, with my ham and cheese sandwich. It dawned on me that Jim had set me up. It wasn't urgent for me to pick up a script for a movie being shot in two months; it was urgent that Max Baer meet me.

Max reminded me of a big goofy dog, who was loveable, but had never been fixed properly.

I avoided his calls for the next few weeks. Max finally got the hint.

15

A few weeks later I found myself with a full day off from work, and it felt so good to be at home.

The overpriced coffee table I ordered three weeks ago finally came today, completing my living room set.

I had walked into Bullock's last month, and there it was. A couch, two oversized chairs with matching footrests, and a coffee table, in colors of cream and rose. I had to have it. Not only was it a beautiful set, but it was from the most prestigious department store. Only the best would do. I had chosen to stay in the world of porn, and part of my acceptance of whom I was, and what I was doing with my life, meant only the finest. To soften the pain, and mask the hurt of my parents writing me off, I would only buy the best quality; the most expensive money could buy.

The commission only salesman walked up to me. "It's a beautiful set, isn't it. Our top seller, can't keep them in stock."

Didn't my mom and dad realize that I was only trying to survive? "Yes, it's gorgeous." I turned to face him.

He was looking at the black leather couch and love seat one display over.

"Uh, this is the one I like, not that one."

"Oh! That set is simply exquisite and a favorite among the ladies. Shall I write it up for you? There is free delivery through today only."

Whichever one I chose, would be the best in some way. What a total salesman.

I did a quick calculation in my head. Two movies, two days each. "I Like To Be Watched", and "Kissin' Cousins" just paid for my new set.

"Yes. Write it up."

I was on my way out to go shopping when the phone rang.

"Hello."

"Hi, it's Michael."

"Hi! How are you?"

"Good. Listen, are you free for dinner tonight? I'm going to be shooting a movie four days after we get back from the CES show, and I want you to play the starring role. It's a five day shoot, and we're shooting on Beta Cam.'"

"What's Beta Cam?" I totaled up the pay in my head.

"It's the highest quality of video available."

"Sure, it sounds fine. Pick me up at seven."

"Great, I'll bring you the script."

Script, like I ever bothered to read them before I sat down in the makeup chair the morning of the shoot. Sometimes, the directors still had to tape them on my co-star, or on a piece of furniture nearby. I don't think viewers really gave a hoot about my acting abilities; thank goodness.

A big fat line of coke and I was out the door.

Next stop, the Beverly Center.

After a two hour shopping spree, I was ready to go home. I passed the food court and wondered when I ate last.

I stepped into the glass elevator, and there she was, my mother. I hadn't seen or spoken to her in over a year. We locked eyes, and the corners of my mouth began to form a smile. She was my mom, Mommy, whom I missed and loved so much. Here she was, two feet away from me, alone, no Marv. I opened my mouth to say hi, just as she turned her face and body away, leaving me to stare at her backside. This was her way of telling me to stay away. This was my mother's way to shut me out and close me off to any contact. Her rigid body told me that I was not welcome or accepted. I stared at her, knowing that she would never turn around. She wore a long olive green skirt, white silk blouse and sweater wrapped around her waist. Her familiar head of curls was now streaked with blonde highlights.

I felt the lump forming deep in the back of my throat. I felt the sensation of tears forming in the corners of my eyes. I thought of the kitten Clair told me that Mom got recently, and wondered if she loved that kitten more than me. Did she turn her back on the kitten when it needed love?

I averted my eyes downward, as the first tear rolled down my cheek, to the blonde kid, licking his red lollipop with such intensity. His mother was pulling him in tight, as close to her body as she could. My mother was pushing her body as far away from me as she could.

I moved my eyes away from the carefree child to a couple in the corner. They were kissing and whispering to each other in a language that lovers used. They were in love, heading home to make love. I didn't even know what that meant anymore. It sure wasn't fucking on film. It sure wasn't standing within arms reach of my mom, who dismissed me by turning her body to avoid any form of contact.

I stood in my corner of the elevator wearing a tan suede dress with matching boots, the finest labels money could buy. Nobody in the elevator noticed me. Nobody in that space cared that there was a girl wiping her tears away with the backside of her hand.

Slowly raising my eyes back to my mother, I realized it wasn't about the best money could buy. The furniture, appliances, clothes, shoes, and even the imported Columbian coke couldn't replace what was right in front of me, close enough to touch, but a million miles away.

I took one last look at my mom and felt ashamed. I couldn't blame her for avoiding me. I fucked on film for a living and everybody knew it and hated me for it in the family. I was a complete disgrace to her. The elevator doors opened one floor below and I got out. Mom never turned around. She kept her body in the far left corner of that small glass elevator. It wasn't the floor I needed, but I had to get out. I held back my tears while waiting for the next elevator. Standing straight, with my head held high, holding onto my packages, holding onto my crumbling pride.

Don't lose it here in the mall I thought to myself while waiting for the next elevator.

An elderly couple waited next to me. Their arms were interlocked, and he was holding a shopping bag from Robinson's department store. They were talking about what to have for dinner. I was having dinner with a porn producer to discuss a fuck film. I moved closer to him. I needed to feel his yellow sweater against my skin. The elevator doors opened, and the three of us stepped in.

Don't lose it here in the elevator.

The recorded voice said P5, which was my floor. Get out and find your car.

Safe in my car, tucked away in the concrete parking structure, I began to weep. I couldn't let Mom see me cry. I couldn't let the shoppers see me cry. It was private and personal. Nobody would care anyway.

I sat in my car for five minutes listening to a Madonna tape before dumping the remainder of my cocaine onto a make-up mirror. My favorite song "Borderline" began playing as I lowered my head to snort it.

I drove home through Laurel Canyon and realized that porn was all I had.

I got home at six o'clock and jumped in the shower, realizing how hungry I was.

My friends in pornography cared about me. They were always there for me.

As usual, there was nothing in my new $1500.00 refrigerator.

I didn't have a mom or dad anymore. My mom had turned her back on me.

Six-fifty, the buzzer rang. My stomach was growling. The last time I ate was yesterday on the set. A chocolate donut sprinkled with peanuts.

Michael and I sat down in a booth at a small, romantic Italian restaurant.

"The chicken picatta is excellent here." Michael said.

I closed my menu. "Perfect, I'll try it."

Michael talked about business; I ate my dinner chiming in the conversation when necessary with a simple "yes" or "sounds great" between bites.

"I even got John Holmes out of retirement to be in this film."

I swallowed the last bite of the lemon and butter chicken, and looked at him for the first time since the food arrived.

Michael was only half way through his dinner.

"John Holmes? I don't have to work with him do I?" Ouch. I didn't think I could handle him.

"No. I've got you with Harry Reams and Ron Jeremy."

The waiter walked over. "May I get you anything else?"

"Yes please. I would like another chicken picata dinner."

Both Michael and the waiter stared at me.

"I seem to be real hungry tonight."

After topping off my dinners with a bowl of fresh berries and cream, I was full, sleepy and ready to go home.

"Thanks for a great dinner Michael. I better get to sleep, I have an early call tomorrow."

Michael was cute, and I knew he had a crush on me, but I had no desire to have sex with him or anybody actually.

I crawled into bed with a full belly, and fell asleep for a full ten hours.

I spent the next week shooting two movies back-to-back with out a day off. "Little Girls of the Street" and "The Enchantress."

We shot "Little Girls of the Street" on the streets of Hollywood. My co-stars and I played young hookers. Standing on the street corners in our skimpy outfits, the director Drea, would shoot the exterior footage from across the street or from a window above.

The window of a black Lincoln rolled down. "How much?"

Heather Wayne, Gina Valentino and I looked at each other. This man wasn't part of the script.

"You, in the black mini-dress. What's the charge?" I was in that black mini. The three of us walked up to his window. A baby seat was strapped into the back seat, and a large bag of diapers sat on the seat beside him. He wore a gold wedding ring that caught my eye. What a louse of a husband he is. He pushed the bridge of his glasses up, and gave a nervous blink at the same time. He was angrily touching himself through his gray wool pants. "I asked you how much." He demanded.

Gina spoke first. "Does the little misses know about this?"

"That's none of your God damn business. I want the one in the middle anyway."

I was the one in the middle. "What do you think Heather?" I asked.

"I think he would look great on film."

He wiped the sweat forming at his brow, "What are you talking about?" He was such a nervous Nellie.

I ducked my head five inches in the window. "We're shooting a documentary on men who cheat on their wives. If you turn around, you can wave into the camera."

He whipped his head around, and Drea, across the street, waved to us and gave us the thumbs up sign. The three of us stood there, choking off the exhaust from his car as he screeched away from the curb burning rubber.

Three days later, with that movie in the can, I dove right into shooting "The Enchantress." Pretty much the same cast, as always. The only difference was the script, and possibly the location. Even location owners were a tight-knit group.

The talent turnover in porno was very minimal. There was a handful of tried and true male performers that worked constantly. A frequently asked question is why there aren't more male performers? Why are there always the same men?

With bright lights, a room full of people, a microphone looming above you, and a camera following your every move, the pressure is on. It looks easy. The pay is decent, and you get to screw beautiful girls every day. Men always tell me, "Oh man, I could do that, no problem. I love sex."

"Action!" is yelled from the set, and suddenly that hard weenie gets smaller and smaller, right before my eyes.

An angry voice yells, "CUT!"

"Give me a second man, I don't know what happened, this has never happened to me before."

He strokes and strokes, it gets smaller and smaller. "Hey, can you just suck it for a minute?"

I shake my head no. It isn't my problem. "Not 'til he yells action." I lie. "I don't want to mess up my lipstick."

The director yells, "Would somebody cut the lights? Is Ron Jeremy still here? We need him as a stunt dick."

The gaffer yells back, "Yeah, I think I saw him at the lunch table."

Whatever little bit of manhood he had left, is now gone for good. No hard-on equals no cum shot. No cum-shot equals no sales. No sales equals no money. No money equals get a new career buddy. He is never to be seen in the world of porno again.

So there I was, having sex with Peter North for the ump-teenth time in my career in "The Enchantress."

I stopped by Boyle's apartment on the way home for two more grams.

I had the next day off, but had to be on the set by ten that night for "The Woman in Pink."

The producer could only rent out the warehouse we shot this in from ten at night, until five the following morning.

By seven that evening, I was exhausted. Heather and I had gone straight from Boyle's to my place.

Party-hardy with our vials of coke, then the unavoidable crash and burn.

"Heather, I'm going to take a two hour nap."

We put away our stash, what was left of it, and crawled into bed. My alarm went off what seemed like minutes later. Nine o'clock at night.

I lifted my exhausted body out of bed, took a shower, grabbed my wardrobe and tried to wake Heather. It was utterly useless.

I reset the alarm for eleven; her call time was midnight.

I sat in Wanda's chair.

"Are you alright?"

"Yeah, I've just been working to much."

"I just love you so much. I hope you're taking it easy on the drugs. You're going to ruin your skin."

I didn't even try to deny it anymore. "I'll be fine Wanda, all teenagers go through this stage."

"I guess that's true, they just don't have the money like you do."

I knew that was true. Working a regular job would never allow somebody my age to frequent their drug dealer nearly every day.

"I hope you're saving some of your money."

"I am." And I actually was. After furnishing my new place, buying clothes, paying my bills, and of course, supporting a drug habit, I had still managed to save quite a bit of money.

I never brought drugs onto the set. I needed to be as straight as possible while making films. I didn't want to lose touch with what was happening to me. I was after all a professional. A professional what, I wasn't sure. Person all around, I guess.

And miracle of all miracles, I always showed up.

Tonight I showed up, had my hair and makeup done, undressed then got redressed and headed to the bed to shoot my sex scene with Tom Byron, who played my husband.

Bed, oh God how I needed some sleep.

"What does this scene call for?" I asked, stretching my body out on the bed.

"Didn't you read your script?"

"Was there a script?"

"Yeah, you had a page of dialogue."

"Huh, that's funny, I don't think I got one." Then I remembered I left it at home. I had made an envelope out of it for Heather's half of the coke.

I closed my eyes, "Just give me a brief run down of the scene, I can just adlib through it." The pillow was so comfortable.

"Christy, are you awake?" Tom was bent over me. "They're ready to shoot."

"Of course I am." I couldn't open my eyes, not for lack of trying, but because the fake eyelash glue Wanda had used was sticking together. "Tom, I can't open my left eye, will you get Wanda?" I laid my head back down until Wanda showed up.

"Christy, wake up, I can't get to your eye if you're sleeping."

Why was everybody bugging me? I sat up, and Wanda poked a Q-tip around my eye.

Tom Byron and I ran some dialogue, got naked and began to have sex.

"Wake up Christy." Tom whispered. "The camera is panning up to your face right now."

I opened my eyes and wondered how long Tom had been having sex with me.

I made some silly, sexy faces into the camera, wiggled my body, moaned a bit and pretended to cum.

"Wake up Christy. It's four-thirty and we have to be out of the building in thirty minutes." Ron's soft, sweet voice was whispering in my ear.

"Where am I?"

"On the set. You passed out after, actually during your sex scene with Tom and we let you just keep sleeping after. I'm so sorry I had to wake you, but we all have to leave."

"Thanks Ron." He was so kind and understanding. "I wish you were my dad."

Seven straight days of work behind me, I could now enjoy two days off for Thanksgiving.

The telephone rang at nine thirty in the morning.

"Happy Thanksgiving!"

"Hi Clair. Happy Thanksgiving to you too." I didn't feel very thankful for much today.

"Dad wants to know if you want to meet him for lunch today." Clair's voice dropped, "Carol said you couldn't come over, but she agreed to let Dad see you for lunch somewhere. So if you can, we would love to see you at noon, Dad said you could pick any restaurant you want; just the three of us, like old times."

But nothing was like the old times. The past year was a very new and different time. Nothing would ever be the same again.

"I can't, I've already made plans."

I had too much pride and dignity to have crumbs thrown my way. Gee, wasn't Carol generous in letting my dad go out to see me for an hour on a holiday. Thanks, but no thanks.

"Dad really misses you. He always asks me how you are. Mom misses you too, but she's so busy taking care of Marv. He's hearing voices in his head now."

Isn't it ironic that my parent's problems went on, even with me out of their lives? Take me out of the equation, and their lives weren't enriched, happier or freer. Daddy was still miserable under Carol's thumb, jumping through hoops to try and please her and becoming more miserable in the process. Marv, still out of work, was now one step away from the loony bin. Karma sure bit him in the ass.

"Let them know that I miss them too. Tell Dad thanks for the offer and to have a good time without me."

"I miss our family being together."

"I do too Clair, but the times not right yet." I didn't know when the time would be right, but I had to believe that one day it would. I had to hold onto any shred of faith I could. If I could make it through the holidays, I could survive anything else in my life.

I snorted a line of coke, and headed out the door for Thanksgiving Day at Bruce Seven's house. Bruce welcomed everybody into his home. A den father for all of us lost souls, me being one of them.

Sitting at his dining room table, I looked around at all the people there. I had had sex with almost everybody at one time or another. But that was it, just sex on film. It was our job, nothing more. Once the cameras stopped rolling, we were just friends, in an odd sort of way. We just sat around eating, talking, laughing and enjoying a holiday together. We were thankful to have each other. There was no illicit sex taking place on the dining room table, or on the kitchen sink bent over the cooked turkey. There may have been yesterday, or even tomorrow, but not today.

Everybody there had one similarity in our lives, a shattered piece that bounded us together, a chip on our shoulder from something or somebody in our past or present. When you walked through the door of World Modeling, you were searching for something that had been taken away; A piece of your heart, pride, self-esteem or self-worth. We bonded together, bearing our souls and bodies on celluloid to get the attention we were lacking. We were paid very well for it financially, and we paid very dearly for it emotionally.

I ate among friends and was so very grateful for the people who took me in under their wing. I had food on my plate and a table in front of me, even if I did have sex on it three days ago.

My phone rang the day after Thanksgiving. "Hello."

"Hi, is this Christy?"

"Yes."

"Hi, this is Jimbo from Wicker Unlimited."

Then it hit me. "Oh no. I forgot to transfer money from my savings into my checking account. I'm so sorry. I'll do it today. Actually, if you want, I'll get a money order and drop it off to you in an hour. I feel horrible. I've just been on locations everyday since I bought the patio furniture from you."

"Actually, I bet we could work something out."

143

"Well, of course we can. Would you prefer cash then?"

"You know, I'm sure you hear it all the time, but you are a real looker."

"Thank you." Unsure of where this was heading.

"I'm a part owner in this store, and I could do some fancy book work to erase your $1700.00 debt."

His little piggy looking face filled my head. His tiny head all scrunched up, with a snout instead of a man's nose. His eyes were like that of the rodent family and his lips were dry and chapped like a reptile.

"I'm leaving right now to bring you a money order. I'll add an extra $10.00 to cover any bank charges you incurred. Have my check ready to give back to me. Bye."

How disgusting, he thought that I would sleep with him for free furniture. Did he think I was a prostitute? Even the thought of his naked, sweaty body on top of me made me feel dirty. I was sure he wouldn't last beyond a few grunts, but the damage to my psyche would linger. I could never sell my body to a stranger. I could never sell my body. I had my pride.

I could justify making films. It was different. It wasn't just a strange body invading me; it was somebody I knew. Peter, Tom, Ron and all of the rest of the talent weren't doing this for pure pleasure, it was their job, and it was my job. We all got paid. We were actors, and our acting included sex scenes. Harry Reams wouldn't have sex with me for free; this was his job, the way he made money to pay the bills. We were friends, who had sex together.

Prostitution was a whole different ball game, wasn't it?

I could justify what I was doing, and in the end, that's all that matters. Jimbo and I exchanged the money order for my bounced check.

"I was just making a suggestion. I wasn't trying to imply that you were anything. Just trying to help you out maybe." His eyes never left his hush puppies.

"If you ever call me again, I'll file harassment charges."

How dare he insult me.

Me, pre-braces in 4th grade.

Clare and I eating dinner at four and six with the mumps.

Me posing in 1984, looking like I'm straight out of 1974.
(Vivid Video)

So proud of my first Porsche in 1989 before it was stolen six months later.

My first box cover for Vivid in 1990. (Vivid Video)

On a box cover shoot with Amber Lynn & Janine.
"Where the Boys Aren't #9" (Vivid Video)

147

My 1984 prom photo. YES, I did have a date but couldn't find his photo.

Hugging the one and only Ron Jeremy whom I love.

Taking a few photos for my website after signing all night in San Diego.

Victoria Paris and I celebrating her birthday in 1999.

Keisha and I comparing in 1989.

Stopping for a quick photo at the LA Expo in 1998.

Victoria and I getting a hug from Mike Horner, one of our faves.

Old school girl – me, vs. new school girl's Lene Hefner and Adara Michaels

They don't make 'em like us anymore! With Nina Hartley & Victoria Paris.

You'll never see the four of us together again. Savanna, Jamie Summers and
Hyapatia Lee in 1992. (Vivid Video)

Grant and I taking a couch break after stuffing ourselves Thanksgiving 2001

16

The weather was changing. Christmas was in three days. The air was cool and the sky was gray. Large Christmas trees sat in the windows of stores and white lights were wrapped around poles up and down my street. I purchased two red poinsettia plants and put them on my doorstep.

I didn't bother decorating the inside of my place. I didn't want to think about the holidays. Holidays meant Mom and Dad. I no longer had that. I didn't want to remember.

I laid out two perfectly straight lines of coke. One went up my right nostril, the other up my left.

My body felt alive. I felt the rush to my brain jumpstarting my tired body.

Taking the plastic bucket and mop out from my broom closet, I began mopping my kitchen floor. Every tile, every line of grout and every inch of the floorboard began to shine. My jaw was moving back and forth with such intense concentration.

The ring from my phone startled me, but a call was welcome. Right about now, I had such a burning desire to talk to somebody, anybody, it didn't matter who. I looked at the clock by my phone. Wow, I had been cleaning my floor for two hours, only taking a break for a quick line and a cigarette.

"Hello." I leaned my mop against the wall and rubbed my lower back.

"Hi, it's Grant."

"Hi! How are you?"

"Good, I'm in San Francisco at school. I just wanted to see if you're okay."

Grant was always watching my back. Two months ago, we went to dinner and I told him what I was doing for a living.

"I already know. Marv told my dad and said you've really gone off the deep end. Your mom and dad are pretty worried about you."

Fuck Marv. I'm sure he was as happy as a pig in shit with my mom all to himself now that I was out of the picture.

Marv and Grant's dad Leonard loosely knew each other from the music business.

Grant held my hand in the car on the way home from dinner.

"I wish I could just take care of you, so you didn't have to make those kinds of films anymore."

"I'm fine Grant, I really am. People can say and think what they want, and I'm sure they do, but I'm actually really happy."

So my mom and dad were worried about me. Well, what in the fuck did they think I would do? How did they think I would survive on the streets after they threw me out? Going home wasn't an option. I did what I could to survive, and I did it as best as I could. At eighteen, I realized that I only had myself to rely on.

Grant came to my apartment, and we made out on my bed, but I cut it off at second base. I had to work in the morning. Somehow, sex in my personal life didn't exist anymore. I had no desire.

"I'm fine. I moved out of that dump in Hollywood since I saw you last. I have a cute two bedroom condo in the valley now."

I moved the receiver away from my mouth and snorted the remainder of coke straight out of the vile. I wondered if Boyle was ripping me off lately. My grams didn't seem to last as long anymore.

"I know, I was there last month remember? You had just moved in when I came by. You showed me around and then told me we would have a slumber party one night, just the two of us."

"Oh yeah, I remember." I didn't dare ask why that slumber party never happened. I'm sure I flaked out on him. I seemed to be doing a lot of that lately with my friends. I didn't want to, I was just so consumed with work.

"I've been so busy with work and getting my place together, I'm sorry I haven't called you."

"It's okay, but I would like to see you. If I get you a plane ticket, will you come to visit me in San Francisco?"

I had to call Boyle soon. This coke high seemed to be wearing off faster than it should. I wonder if he's been cutting it with something recently.

"Yeah, that would be great Grant. I would love to come down and see you."

I tilted my head back, put a few drops of water down each nostril trying to loosen up any traces of coke. A bitter taste filled my throat, my head buzzed.

"It's actually up to see me, not down."

"Yeah, great!" I said. My body feeling jittery, my heartbeat pounding in my chest, I tried to think of what Grant just said to me. Shit, what did I miss? I couldn't concentrate anymore. I had to get off the phone and sweep off my patio.

"Call me when you book my flight." My eyes focused on the broom.

"Well, when can you take time off of work?"

"Anytime. I make my own schedule. Just book it, and I'll be there."

"Hey, are you okay? You sound," Grant paused, searching for the right word, "different."

"No, I'm great." Just as high as a kite.

"Alright, I'll call you tomorrow and leave the flight info on your

155

machine if you're not home."

"Great, see ya soon."

The next day, I got home from shooting "Educating Mandy". Grant's message let me know I was booked on a flight to San Francisco on Friday in two weeks. "If we don't get a hold of each other in the meantime, I'll just see you at the airport."

The next morning I opened my date book to the weekend we were supposed to meet.

I was already booked for four days on a major production for Video Exclusives', "Holly Does Hollywood". I was cast as Holly, the lead role.

I couldn't fly to San Francisco. I had to work. I would call Grant tonight when I got home from the set. I'll just see him the following weekend. He'll understand.

That night, I came home from work exhausted. I took a bubble bath, climbed into bed and passed out watching TV.

For the next two weeks I forgot to call Grant.

17

Even the world of porn came to a halt between Christmas and New Year's. Everybody needed to be with somebody. A real family or not, it didn't matter. Everybody clung to somebody to survive the holidays.

Michael called me Christmas Eve. "What are you doing for Christmas?"

I looked around my pad. No tree, no presents, no plans. "I was just going to spend it with Wanda and Ron."

"Do you want to go to Hawaii for eight days? I've got an extra ticket."

Hell yeah. "I would love to."

"Great. I'll pick you up tomorrow morning at nine. With the time change, we can be on the beach by noon."

Michael was a nice guy. Since I had shot two movies for him, we had become friendly. A dinner here and there and phone calls every few days.

I snorted two larger than usual lines of coke. Figured I better use it all up before my trip. I certainly didn't want to be busted at the airport for drugs. I could always save it for when I got home. The familiar bitter taste filled my mouth. Yeah right, I would save it.

Three hours, and one gram of coke later, I was packed and ready for Hawaii; which island, I had no clue. I forgot to ask. It didn't matter, Hawaii is Hawaii, and a free trip is a free trip.

If I hadn't been so hyper from the drugs, there was no way I could have lugged my three bags to the front door. I had packed like I was taking a three-month trip. Five different outfits a day to choose from, with all sorts of shoes and purses to match.

1a.m.: - I was wide awake. I spent the next hour picking out what I would wear on the plane, rearranging my closet while I was in there. May as well Windex off the mirrored closet doors while I was at it. I changed my sheets. Who wants to come home to dirty linens? I tackled that linen closet while I was thinking about it.

I checked out that sock and underwear drawer, what a mess. It wasn't thirty minutes later.

5a.m.: - Beginning to unwind, I took a shower, dried my hair and got dressed. Bermuda shorts, a pink and black checkered shirt, and black heels. I was as white as a ghost, dark circles under my eyes, and twenty pounds too thin for my five foot six frame.

Checking myself out in the hallway mirror, I thought, damn I'm looking good.

Three hours until Michael came to pick me up. I wasn't very sleepy, so I just sat down on the couch to watch a little TV.

The telephone and security buzzers were both ringing at the same time. My bleary eyes focused in on the VCR clock. Nine fifteen in the morning; SHIT!

I said Hello into the security intercom and the telephone at the same time.

"It's me, Michael. I've been ringing you for fifteen minutes."

"Oh, I was just drying my hair, come on in."

I must have dozed off. It's a funny thing how the body seems to need a couple of hours of sleep every week.

I opened my front door and waved to Michael who was walking down the long corridor. He was actually very handsome; tall, well built and with curly dark brown hair.

"Hi. Sorry about that."

"Don't worry about it. I just got worried that maybe you weren't here."

What, me flake? Yes, but not on a trip to Hawaii.

He looked at my luggage, then at me. "You've got to be kidding."

"Oh no, I'll need all of it."

After heaving and hoeing, Michael had finally wrangled a huge suitcase under each arm.

"Oh, let me get that last piece Michael." I bent down and picked up my makeup bag.

I locked my front door, and we were off to the airport.

"We're here." Michael nudged me awake.

I could barely get out of the car. My body felt like it weighed five hundred pounds. "I must have fallen asleep."

"Yeah, and snoring the entire way."

I stumbled, literally in my heels, to our gate. We had five minutes before the flight left.

We found our seats, and I buckled up for the five-hour flight.

Michael began looking through the airline magazine. "Let's see what movie is...."

His voice became more distant with every word spoken.

"We're here." Michael nudged me awake.

I wiped the drool from my left cheek. "That went by so fast."

"Yeah, when you're in a coma, it usually does."

"What island are we at anyway?"

He stared at me and cocked his head. "Maui."

"Cool."

We got off the plane, and I felt the warmth of the sun surround my body. God, it felt so healing on my skin.

Michael grabbed his duffle bag off the belt. My two suitcases, which now sported decals reading "heavy", were the last to come down.

Michael looked at me, and realized that I was quite useless in helping him out. He yelled "Porter."

Ten minutes later, we pulled into the Sheraton. One room, one bed.

I opened a suitcase, and pulled out one of my many bikinis.

"I'm going to the beach Michael, I'll see you there."

He was on the phone, not looking very pleased with his conversation.

Five hours later, I woke up as the sun was setting. I found my way back to the room. Michael was sitting in bed watching a ballgame on TV. What a dud I thought.

"Hey, why didn't you meet me out there?" I asked.

"I was out there 'til about half an hour ago with you. I just couldn't wake you up to save my life."

For the next six days, I ate and slept.

On day seven I walked into our room after a massage and the phone was ringing.

"Hello." There was a moment of silence from the other end.

"Put Michael on the phone." A very angry female voice demanded.

"I don't know where he is, I just walked in."

"You tell him Jenny called." I knew the slam was coming, so I pulled the phone away from my ear.

As I was writing the message down, Michael came through the door. God he was good looking.

"Some girl just called named Jenny. She didn't sound too happy to hear me answer."

"Oh, she's my ex-girlfriend. She was supposed to be on this trip with me, but we got into a huge fight, so I told her not to come. I just hadn't told her that I was bringing anyone else."

"Well, I think she figured it out now."

Most girls would have given him the riot act. All that sisterhood, female-bonding bullshit. Not me. We had sex that night for the first time.

It was the first time I felt like having sex since I started making films.

18

At the end of March, I was booked for two days on a Video Exclusives production "Savage Fury."

I was so tired. My body was exhausted, depleted and drained. My brain could only concentrate on the immediate activity in front of me, nothing one minute ago or one minute ahead. I was worn out, overworked and over fucked.

The red neon numbers on my clock read nine thirty, which meant it was time to get up and get ready for work. I rolled over and touched Michael's shoulder. "I have to get ready for work." I understood why bears chose to hibernate. One night wasn't enough, my body craved weeks of endless sleep.

"Oh great, my girlfriend is going off to get screwed all day." He moved his body away from my touch.

"But you knew what I did for a living when we started to date." I sat up in bed and felt the onset of the now familiar headache that greeted me every morning. "Don't forget we met on one of your productions." I got out of bed and held onto the brass footboard until my dizzy spell passed. "And I even made a film for your company after you moved in with me last month."

Michael began to snore, and a very fake one at that.

I walked into my kitchen and made a pot of coffee. "Hello my sweet kitty cat." I wondered if my cat and sister were the only two people who really loved me without criticism.

Michael said he loved me, but his next breath was always a put down. "Do you know how embarrassing it is for me when I have to tell my friends that my girlfriend is a porn star?"

I sat down and took a sip of coffee, pet my cat and wondered when our three-month relationship turned so ugly. I didn't care what my friends thought about Michael producing and distributing porn films, I was in love. Why did he care? And if he cared so much, why didn't he make me a better offer? I would have married him in a heartbeat. He on the other hand, said he could never marry a porn star.

And that was me. A porn star. A very confused, lost soul who happened to make her living by having sex on film.

He, Michael, was a very self-centered soul who happened to become a multi-millionaire by hiring girls just like me to have sex on film for his company.

Between the coffee and a hot shower, enough cobwebs were cleared out of my brain to make it to the set on time.

"Hey Tina." Tina was the director on this movie as well as one of my best friends.

Tina stopped arm wrestling the soundman when I walked in. "Are you okay Christy?"

I put my wardrobe bag down. "Same old same old." I smiled, but I felt like crying. "It's show time and I can't disappoint my fans."

"You never do." Tina looked me in the eyes. "The sooner you dump him, the better."

"I know." But I also knew that he was all I had.

The two days flew by like a blur. Scanning my script in the makeup chair, I got the gist of the plot. I played a college girl who got raped with my friends by a group of guys, and one year later we seek revenge. Pretty simple stuff. I fucked. I got fucked. I gave head. I got head. It was suddenly just a job and I went through the motions. I did some dialogue, had a three-way sex scene, did some more dialogue, pretended to shoot and kill the bad boys, shot the breeze with my girlfriends and what the fuck, had some more sex. It was a wrap. I got paid and went home.

Michael wasn't home when I got back from my second day on the set. Was he home last night? I had fallen asleep at eight after my first day of work and didn't get up until my alarm went off at ten. I slept for fourteen hours and I still couldn't think straight. My head hurt and felt like it weighed one hundred pounds.

By eight fifteen, I crawled into bed and called Wanda.

"Hey Wanda, what are you doing?" Wanda was my other best friend.

"Just replenishing my makeup case. I got this new blue eyeliner that will look gorgeous with your skin color. I'm going to try it out on you this weekend for the Hollywood Video shoot."

"Which shoot is that?" Was I working this weekend?

"Duh Christy! It's the two-day shoot you're starring in. Don't tell me you forgot."

"No, of course not." I grabbed my date book and opened it up. "I thought it was the following weekend." But of course I was wrong. The weekend after this, I was booked on a Four Play production, and Monday through Thursday I was booked with Essex leaving me with only Friday off. One glorious day off.

"It's the boom of the video age," Jim said one day last month. "We're all here to make hay while the sun shines."

"No, Hollywood is definitely this weekend Christy. Don't forget my dad's shooting you on Friday for a layout."

There goes my one day off. "How could I forget?" I grabbed a hotel pen off my nightstand and wrote it down. "It's right here in my book." Along with every other day marked off. Between video shoots, box cover shoots and magazine layouts I didn't have one free day. I turned the page to May, and saw that I had the second Tuesday of the month off. Now, if my eighteen-year-old body could just hold out for a few more weeks. I didn't think to worry about my mind.

"Are you okay Christy?"

"Oh sure, fine, just a little tired." That was a complete lie. I was far from fine.

"Who did you work with the last two days?"

"I have no idea." I couldn't even remember who I was having sex with just hours ago, let alone yesterday.

"How's Michael?" Wanda asked with concern.

"I have no idea."

"Are you okay Christy? Do you want me to come right over?"

"No, I'll be okay, I just need to get some sleep. I love you so much."

"I love you too. Call me anytime tonight and I'll be right over."

"Thanks, but I'm sure Michael will be home soon."

"I think Michael," Wanda stopped. "Oh Christy, I know you deserve better."

Unfortunately, I didn't think so.

"Well, call me if you need me Christy. I don't care what time it is."

My head hit the pillow for the next thirteen hours.

10a.m. and there was no sign of Michael. I reached for the phone and called his office. "Hi Kelly, is Michael in?" I knew that Kelly wanted Michael. I saw the way she looked at him when I stopped by his office. She made me sick with jealousy and fueled my ever-growing insecurity. She wanted my man.

"Hold on Christy."

I just didn't bother to notice the way he looked at her.

"What's up?"

My heart skipped a beat hearing his voice. "Hi. Have you been home in the last two nights?"

"Naw, I knew you would be working, so I just hung out at Gordy's house and fell asleep there."

I could have sworn Michael said his partner was going out of town this week. "I thought Gordy went to Hawaii." As exhausted as I was, I knew this was the week.

"What? Are you questioning me? If you pull that shit on me, I'll just never come home."

"No, no. I guess I thought it was this week, but you're right." But I knew he wasn't right. Five nights ago we took Gordy and his girlfriend to the airport. "Are you coming home tonight?" Oh please say yes.

"Maybe, we'll see. 'Til then, have fun getting fucked today."

"I'm not making a movie today, I'm shooting a layout." But he didn't hear me. All I could hear was a dial tone. I sat in bed frozen with the

162

phone in my hand. He just hung up on me, and said he didn't know if he would be home tonight. Gordy was out of town, so where had Michael been for the past two nights? Was he with another girl? Of course he was. Would I confront him? Of course I wouldn't. He was after all, all I had. He had said it himself. What could I do to make him love me more? I never thought about what I could do to love myself more. Did Michael think I liked my job? Did I even like my job anymore? There were so many questions that I couldn't answer. I didn't even know where to begin finding them.

I dragged my body from under the warmth of my comforter and stood in front of my mirror. What could I do to make myself prettier for Michael? For starters, maybe I should get rid of my long white nightshirt and get some pretty silky lingerie. I had a drawer full of some that I had worn on movie sets. I bent down and opened up the bottom drawer and pulled out a pink silk teddy that I bought at Judy's. I took off my nightshirt and slipped the silk fabric over my head. I stood up and looked at myself in the mirror. I immediately thought of a sex scene I had worn it in when I worked with Peter North two weeks ago. I took it off and shoved it back in the drawer. To me, it was now tainted, along with every other piece. I looked at my hair that was still curled and sprayed from yesterday's shoot thanks to plenty of Aqua Net Super Hold. Maybe if I put some blonde highlights in my hair he would notice me more. I moved my face one inch from the mirror and checked out my nose from every angle. Michael was always telling me that my nose looked like a birds beak. Maybe a nose job is what he was hinting at. I'll have to ask Wanda the name of a good plastic surgeon. I pushed up on the tip of my nose up to see what it would look like but it just made me look like I had a pig's snout. I pinched the bridge of my nose and pulled it back but that just made me look like a donkey.

I went into my bathroom and turned the shower on. While I was waiting for the water to get hot, I took one last close look at my nose.

I actually liked my nose the way it was. Besides, if the doctor screwed up, then Michael would definitely drop me.

I threw my nightshirt in the hamper and realized how comfortable it was. If Michael wanted me in sexy lingerie, he would just have to buy it for me.

I ran a brush through my hair and noticed how pretty my natural chocolate brown hair color was.

I stepped under the hot water and felt the cobwebs begin to disappear. Maybe I wasn't such a bad package deal after all. Maybe, just maybe, it was Michael who needed an overhaul.

I stepped out of the shower and looked in the mirror. It didn't really matter what Michael needed. I needed help in finding my long lost self-esteem and pride.

I drove up Laurel Canyon heading into Hollywood and thought about my job, my boyfriend and my parents. These were the three main things in my life that I had to change. I got to the top of Mulholland and Laurel Canyon and pulled over. I looked up at the beautiful blue sky and green trees surrounding me, and began to cry.

Why is it I wondered, that I could be looking at such beauty in this world and yet feel so sad and lonely? Wasn't it enough that the sky was blue, birds were singing in the green treetops, and I was alive and breathing? That is what I needed to figure out, and fast.

I looked at the clock on my dashboard and realized that I was already fifteen minutes late. So, as I had learned to do so well, I shoved my troubles to the back of my mind. What would be the harm for one more day? The problem was, that I was like a pressure cooker about to explode at any minute.

I found the photographer's address on Hollywood Blvd. above the Loves restaurant.

Today I was working with a new photographer named Ed. I was shooting a simple single girl layout with a Hawaiian motif. I grabbed my thongs and a Hawaiian print shirt from the trunk and headed up the piss-smelling flight of stairs.

I got to Ed's door and let myself in. Standing in the center of a Hawaiian backdrop, which resembled a kindergartener's portrayal of the tropical island, was a tall bald man.

I plastered on that big fake smile and lied, "Cool set. I'm Christy and you must be Ed."

He stood back to admire the infantile backdrop. "Yes, I stayed up all night painting it."

I looked at his fingertips for paint residue, but I didn't see any. "So, Jim tells me you're a new photographer in the business."

"Yes."

He was a man of few words which suited me just fine today. I didn't feel like being here, let alone making small talk with Baldie. "Great, lets get started then."

Ed pulled an office chair to the center of the set. "We'll start with you sitting in the chair in your Hawaiian outfit."

"All I brought was a shirt." He had to be joking. No sand or trees as scenery? "If this is supposed to be Hawaii, don't you have a lounge chair or something Hawaiian looking?"

The tip of his head became red. "What do you mean all you have is a shirt?"

"You guys are supposed to have wardrobe, not the models." I was getting a real bad feeling. I eyed the door. "Hey Ed, I need to get paid

164

before we start anything since you're new and all." I could hear traffic from two stories below and felt a bit of comfort when I heard somebody from the street yell, "Fuck You asshole, learn how to drive." At least I knew I wasn't totally alone.

"What? I was told you get the cash afterward."

"No, ask Jim." I lied, "He's the one who told me to get it up front." I shrugged my shoulders. "You know that crazy Jim." Yeah, about as crazy as a dead fly. "So, do you have a bottle of lotion I can spray on me for a prop or anything?"

"No. Jim didn't tell me much of anything."

We stared at each other for a minute, and I could hear a car crashing into another. "You stupid fuck," came through the open window in Ed's studio.

"It's up to you Ed." I almost wished he wouldn't pay me up front so I would have an excuse to leave. Jim would be furious, but suddenly, standing in this hot studio above Hollywood Blvd. with an idiot who couldn't even do a set right, I came to the realization that I could care less if Jim was pissed at me. In fact, I was pretty fucking pissed at Jim for sending me to this loser. "Do you have anything else for this set?"

"No, we'll work with what we have."

Neither one of us moved.

"You need to pay me now."

He dug into his pocket never taking his eyes off me. He pulled out eight crisp one hundred dollar bills.

"Cool, thanks. I'll be sure to tell Jim you followed through!" I shoved the money in my own pocket. "I think you should run down to the drugstore and get a few props like a beach ball, lotion and maybe even a towel."

I didn't give a rat's ass what he got at the drug store; I just wanted to deposit this money up the street. "I'll go down with you."

"Does it really make that much of a difference? With what I'm paying you, I'm already way over budget."

Did this man ever blink? "If you want to be in the Vogel or Randall league of being a photographer, you better get some props." I wasn't even sure if this creep actually knew how to load a camera. "I'm going to run down with you and grab a burger. Do you want one?"

He eyed my pocket with the money. "You're leaving?"

"Yeah, do you mind if I leave my wardrobe here?" I didn't want him to think I was bolting. "I'll meet you back in fifteen minutes." I hung my thrift store Hawaiian print shirt on the chair. "Don't want it to get wrinkled."

We both eyed the already wrinkled shirt. "I'm going to leave my date book here too."

He looked at his watch. "Fifteen minutes."

"Great. And maybe pick up a paperback novel, so it looks like I'm reading on the beach." I smiled, "Just another option." With that backdrop, it will look like I'm reading in the eye of a hurricane.

Ed and I walked down the flight of stairs. He went right, into the drugstore and I went left, into the bank two doors down.

Fifteen minutes later we were both back in his dump of a studio and I was dreading the shoot from the tips of my toes.

Ed threw the drug store bag down on the ground. "Let's get started, we're already forty-five minutes behind schedule."

Like it was my fault. "Let me just change." I turned my back to his now leering eyes, which still hadn't blinked and undressed down to my underwear.

Ed was standing too close for comfort. "Here's your shirt."'

I did a quarter of a turn and put it on as fast as I could. "Thanks."

I don't know why I was so modest undressing. After a handful of frames, I was going to be stark naked in front of Ed.

I draped the neon yellow towel over his office chair, put my sunglasses on and held the paperback a foot away from my face. Snap, snap. I lifted the glasses up, put them on my head and smiled for the next two frames.

He pulled the camera away from his face. "Get naked now."

"You don't want to set this beach..." What was it exactly? "...Scenario up anymore? Vogel usually uses a full roll of film to set the scene up."

He looked at the camera lens, "I don't really care about Vogel. This is my shoot."

He was an arrogant little fucker. "Sure is." How dare he not care about Vogel. Vogel was like a father to me. "Do you want the chair in the picture still?" I was stalling.

"Of course, it's perfect with that towel over it."

I began to unbutton my blouse and he began to shoot away. I turned my back and stepped out of my underwear. I could hear the camera clicking away. I looked over my shoulder. "Want to wait 'til I'm ready to pose here?"

"No, I just love these candid photos."

Yeah, of just my white ass. "Okay, how about some standing poses?"

His voice came out in a whisper now. "No, get in that chair and point your ass to me, don't even bother turning around."

I sat backwards in the chair, my legs tucked under me.

"Point it out even further and spread your cheeks open as far as you can."

I thought of the money I had just deposited, and did as I was told.

"Your cunt looks dry."

"I think it's the hot lights blaring down on it." And because I'm anything but turned on. Did this idiot think girls' pussies were just oozing out liquid all day long?

The room became silent. And then I felt it. I felt something wet and hot against my private parts. I held onto the back of the chair for support while the top of my pressure cooker finally exploded.

"WHAT THE FUCK ARE YOU DOING?" I screamed as loud as I could. I hopped over the back of the chair like a bunny rabbit. "Who the fuck do you think you are?" His zipper was up, so it must have been his tongue. And suddenly, Ed got all of the anger, sadness and misery that I had built up in me for the past year.

"You piece of shit, how dare you touch me. Get away from me or I'm calling the cops." I wasn't even sure if he had a phone. "How dare you try to rape me. Make one move towards me and I scream as loud as I can." I looked down at my bare breasts. "And I have one set of loud lungs." I hated Ed for my mom choosing that piece of shit, no good Marv over me.

"I wasn't trying to rape you." Ed finally blinked, and made up for lost time. He blinked like a butterfly and stammered, "It's just that you're a porn star and all."

I was shaking with rage. "So that gives you the right to invade my body?" I picked up the office chair and threw it against the Hawaiian backdrop. "IT'S MY JOB!! IT'S NOT WHO I AM!" The chair connected and tore through the center of the backdrop, "You stupid moron." The metal chair landed on the ground, taking out a light stand on its way. Hawaii had just been hit with a tsunami named Christy. "I HATE YOU." I hated Ed for my dad choosing that fake, phony cunt Carol over me.

Ed cried. "My set."

I dressed in record speed never taking my eyes off Ed. I hated Ed for my sweet sister choosing a stupid college in London over me. "Fuck you and fuck your set!" I looked around to see what else I could damage.

His face was buried in his hands. "I'm sorry, I didn't realize..."

I grabbed my purse. "Well you should have." I hated Ed for my mom and dad not speaking to me.

Ed looked up from his hands, "But what about the shoot? Can we finish it? I promise I wont try that again."

I slid into my thongs. "Shoot's finished." I hated Ed for the abuse I took from Michael.

"But I can't sell twelve frames for a layout."

"Too fucking bad." I grabbed the plastic bag of lotion and shoved the paperback in it. I hated Ed for Marv coming into my life. "I'm going to call Jim and tell him never to use you again you moron." I slammed the office door in his face as he was asking for a portion of his money back.

I hated Ed for everything.

I hated my life.

I took the stairs three at a time and jumped over a passed out drunk at the bottom. I unlocked my car and took one last look up at Ed's office. He was sitting in the window, watching me. I flipped him the bird and called him an asshole one more time at the top of my lungs. Nobody on Hollywood Blvd. even took notice. It was just another day in the heart of "Hollyweird".

I drove home shaking from anger that somebody would think that just because I was a porn star, they had free reign to my body. It was my body. I couldn't wait to get home and call Michael. He would know what to do. He would probably want to call Jim personally.

I opened my front door and knew something was wrong. I stepped in and closed the door behind me. My TV and VCR were still in the living room, so I knew I hadn't been robbed. I turned to my right and saw a big empty space where my washer and dryer were when I left this morning. I dropped my purse, ran into my bedroom and opened my closet door. The right side was empty. Michael had moved out.

"Put Michael on the phone." I was in no mood for that bitch Kelly today.

"He's in a..."

"NOW, or tell him I'm coming down and camping out if I have to."

"Hold..."

"I will, but not for long." I sat on the edge of my bed and listened to three bars of elevator Muzak.

"It's me." Michael said. "That was a pretty rotten thing of me to do, huh?"

"Yeah, it was pretty mean." I began to cry. "You could have told me."

"I didn't want a scene, I just wanted to leave."

There were a few moments of that awful silence until I blew my nose. "So this is it?"

"No, we can still date, I just got my own place."

"Where did you move?"

"My tenants moved out of my condo in Brentwood, so I moved in."

There was more silence until two things hit me. "So you must have been planning it for a while."

"For about two weeks."

"But you still want to date me?" What a loser I was, the Big Kahuna agreed to still see me.

"Well, yeah, why not. I just needed my own place."

"Oh, Okay." The tears began to dry, for now. "Can we go out tomorrow night?" Work never went past six or seven with an eight o'clock call time. Two quick scenes and I would be out of there.

"No, I've made plans, but I'll see you Monday." He didn't ask, he just told me.

"Uh, okay." One more blow of the nose. "Michael, why did you take back the washer and dryer you bought me?"

"Yeah well, I realized I needed a set at my new place."

"Oh, okay, I'll see you Monday night."

I hung up the phone and started to move the clothes around in my closet. Maybe if I didn't have to stare at a big empty space, it wouldn't hurt so badly. Wrong. Nine hangers into it and I began to cry. I sat on the ground and hugged my knees into my chest. I thought about one of my father's adages. "Some days, when it rains it pours." And I cried even more. God I missed my parents.

I woke up to my telephone ringing. Who would be calling me so early in the morning? I rolled over in bed and looked at the clock. Twenty minutes after nine. My call time for Hollywood Video was over an hour ago.

"Hello."

"Christy, it's Jim. What's going on? Hal is having a hissy fit. His star was supposed to be on set almost two hours ago."

Hal hasn't even begun to have a fit.

Jim continued and I lit a cigarette. "If you hurry up and fly to the set in the next thirty minutes, everything will be alright."

No, everything will not be all right.

"Christy? Are you there?" His voice softened. "Please tell Uncle Jimmy you've got one foot out the door."

"I don't think I'll be making that shoot today."

Silence. "What did I just hear?"

"I said, I wouldn't be making that shoot today, tomorrow or any other day. I quit Jim."

Jim gave a small yelp. "But you can't just quit. Is there anything I can do? How about if I tell Hal you wont be able to make it today, but will shoot all of your scenes tomorrow."

Maybe I would feel different tomorrow.

"Christy, are you okay?"

That was the million-dollar question. "No. I'm not okay. My parents have disowned me, Michael packed up and moved out yesterday and that mother-fucker Ed tried to stick his tongue in me yesterday."

"Oh yes, Ed called me. I was going to call you about it."

Sure, when pigs began to fly Jim would care about Ed touching me. "No Jim, I quit." Jim's only concern about the Ed incident was that I might not show up today, or ever again. "There's nothing you can do about Ed now. I just can't believe you sent me to a new photographer. You didn't know a damn thing about him and you still sent me. I counted on you to

169

protect me Jim."

"So, just like that? You quit?"

That's right, this body is no longer for hire. "Yes, I quit." In the end, I realized that I was just a fifty dollar a day fee to him.

In his last ditch effort, "But Hal has you booked, you're breaking an oral contract."

"Find me a judge who will make me fuck." You got away with that once pal. "Goodbye Jim." I hung up the phone, pulled the covers over my head and fell back asleep until eight o'clock that night.

The following month I slept, ate and saw Michael when he had time for me.

My second week into retirement, Michael asked, Do you miss the business?"

"Not one bit." And I didn't. "Aren't you glad I quit?"

"Sure, what ever makes you happy."

He sure didn't make me happy. I just needed a brick to fall on my head to realize it.

19

Two weeks later, Michael asked me if I wanted to go to San Diego with him for the weekend and his nephew Kevin who was visiting from New Jersey.

"Clair's just got home from London, and I want to spend the weekend with her before she leaves for college to Sacramento next week."

"Fine, I'll call you Sunday when I get home."

I wondered why he seemed mad. Didn't he realize that Clair would always come first? She was my priority in life.

I spent the next three days with Clair. I had missed my sister so much. She was the only one who had stuck by my side through everything; the drugs, porn, and even flaking out on her at times. She understood what I was going through, and never once judged me. My one constant in life was always and would always be Clair.

"What are you going to do now that you quit the business?"

"I don't have a clue Clair."

We spent the weekend being girls, sisters and best friends.

Michael's call came in Monday morning, not Sunday as he promised. "You sure missed out on a great weekend."

"I'm glad you had fun. I also had a great weekend with Clair." I was about to tell Michael about my fun weekend with Clair, when he told me that Jenny had joined them for the weekend at the last minute.

I went numb. My body began to tingle with rage. My stomach felt hollow, like I had just been kicked.

"Why?" was all that came out of my mouth.

"Well, she's known Kevin so long and all. It just worked out that way."

"I can't believe you. How could you do this to me?" I was screaming by now. But I knew he was doing it to me because I was allowing him to and that's what made me so angry.

"Whoa, calm down. You could have come you know, but you didn't want to."

"But Clair..." Oh fuck it. This was going nowhere.

"I've got to go Michael, I'll talk to you later."

"Hey wait a second, it's not like I had sex with her or anything. What's the big deal?"

He just didn't get it. It was a huge deal to me. My boyfriend just spent the weekend with an ex who was still pining for him.

"I've got to go Michael."

"Suit yourself. But just remember, you could have gone with us."

171

I hung up but held onto the phone, wondering what my options were. I had to talk to somebody; somebody who cared and loved me. I ran through the short list in my head. Clair was leaving for Sacramento tonight to check out her new college, and I didn't want to burden and worry her.

Wanda was on a five-day shoot in San Francisco without a phone all day.

I looked over at my TV, and saw Bob Barker on the "Price Is Right". The sound was muted, but a heavyset girl was jumping up and down, with her arms wrapped around Bob's waist. Bob was trying to keep his balance and shake her loose at the same time. She finally let go, and ran over to her new pullout couch and grandfather clock. Bob straightened his tie, and adjusted his neck, while talking into the camera. A commercial for a motorcycle accident attorney came on.

I punched in an area code and phone number.

"Hi Tina, it's me."

"Hi honey! How are you?"

"Actually, not too good. When are you coming back to LA?"

"Not for two weeks baby, what's wrong?"

I filled her in on the latest Michael saga.

"Sit by the phone, and I'll call you back in five minutes."

One cigarette later the phone rang.

"Hi."

"American Airlines at two-twenty this afternoon out of LAX. There's a prepaid ticket under your name at the counter. You're coming to Indiana."

"I love you Tina."

"I love you too Christy."

That afternoon I got on a plane and headed to Indiana. Tina was waiting for me when I landed at O'Hare airport in Chicago. She was my best friend. Tina and Wanda were the only two friendships I kept in the business.

"Let's get your bags."

"I didn't bring anything, just this duffel bag." I looked down at my shoes and felt a tear roll down my cheek. "I just left Tina."

"That's okay, we'll share all of my stuff, just like best friends do."

So off we drove to Gary, Indiana, which was the headquarters of Video Exclusives. Tina and Mark kept a condo there.

I spent my week in Gary looking back on the past year of my life; Jim, modeling, films, Michael, drugs, and no parents.

Had my life come to this because of a stolen credit card and a night of drunk driving? No, it had to go much deeper than that. It had to start long before I turned seventeen. It had to start with feeling left out, searching for approval. I was desperately seeking attention from the male race and

172

validity from my various stepfathers. I was searching for love and sanction from my real father. I wanted to be noticed and put first in his life. I wanted, for once in my life, to be put before Carol and Eve without a fight, or a struggle. It should come so naturally for a father with his daughter; but it didn't.

* * * *

JUNE 1981
Fourteen years old

As the weeks, months and following few years went by, Clair and I saw less and less of our father. His new wife and her teenage daughter now consumed his life. The weekly phone calls were coming in every few weeks now, and our monthly weekend overnight visits became a Saturday night every five to six weeks. On a rare good month, our father would pick Clair and me up for dinner, sans Carol and Eve, and catch up on our lives over a hot dog and chili fries at a hole-in-the-wall located between our two houses.

"I'm having nothing but trouble with Eve at home." My father roared while licking the chili off his upper lip with his tongue.

"I politely asked her NOT to open up charge accounts under my name, forge my signature illegally, charge the card up and over its limit, and then throw the statement away when it came in the mail." Dad paused long enough to shove the rest of his wiener in his mouth before plowing ahead with his bellyaching to his two barely teenage daughters.

"I got a letter from a collection agency last week telling me that I owe over $800.00 to Joseph Magnin's. 'I've never even stepped foot into that Goddamn store' I told them." Dad pounded his fist on the worn out wooden table, causing the couple behind us to turn around. Clair and I were used to his dramatics and kept on eating. Dad was oblivious to anyone but himself.

"Yesterday, in the mail, they sent me a copy of my application along with my forged signature on sales receipts. I told those sons of a bitches I never purchased four pairs of ladies shoes and a handbag. So when I casually asked Eve if she knew anything about this, she told me to fuck off and slammed her bedroom door in my face. She repeated this until the door finally fell off its hinges. Did her mother do anything about it? NO! She told me to stop harassing her daughter. That woman never stands behind me." Dad paused for another breather while his lips pursed like a duck for a moment before he belched.

You never stand behind Clair and me.

"Last month, when Eve took my car out without permission, she

173

returned it with the bumper shoved in the back seat. When I asked her ever so kindly if she knew how the bumper found its way into the back of the car, she told me she hated me and threw our gumball machine across the kitchen. There were pieces of glass and gumballs everywhere. Did Carol punish her? NO! She told me not to be so harsh on her daughter. She said that Eve was just going through a tough stage at seventeen. That's bullshit if you ask me. Those two treat your Daddy like shit."

And you treat Clair and me like shit.

Daddy paused for the dramatic finale. "This afternoon when I was looking through our trash bins, do you know what I found?" Dad looked from Clair to me and then back to Clair. "Four empty shoe boxes."

Empty, just like your relationship with Clair and me.

Daddy finally stopped ranting and focused his tired, watery eyes on us.

"How's eighth grade going honey?" Dad asked while grabbing a handful of my chili fries from my red plastic basket.

"I'm in ninth grade Daddy." How could he forget?

"I was just voted best figure and my photo will be in the ninth grade yearbook standing next to a guy named Willie who won for best physique."

Dad's mind was a million miles away.

"Don't forget my graduation is June 15th at 11a.m. Mommy bought me a beautiful pink dress with gold beads on it and a gold snake belt. She's going to let me wear her gold high heels. Then, we're going to go to dinner afterwards."

Dad grabbed my white Styrofoam cup and shook it from side to side. He took the lid off and emptied the remainder of my orange crush soda into his mouth leaving him with a sticky orange mustache.

"Daddy wouldn't miss it for the world."

Daddy never showed up for my ninth grade graduation, or Whomphoppers for that matter.

* * * *

After eight months in the adult business, I got their attention. Dad heard me loud and clear. I'm not sure what the message was, but he got it. Something, anything, it didn't matter. To Marv on the other hand, I was even lower than he could have ever dreamed possible. Yet it caught his attention too. I'm sure Joel didn't even know what happened to Clair and me, or care. We heard through the grapevine that he had remarried since Mom. Twice.

Now what? Where do you go at eighteen after an eight-month stint in porn films looming in your young background? Somewhere, I just had to

174

figure it out.

A week with Tina, away from reality is what I needed. We went bowling, shopping, had BBQ's and played double solitaire late into the nights drinking hot chocolate. Not one call to Michael. Nobody knew where I was and come to think of it, nobody really cared.

It was Saturday night. Time to fly home and Tina was coming with me.

Mark took us to dinner on the way to the airport at Ruth Chris' Steakhouse, in the heart of Chicago. Sitting in our booth, I began to cry.

"Honey, what's wrong?" Tina asked.

Mark, already living with a drama queen, ignored us and ordered a filet mignon.

"I miss my family."

There, I had said those four words for the first time since I left home. Pushing it down and away. Pretending I didn't care. Thinking I was a big girl now. I didn't need them; I was just fine. Not allowing those thoughts to enter my mind, but they had finally surfaced.

I was fine; I could take care of myself. Hadn't I proved that? In my own way, yes I had. But I wanted my dad. I needed to heal my hurt, anger and sorrow with my father. It was time to mend nearly two decades of lost time and love.

I had been searching for a father figure in all of the wrong people. Jim South, Bruce Seven, or any male I dated would do. Any man that crossed my path was fodder for a father figure.

None of them were the right people. They couldn't fill the gap or feed my deepening emotional needs. I sought them out in my life; they didn't come looking for me. They were not bad people, just the wrong people.

I thought of Jim and our final conversation. I just couldn't do movies or magazines anymore. I was finished and eventually he understood. He had seen it before, and he'll see it again as an agent in this business. It was a classic case of burn out. I never thought he was a bad person. After all, I went to him. He didn't come looking for me.

Jim wished me luck and told me his door would always be open.

I was nobody's victim. I loathe victims. I was not a victim to Jim or anybody else I worked for. I learned and I grew from my eight months in the adult business. Now it was time to take steps in salvaging a relationship with my father.

Clair told me Dad had finally moved out again. Carol was having an affair with another man. How classic I thought.

Repairing my relationship with Mom would come later.

"Tina, can I use your calling card?"

I found the phone booths at the back of the restaurant. I closed the wood and glass door, and sat down on the wooden seat. It was Saturday night, and the restaurant was packed.

Busboys hustled by carrying trays of dirty dishes. Servers whisked by, delivering dinners to hungry families, friends and business associates.

Muffled laughter and talk filtered through the closed door.

I turned the plastic calling card over. Dial the 800#, a code and then the number you want to reach. Dad's number was still the same.

With the receiver in one hand, I punched in the numbers with the other.

Daddy, as always, picked up before the first ring finished.

"Hello?" It was always a question.

"Hi Daddy." I answered like I had just spoken to him last week.

"Well hello sweetheart." His voice was sooth and calming.

"How are you?" Maybe he thought I was Clair. We sounded exactly the same on the phone.

"I'm fine. Where are you?"

"At a restaurant." I could feel the lump forming in my throat. Oh boy, the waterworks were starting. "In Chicago." The "O" in Chicago was trailed for a few seconds.

"Chicago is a lovely town. I went there once when a was a young boy. Did you know its nick name is the Windy City?"

"I'm coming home tonight."

"Oh? And what were you doing in Chicago?" Unsure of where this conversation came from, and was going, Daddy kept a calm and even tone.

"Visiting my friend and her husband."

"Does your friend live in Chicago?" Treading on thin ice as to where this was going, he pulled out information one line at a time.

"No, they actually have a house in Gary, Indiana." I answered with hesitation. At any minute, Dad might throw me a curve ball and tell me I did something stupid, but so far, nothing but kindness.

"Gary, Indiana? Are they black?"

"No." I wondered why he would ask that. "Dad, I quit the business."

"What did you quit honey?"

He knew. He just wanted to hear it.

"The business, Daddy." There was such comfort in calling him Daddy, even if I was almost nineteen.

"Why did you quit? Was there a problem? Did somebody hurt you?" A slight huff was detected in his voice now.

Just you and Mom I thought. "No. It was just time, that's all. Now what? What am I supposed to do now?"

"Well, it's funny you should call and ask. My secretary just quit on Wednesday. I was going to put an ad in the paper Monday morning, but if you want the job, it can be all yours."

"I'll take it." I blubbered into the phone.

"Be at my office Monday morning at nine sharp."

"I will Daddy. I miss you and love you so much. Thank you." I paused, "Uh, Daddy, I don't know how to type. I cheated in tenth grade."

"You can do anything you set your mind to."

After hanging up, I sat in the booth and knew my dad was smiling like the Cheshire cat. That was the call he had been waiting for. At this point, who cared? I was too tired to prove anything anymore. The call felt great. I was going home.

Tina and I flew home. Like a true best friend, she stayed with me the next two nights.

Monday morning came and Tina left to stay with her mom a few nights before Mark flew in for business.

I, on the other hand, headed out the door for my first day at the office, a job that I kept for the next four years.

Dad had two seasonal businesses, an income tax practice and a wholesale/retail Christmas tree business.

Jake worked the computer at my dad's office. Once a week, Dad made Jake show me how to use their computer system, Lotus 1,2,3.

Other than my computer lessons, I learned how to run an office. I booked his appointments every thirty minutes, filed, and ran the Xerox machine. I could calm a client when they got an audit letter from the IRS, and believe you me, many of Dad's clients seemed to get those. I could explain with ease, to the hotel manager why they received two eight foot Christmas trees instead of the three ten foot trees they ordered. I knew when and what my dad wanted for lunch and the exact amount of sugar he liked in his coffee. I finally mastered the typewriter. I could set margins, change the ribbon and type out Dad's checks like nobody's business.

Now I just had a few loose ends to clean up with Michael.

I was still seeing Michael on weekends. The more I bonded with my dad, the less I saw of him. It was time to sever the ties on our toxic relationship.

In one week, Michael's sister and her kids were coming to LA for their yearly visit.

"Can you come over tonight and clean my place? It's such a mess, I would hate for them to see it this way."

"No I can't. Why don't you hire a maid?"'

"Why should I pay somebody? If you won't do it, Jenny said she would."

I cringed at the mention of his ex-girlfriends name.

"Then get her to clean up after you." Where did that come from? I was finally standing up to him. Now I just needed that final shove in the right direction to dump him once and for all.

"Okay then, be that way. I'm going to call Jenny right now. Don't say

I didn't warn you."

I wasn't sure what the warning was, but I'm sure it involved rekindling something.

It was four o'clock Tuesday, and Jake and I were alone in the office.

"Hey Jake, what was the secretary like before me?"

"Sara? She quit six months before you started. I was doing everything here myself. It was getting pretty tough on me, I kept telling your dad I needed help, but he...." The big lug droned on, but I learned to tune him out by now. He was quite the big baby when he got on a roll.

I realized that there was no one that quit the week before I called my dad. He was just there for me. I tried to remember when the last time was.

* * * *

1982
Saturday Afternoon

My driving instructor Roberto was picking me up in twenty minutes for my final day of driver's education. Today was the day that I passed and went straight to the DMV for my license, or failed and had to retake the entire course. Roberto was always giving me goo-goo eyes in class. I knew, of course that I would be passing.

Driving meant freedom. Now all I needed was a car. Dad was matching the money I had managed to save. The balance would be financed, and I would pay the monthly payments from the money I made from my part time job.

A brand new, gold convertible Rabbit was what I wanted.

I opened our front door.

"Hi Roberto!"

Roberto stared at my tan, thin legs that flowed from the red and white shorts I was wearing. His eyes then zeroed in around the middle of my red tank top. "Hello to you too lady."

We got into his car and headed down Coldwater Canyon.

Roberto was driving while I looked through a box of cassettes I brought along.

"Hey Roberto, do you like Devo?"

"Is he in our driving class?"

I popped the tape in and "Whip It" began to play.

"No, I don't think so." No need to humiliate him. He was after all, giving me my passport to freedom.

"Where are we going to drive today?"

"Actually, I'm kinda hungry. How about if I take you to lunch at El Torito?"

178

"That sounds perfect Roberto." I was always up for a good enchilada.

One hour later, we were back in Roberto's car.

"Well Christy, I better get you back home. My next appointment is in thirty minutes."

I panicked. "But I didn't get a chance to drive yet. I need my certificate on Monday to take to the DMV"

Roberto reeked of one too many margaritas at lunch. "Do you feel comfortable with what you've learned so far in my class?"

I tried to remember what I learned. "Yes, totally." I lied.

"Well then pretty lady, that's good enough for me." With that, Roberto signed off on the dotted line to a very inexperienced driver.

MONDAY AFTERNOON.

Four o'clock and it was time for my written exam at the DMV This was my final step to freedom and my new car.

"Just answer these twenty questions without getting more than four wrong, and then bring it right back to me." He handed me the test with a wink and a smile. "Mikey is the name."

I stood at the worn out wooden table, and just stared at the questions. Shit, I knew I should have studied for this. I hardly knew any of the answers. They all sounded like they could be right. I looked around the table to read what people had carved in the wood. "Jose loves Maria", "Fuck the DMV" and a few gang numbers and signs, still didn't give me the answers I needed.

Where was Grant when I needed him? I could always count on him to let me cheat off his exams at school.

Thirty minutes later, in my skintight jeans, tight T-shirt and a big flirtatious smile, I handed Mikey my paperwork.

Mikey scratched his beefy neck with the tip of his red marker, while scanning my answers. "Did you study for this test?"

I thrust my chest out. "Yes. Very hard!"

"I think you should take one more look at answer number eight."

"Oh! I meant the car on the right has the right away, not the left. Sorry."

Mikey looked around, and slid my test back to me. "Uh, you may want to study the answers you marked off on numbers 8, 12, 19 and 20. Here's a fresh eraser." He whispered.

"Yeah, I will. I got a little confused at the end there."

Again, for the second time that hour, Mikey handed me my failed test back, with a wink and a smile.

Ten minutes later, Mikey signed off on the dotted line to a very inexperienced driver.

It was amazing what the right outfit, flash of a smile, and the show of some leg could accomplish. Almost.

Two days later with a legal driver's license, I was pulled over.

In my rearview mirror, along with the flashing red and blue lights, a cop was walking towards my car.

The song "I Love A Man In A Uniform" by Gang Of Four, popped into my head. Oh yes, with the nightstick, gun, black combat boots and handcuffs hanging from his belt, I totally agreed with the song. SEXY. No problem I thought.

I unbuttoned my shirt to show a little more cleavage.

I smiled, "Did I do something wrong officer?"

"Do you mean to tell me that you don't even know why I pulled you over?" The black book he was carrying flew open.

Look down at the cleavage officer.

"No." I was still wearing the plastered smile, but a bad feeling was creeping in. I don't think he pulled me over because he thought I was cute. I just had no idea what I had done wrong.

"I will need to see your driver's license."

Now I was really confused, my charms weren't working on him. I handed him my license, letting my hand brush against his. No wedding ring, was a good sign.

A pen materialized out of nowhere, and he began writing in his book and I didn't think he was giving me his phone number.

Still unsure of what crime I had committed, I asked, "Am I getting a ticket for something?"

He snapped the book shut and lowered his sunglasses to the bridge of his nose. "You cut me off with your right-hand turn two blocks back is what you did wrong. You didn't even stop at the red light; you just sailed through like you owned the road. I had to swerve into the left-hand lane to avoid a collision with you. If there had been a vehicle in that left-hand lane, I would have been deceased on my motorcycle right now. That, little Missy, is what you did wrong in a nutshell."

His face was beat red right by now. He pushed his sunglasses back up, and flipped his black book back open simultaneously, and began writing again.

With a new tactic in mind to sway him my way, I began to cry. "But officer," I looked at his name tag, "P. O'Mally, you can't give me a ticket. I just got my license and my parents will be so mad." I sobbed a little louder for the sympathy effect.

"You're a cry baby, and cry babies shouldn't be allowed to drive." He handed me my license back, along with the ticket, with out ever looking down my top.

"Have a nice day," was all he said.

180

Gang Of Four had obviously never met this officer.

Mom was livid when I told her that night.

You what?"

"Well, I didn't see him Mom."

"You didn't see him, because you didn't stop. No driving besides school and back for the next two weeks."

"But Mom."

"No buts about it. And tell your father that he has to take you to court on this. I'm too busy."

Three weeks later, Daddy came to pick me up.

"Hi Daddy!"

"What are you wearing?"

"A mini-dress."

"You march right back into the house and put on a presentable outfit. You need to learn how to dress like a young lady. Enough of this flashy-washy attire that you always seem to be wearing. Short shorts, tight tops, and tight blue jeans." He mimicked me, "Oooh, look at me boys, aren't I cute?" in a fake high pitched voice. "I can't believe your mother lets you dress like you do. We're going to see a judge today for Christ's sake, not a John Elton concert."

"It's Elton John, Daddy, and I don't talk like that."

"Please just go in and change with out making Daddy upset. I don't have all day."

Five minutes later, I came back out wearing a turtleneck and wool slacks.

"That is much better. Now get in the car, we have to see the judge in fifteen minutes."

It was the end of June and I was burning up trying to look like a presentable young lady, but I kept my mouth shut.

It was our turn to see the judge.

"Keep your mouth shut, and let Dad do all the talking."

The first thing Dad did was hand the judge his business card, with a shake of hands before we sat down in his office.

Dad's eyes focused in on some horse trophies proudly displayed behind the judge's desk. In the center of the awards, was a photo of the judge, standing next to a horse with a ribbon around its neck. The judge was beaming from ear to ear in the photo, so proud of his beast.

Daddy got a far away look and smiled. "I once owned several race horses myself. 'Raggedy Ann', 'Bundle Of Joy' and 'Lady Luck' were my poisons."

And our child support I thought.

Dad and the Judge got to talking, and realized that they had used the same trainer.

"Richie is a good man." Dad said.

"Salt of the earth." The Judge shot back.

Twenty minutes later, bored out of my mind, the intercom rang on his desk.

"Your next two cases are here."

His finger hit a button; "I'll be ready in a minute."

The judge looked at me for the first time. "Did you learn your lesson?"

"Oh yes, I'm so sorry."

"Good. I never want to see you in this office again. Case closed."

My luck had returned. My luck and Daddy's ability to sell anything to anybody.

That was the last time I could ever remember my dad sticking up for me.

* * * *

"Hey Jake, do you mind if I leave a half hour early today?"

"Naw, go ahead."

Instead of going home, I headed in the other direction. Remembering a sign on a building last month, I finally found it. "Marriage and family counseling." And below that, "We work on a sliding scale."

I parked my car and went in.

"May I help you?"

"Yes, I need help. Today if I can start."

I filled out the paperwork, and with my income level, I was put in the ten dollar per session range.

During my twenty minute wait, I read a pamphlet on the dangers of cocaine use.

* * * *

February 1985:

Heather Wayne and I were at a club. It was two in the morning, and everything was shutting down, except for our cocaine filled systems.

"Hey Christy, you know that guy who recognized us?" She wiped her nose, then waved to a guy at the bar. He smiled and waved back.

"Yeah, the real slimy looking one."

"That's the one! Well, he just showed me a bag of coke. Can we invite him over to your place with us?"

"Sure, why not." He was creepy looking, but he had the goods.

Heather gave him a shaky thumbs up, hopping from one leg to the other. "This is so much fun Christy. I'm so glad you're my best friend."

Coke and porn, not a deep foundation for a lasting friendship, but what were my other options? I had alienated all of my school friends.

So my new best friend, "Cokeman," and I all piled into my car.

For hours, we talked about absolutely nothing in my living room. We were all going to go on a trip together. "Hey!" Heather said, "Let's all go to the Grand Canyon! Get it Christy?" The weather, politics, and any other meaningless chatter, that would never be brought up again, were discussed in great detail.

Four hours later, the drugs were gone, the sun was coming up and I couldn't remember the guy's name for the life of me.

"Shit man, don't you have any more?" Heather asked. Her eyeballs looked like they would pop out any second.

"I've got some at home, but I'll need a lift."

"Christy will take you!" At nineteen, Heather never bothered getting a driver's license.

With no cars on the street at 6a.m. Sunday morning, the drive from the valley to Hollywood took fifteen minutes.

He lived in a one-room guesthouse behind a liquor store off La Brea and Hollywood Blvd.

He unlocked and opened his front door. The smell of old booze, stale food and cigarettes that emanated from inside nearly knocked me over. I stepped inside and did a quick survey of this one room hovel. It looked like a bomb had gone off.

Stacks of filthy dishes were piled in the sink and on the counter. A heap of clothing filled an entire corner. Dirty overflowing ashtrays, fast food wrappers, newspapers, used socks and underwear were strewn across the floor. A single mattress was in the far corner. No box spring, no sheets, no covers and no pillows. Just a dirty, stained, torn up mattress.

I was getting a real bad feeling.

He closed his front door and locked it with a key. With a key! There was no knob I could turn to just escape this nightmare. I needed a key.

He slid the key deep into the front pocket of his Levi's. He put his hands on my shoulders. "It's time for me to collect payment on all of that coke you and your girlfriend snorted." He began shoving me in the direction of the mattress.

The alarm bells were sounding off in my head. I was about to get raped. And for what, drugs? Think God damn it. You're a survivor. THINK! After a twelve-hour binge of coke, I suddenly sobered up in two seconds flat. I mustered up all of my acting skills and turned around to face this piece of shit. Pretend you're on a movie set. It's just dialogue this time; no sex scene is involved. Get into character, the role to save your ass.

Suddenly I transformed myself into Traci Lords.

I pouted my lips and looked at him seductively. I ran my index finger up his chest. In a baby voice I thought only Traci had mastered, I heard myself say, "I'll be right back. I just have to go pee-pee."

My heart was pounding. Oh fuck, did he buy it?

"I'll be waiting in bed for you. Hurry up." He unbuttoned his jeans and began lowering them.

"MOVE!" My head screamed.

The window in the bathroom was small, but after the past four months of heavy partying, so was I. I turned on the faucet, and slid the window open. I flushed the toilet and punched out the rusty screen. Standing on the rim of the tub, I put my arms in the open window and hoisted my body up, and halfway out of the window. From the waist up, I was hanging three feet above the concrete outside. My car was six feet in front of me.

"Hey, what's taking you so long?" He was pounding on the thin door. My voice shouted in the direction of La Brea, not his hovel,

"Oh! I'll be right out." One final heave-ho, and I was out, hands first onto the pavement. I could hear his body slam against the thin bathroom door.

"Hey, what's going on in there?"

I got off of the ground and ran to my car. I jumped in, and locked the doors.

I looked in my rearview mirror, and saw him standing in the doorframe, cupping his hands around his mouth, yelling something in my direction. He was wearing his filthy jeans, unbuttoned, and no shoes or shirt. With trembling hands, I fumbled for the ignition key on my keychain and saw him take three large steps towards my car. I shoved my key into the ignition, and turned it to the right. I could now hear his voice, but couldn't make out what he was saying. I think I heard the word bitch in there.

My car hesitated for a few seconds, before the engine finally turned over. I cursed myself for not getting that long overdue tune up. I pressed down on the clutch with my left foot. He was inches away from my rear bumper. I shifted into first, and pressed my right foot all the way down on the gas pedal. My car lurched forward several feet and I took one last look in my rear view mirror. He was flipping me the bird through a large black cloud of smoke from my exhaust. I thanked myself for not getting that tune up after all.

I made a left hand turn onto La Brea, tires burning rubber, and headed home.

Half asleep on the couch, Heather lifted her head, "Did you get more?"

"No. You have no idea what I just went through Heather."

But after hearing the word no, she fell fast asleep on my couch.

That wakeup call in February 1985 was the last day that I ever put cocaine into my body.

* * * *

A beautiful Asian woman extended her hand out. "Hi, my name is Lois, and I'll be your counselor." We shook hands on a relationship that was the beginning of my new life.

20

Day 1:

I followed Lois down a hallway, with three wooden doors on each side. The third one on the left was hers. This was the door I was walking through to change my life, and take control again. I hated that I felt so lost, alone and scared at nineteen. What happened to that self-confident, cocky girl who could do or get anything she wanted? Why did I allow people to beat me down so emotionally? That I deserved less than the best? That's what I wanted to find out and change. Change it back to the time when I was self-assured, independent and strong.

I could only rely on myself and hopefully Lois would help me.

I definitely needed help.

Her room was a small box with off white walls and a multicolored shag carpet in tones of tan, brown and gold. I sat in a black leather love seat for my fifty-minute session. Lois was in a wooden chair opposite me. The fake wood coffee table had a spider plant in the middle, yellowing at the tips, and a large box of Kleenex to the left.

We sat down opposite each other.

Lois looked at me, an empty pad of legal paper sat in her lap. "Why are you here?"

There was so much I needed to talk about, that I wasn't sure where to begin. I envisioned Joel's face and began to cry. "Joel left us when I was eleven." I grabbed for my first piece of Kleenex.

"Who is Joel?" Her voice warm and full of concern.

"Our first stepfather."

"Tell me about him."

I thought back to that cold dark day in January, 1977.

* * * *

The sky was filled with huge black rain clouds, but no rain was falling. I missed my mom. Where was she? Late as usual. Finally there was a knock on the door and she was here to pick us up.

Clair and I ducked our heads as we got in the bright orange VW Bus. The bus's weak heater hissed and spit before the hot air came through, then there was the odd smell of burning rubber that the heater always emitted for the first few minutes.

Mom was sitting high in the black leather seat, holding onto the stick shift with her right hand. Clair and I sat side by side on the bench behind

Mom. My right thigh was pressed against Clair's left thigh to help keep each other warm. The only heat we could feel came from a small vent in front and below the AM stereo.

"Mommy, where's Joel?" I asked.

Mom looked straight ahead and shifted from third to fourth gear. "We're getting a divorce."

Clair found my hand and held on tight.

"What Mommy?" Surely I hadn't heard right.

"I'm so unhappy with him girls."

Rain began to fall.

I started to cry, and could feel Clair's body shaking next to mine.

Mom was softly crying too, not for Joel, but because her babies were sad. As the bright orange bus pulled into the carport, we could see Joel packing. He had been our father for the most part, since I was four.

Joel slammed the trunk of his car, and turned around to look at us. "Come here girls." He crouched down to our height. "I'm going to call you two munchkins real soon." He wrapped his arms around us, hugging our bodies in tight, and kissed each of us on the cheek.

"We'll go to dinner at Shakey's Pizza next week." He released his grip, stood up, and got in his car. He unrolled his window and waved at us. "Goodbye girls." Clair and I kept waiving, until he made a right hand turn and we couldn't see his car anymore.

Day 2:

I sat down in the center of the couch.

"How are you feeling today?" Lois asked.

"Better. It felt so good to cry." I wept for the loss of Joel, and then for all of the years I grew up without my real father to count on, the shitty relationship I had with Michael, and finally for my mother who I hadn't spoken to in almost two years.

"I think I should tell you something else about me." I looked down at the carpet. Oh God, here it comes. Once she hears about my past, she'll never want to see me again.

"I am your therapist, and I want you to know that you can tell me anything."

"But this is pretty major."

"Whatever you tell me goes no further than these walls. Everything we talk about is confidential."

"I got into porno right after I turned eighteen." My eyes never looked up. I didn't want to see the rejection in her eyes when I told her my dark secret.

"What were your other options for survival at that age?"

187

"None." I stopped pretending to examine the carpet and looked at her. She was still looking at me with care and concern in her eyes. "That was the only way I knew how to survive."

"So you did what you had to do. You proved to yourself and your parents that you could survive just fine with out them."

She was so calm and nonchalant about it. She didn't even flinch at the word porn. Maybe she didn't understand the full extent of it.

"I actually made X-rated, hard-core films." She couldn't misunderstand that. "With men and women."

"That would be a facet of the adult business, wouldn't it?"

She reacted like I had just told her that I worked at McDonalds.

"How do you feel about making films and posing for magazines?"

She took it in such stride.

"I'm okay with it. It was actually kinda fun." I felt myself smiling. "I just burned out and couldn't do it anymore. Then there was this guy I started dating named Michael."

The thought of Michael made my smile go away. He was a whole new can of worms. "I'm still seeing him but I don't want to."

Her eyes never left my face. I had just told her about me being in porn, and she accepted it and me.

"Tell me about Michael."

"I met him on a movie set. He is a porn producer."

Eight minutes into the session I began to cry. "He told me that if I didn't clean his apartment, that his ex-girlfriend would."

"How does the mention of his ex-girlfriend make you feel?"

"Scared."

Lois leaned forward in her chair. "About what? What are you afraid of?"

"That he'll leave me and go back with her."

"Are you a part time maid?" She sat back again.

"No."

"So why would he expect you to clean up after him?"

I shrugged my shoulders. "I don't know."

"Doesn't he respect you?"

I shook my head no. "I don't think so."

"Do you respect yourself?"

I shook my head no again. I began crying deep, heavy sobs. I was sad that I had let my self-esteem become so depleted, but I was also relieved that I was about to change and make myself better.

"Why not?"

"I don't know."

"Well, that's what we're going to find out, and then change it."

"People seem to put me last."

"Who?"

"Everybody. Mom, Dad, all of my stepparents and Michael."

"Did the people in the adult business put you last?"

"No, never. They always put me first."

"So it felt good to finally be put first. People listened to you, respected what you said. You felt worthy, pretty and important."

I shook my head yes. I was crying so hard, I couldn't even speak.

"What I am about to tell you is very important. Don't ever lose that good feeling. Always cherish it, no matter what you choose to do in life. Just remember that it was time to move on from that business, and that's why you quit. Don't ever have a negative feeling about what you did. Ever. Whoever you allow into your life must accept every aspect of you. Do not accept anything else or you will be selling yourself short." Her voice was intense for the first time.

Clair accepted me. Lois accepted me. Dad even was starting to accept me.

"Why are you still with Michael?"

"He said that with my past, not many men would want me. That I was tainted...damaged goods."

"Do you believe that?"

"Kinda. Marv told me the same thing."

"Who's Marv?"

Oh boy. "My current stepfather." There was so much ground to cover.

"Do you like him?"

"No. Not one bit."

"Why not?"

"He was never nice to me, and he was always competing with me for my mom's attention." I took another piece of Kleenex. "And I guess he won."

"What do you mean he won?"

I looked at Lois. "Because my mom picked him over me." Why didn't mom throw him out instead of me?

"Did he abuse you?"

"No. I have never been sexually abused by anybody."

"Abuse doesn't just mean sexual. There's physical and emotional as well."

She took in every word. She cared, above and beyond her ten-dollar fee.

"I've never been hit by anybody, but emotionally, yeah, I guess so." Marv was the straw that broke my spirit.

* * * *

1982

189

It was Sunday morning. Marge and I were sitting on the couches talking in the living room, while my mom made breakfast. Marv came in and put his arms around Marge. "Good morning honey. I love you so much. I have the best daughter in the world."

"Dad! You're hurting me. Let go."

She jerked away from his embrace and smoothed down her hair.

Marv sat down on the couch with her. "Oh honey, let me just hold you for a minute. I don't get to see you enough, you're growing up so fast."

Marge laid back into his open arms. They began talking in a father-daughter lingo, the kind that only they understood.

I sat on the opposite couch; alone, envious of the attention her father gave her. I wondered what my father was doing right now. Was he telling Carol how much he loved her? Did he ever stop and think about me? Somehow I didn't think so.

Mom came in and told us it was time for breakfast.

Marv hadn't even said good morning to me.

* * * *

"Are you looking at Michael as a father figure?"

"In a way, yes, I am."

"But you have your own father, you don't need him."

Lois didn't finish the sentence with "as a father." I just didn't need him for anything.

I left Lois on the second day and drove straight to Michael's apartment. I gathered up everything I had there, locked his front door and slid the key under.

I would never allow myself to go back there.

The message light was blinking on my answering machine when I got home.

"I can't believe you took your dishes back right before my sister's visit. Now I'm going to have to go out and buy some."

So there was my answer. He didn't miss me. He was pissed because now he had to buy dishes.

I sat on my hands all night and wouldn't answer the phone. Not that he ever called back.

Around midnight, I crawled into bed. Nobody knew I was seeing Lois. Not Clair, not my father, not even Wanda and Tina. This was mine, and I wasn't ready to share it with anybody.

Day 3:

190

I got to Lois's office thirty minutes early on my third day. Just being near her made me feel safe and secure. She was my savior, my healer, my own personal God.

"I'm ready for you Christy." Lois was smiling at me and I felt myself smile.

I followed her down the hallway to her room and we sat in our usual positions.

I began. "I took all of my stuff from Michael's yesterday after I left your office."

"How did it feel?"

"Good and sad at the same time." I began crying. Shit, I didn't know anybody could cry so much in three days.

"Good, bad or indifferent, change is always scary. Have you talked to him since?"

"No. I didn't answer the phone, or return his call."

"I'm proud of you."

This woman I respected and trusted with my life was proud of me, regardless of my past.

"Will you be okay over the weekend?"

"Yes." I knew I had to be. "I'm working Saturday." I was strong and worthy. "Sunday, Dad, Clair, Mark and I are going out." I could do anything I set my mind to.

I booked an appointment with Lois for Monday, Wednesday and Friday of the following week. By Wednesday of my second week, I boxed Michael's shit and mailed it C.O.D.

I saw Lois two times a week for the next three months. We started working on my relationship with my mother.

I was determined to be the strong person I once was and take charge of my life again. I needed to learn how to never become a victim to anybody or anything. I wanted to make peace with my past.

21

I was in the process of lugging the postage machine two blocks back to the office, when I heard my name from across the street. There was Grant, waving to me. God, he was cute. He waited for a car to pass, then ran over.

I put the machine on the sidewalk and gave him a huge hug. "Hey, how are you?" His arms felt wonderful around me. A piece of my past was reassuring, and for some reason, I smelled the back of his head when we embraced.

He hesitated before asking the million-dollar question, "What are you up to these days?"

I had become so accustomed to people from my past never asking me what I was up to. "I've been working for my dad for the last year." Nobody wanted to talk about me being in porn. "His office is right down the street." I never knew if it was because they were uncomfortable, or didn't want make me feel uncomfortable. I cast my eyes down to my shoes. "I quit the business." I felt shame at the thought of having sex on film in front of Grant. We kinda liked each other at one point, several years ago, and I think I screwed something up. I just couldn't remember what it was for the life of me. We had kept in touch for a while, and then the calls had abruptly stopped.

"You're totally out of it?"

"Yes." Hadn't he heard me? "For the last year."

"That's great to hear." It was his turn to look down at his shoes. "You know, I forgive you for not showing up in San Francisco."

"Thanks, that means a lot to me." I had no idea what he was talking about.

"Do you still have that condo down the street?"

"Yeah, I do." I wondered when he was there. Hurry up and change the subject. "I have a roommate now."

"Hey, um, would you like to go to lunch with me sometime or something?" He dug his hands deep in his pockets.

He was so cute. His personality was like that of a little boy.

"I would love to. Right now I have to get this machine back to the office, but here," I took out my very own business card from my purse. "Call me at work, or at home. The number is still the same."

"I threw your home number away."

"Oh." I wonder why he did that. "Well, let me write it down for you."

The following week, we went to lunch at a little Thai restaurant across the street. We reminisced about school and he filled me in on what a lot of our classmates were up to. Grant seemed to keep in touch with everybody. I on the other hand, was not in touch with a soul from the class of eighty-four.

We kissed goodbye, and promised to call each other in a few weeks.

We never did.

22

On my lunch-hour one day, I went to get a manicure. While applying my base coat, my manicurist, Kathy, asked, "Have you ever heard of that actor Max Baer?"

"Yes. I actually went out with him years ago." I picked out a shade of pink polish. "Why?"

"Because he's in tanning bed number five."

"He's here? Now?" I turned in my seat and looked at the closed door to bed five. Just then, the bulb above the door went off. His thirty-minute session was up.

"Hey Barbara," Kathy whispered to the owner three feet away, behind the reception desk, "Isn't that Max in number five?"

Barbara, a middle aged woman in her fifties, looked up with a big smile. "Yes, isn't he handsome? I would love it if he asked me out."

So long as you don't mind screwing all of his friends instead of him I thought.

"He's always flirting with me, I think he's going to ask me out." Barbara fluffed her hair in the mirror behind her, and applied a fresh coat of some god-awful color lipstick.

Maybe two decades ago. "Why don't you ask him out? It's almost the nineties after all." I never did like Barbara. She somehow found out what I used to do for a living, and was never nice to me. If Kathy wasn't here, I would never come to her overpriced salon.

"Do you think?" Barbara was suddenly all giddy at my suggestion, forgetting her usual coldness towards me.

I plastered on a big fake smile, "Absolutely." And run right into a brick wall. Bitch!

"Christy, is that you?"

It was his familiar voice that I would never forget. That sure, self-confidant voice that took over and demanded the room. It was the voice of Max behind me.

"Hi Max! Kathy told me you were here!" It was actually fun seeing him. He looked the same, tall, dark and handsome. I got up from my seat, wet fingernails and all, and gave him a hug, nails spread apart, inches away from his body. I glanced over at Barbara, who sat with her mouth open in disbelief.

"How have you been?" Max took a step back and looked at me. "You're looking great."

"Thanks. I've been doing really well. I've been working for my dad for the past few years."

Max bent down and whispered in my ear. "Your tits still look great too." He let out a hearty laugh. Still the same old Max. "Do you ever talk to any of the old gang?"

"Not really, just Wanda and Tina Marie."

"God, I would love to take you out one night."

I moved one foot closer to Barbara. "What?" I pretended I didn't hear him.

"We should get together one night and catch up on old times."

"That would be great." I didn't really care, but I knew my dad would want to meet him. It also didn't hurt matters that Barbara was fuming by this point. "I can't write my new number down, my nails are still wet."

Max smiled at Barbara, "Barbara honey, do you have a pen and a piece of paper I may borrow?" He had no idea that he just twisted that knife in her.

She fumbled around and found a scrap of paper. "Here Max." She looked to be on the verge of tears. Her secret fantasy, Max, was asking this young ex-porn star out.

I gave him my number and we talked for a few more minutes. Max looked down at his diamond-faced watch. "I've got to go, I have a meeting in thirty minutes about a theme park I want to open. I'll call you later tonight." He gave me a kiss on the cheek, and left through the back door.

Kathy told me several appointments ago that Barbara told any guy she fancied, who flirted with me in the salon, what I used to do for a living. Like that would turn a guy off. The dum-dum only got them more interested.

Kathy took the opportunity to get back at Barbara. "How long have you known him?"

Our eyes locked, and I knew where she was headed. "Oh for years now. We used to be pretty hot and heavy, but I was only eighteen, too young to be thinking about marriage."

Barbara was trying to act preoccupied with paper work.

"He's a good looking man." Kathy continued.

"Yeah, he is. I can't wait to go out with him again." My nails were dry, and I was already ten minutes over my hour lunch break. "I better get back to work, I'll fill you in on all the juicy details." Yeah, real juicy. I already planned on bringing my dad along.

That night, Max called me at home. We made a date for the following night at a sushi restaurant near my father's office.

The next day at work I asked my dad if he had ever heard of Max Baer.

"Why sure, he's been dead for some time now. He was a damn fine boxer though."

"He's not dead. We're going to dinner with him tonight." What was he talking about? "He's not a boxer either, he's a actor. Remember, he was Jethro on "The Beverly Hillbillies".

"Oh, you mean his son. Why sure I remember him, That was one of my favorite shows. I still catch it on reruns every so often. It's been a while, but the last one I saw was several months ago. I think Max was sitting in a corner with a big dunce cap on." Dad looked at me, "What do you mean we're going to dinner with him?"

"I bumped into him yesterday, and he asked me out, but I don't want to be alone with him."

"Why? How do you know him?"

"A friend introduced us a few years ago."

Dad calculated the time frame in his head. The porno years. Dad let it go. "Well, sure I would love to go."

"Perfect, we'll go after work."

Dad and I worked an extra hour in the office, and met Max at six.

"Max, I would like you to meet my father."

I saw Max flinch for just a second. The romantic evening that he fancied just flew out the window. "Nice to meet you." Max said and gave my father a good hearty handshake.

I must say, Max was a great sport. The three of us sat down at a table, and Max began to thrill my father with stories about the cast from the show.

My father was grinning from ear to ear. " Max I cannot tell a lie." Dad shoved a piece of yellowtail in his mouth. "I always had a crush on Elly Mae." He licked the soy sauce from his fingers.

Oh brother, like anybody asked him to lie. Dad could be so dramatic. But it was fun to see my dad's eyes light up, like one of his very own, overpriced Christmas trees. He couldn't get enough.

Max poured a cup of tea. "I think the whole male population had a crush on her."

I felt a hand rest on my thigh. It felt good until I remembered his bedroom wishes. "I have to go to the ladies room." I excused myself and called my roommate from the payphone. "Hi Keri. I should be home soon. I ordered some extra food so I could bring it home for you. Do you still want to go to that club tonight?" Five more minutes of talking to her about some guy I had a crush on, and I realized that I better get back to the table. "I gotta go, but I'll be home soon. Gross! He put his paw on my leg. I'm glad I wore pants today."

I sat back down and picked at a piece of California roll. Fortunately, Max was using both hands to draw a diagram on his place mat of some attraction he wanted to build at a casino based on "The Beverly Hillbillies".

"That's going to be Granny's shotgun wedding chapel. People will actually be able to get legally married, right there in the theme park."

Dad's head was spinning from all of this inside information and gossip.

Dinner was finally over. We said our goodbyes, and I knew mine was for good. Max was nice and very attractive, but sexually, we would never work. I was into monogamy and he was into voyeurism.

The following day at work, Dad could not stop talking about Max. Max this and Max that. I even heard him on the phone to his brother Popkin, bragging about his dinner with a star. "Oh sure, we had a wonderful dinner. He confided in me about a theme park that he was opening. He's a good man Popkin, the kind of person you should be surrounding yourself with, unlike those losers you loiter among. Max knows a smart businessman when he meets one, I'm sure he'll ask for some advice once the park takes off. He's a sharp dude."

Oh brother.

Dad hung up after bragging to Popkin, and called me into his office. "Sit down honey."

I prepared myself for a father-daughter talk of some sort.

"What I can not understand, is why you do not choose to date a man like Max. He is smart," Dad began ticking off Max's attributes on his fingers, "he's successful, he's well educated, he has fine tastes, and he's going places baby, that man is going places." Dad came to the end of the line on his fingers. With that, dad pounded his fist on the desk.

"He's too old for me."

"Oh age is just a chronological number. It doesn't mean a thing." Dad pointed all ten of his fingers to his chest. "Take me for example. I can run circles around most men half my age. I may be fifty, but inside, I'm younger than a twenty year old."

"Still, I'm not interested." I stood up. "Want some coffee?" Hearing him grumble something under his breath, I left his office and sat down at my desk.

Every day that week, Dad would find a reason to bring up Max's name. I tried to ignore him, and only answered a question if I had to. Sometimes just a grunt would satisfy him. By the fifth day, once again, he called me into his office.

"Darling, I really do not understand why you do not want to date a man like Max. He's obviously crazy about you. He wouldn't stop looking at you during dinner, and I hear him calling you at the office four, maybe five times a day." Dad paused, preparing for a grand finale of some sort. "You're twenty-one now." Dad took off his glasses and rubbed the bridge of his nose. "Have you put much thought into a family? You are nearly a quarter of a century old."

I mustered up some of my old acting abilities and put on a look of confusion. "But I have a family. You, Clair, Mark, and I guess Mom too."

Dad was getting agitated. "Well of course we're your family. I meant children, babies, a husband." Dad paused, his mind filling with visions of a real star in the family. In a dreamy voice he said, "Like Max."

"Max? A husband? Oh Dad, please."

He snapped back to reality and sat up taller in his chair. "What? What's wrong with Max?"

"For starters, he's several decades too old for me." Oh what the hell, may as well get it all out. "I used to have a huge crush on Max."

Dad's eyes sparkled.

"But he couldn't keep it up."

Dad's eyes clouded.

"You know, in bed. He couldn't do it with a girl. He just likes to watch her with somebody else." I feigned a look of disgust. "That is just not my style Daddy. It's not my thing at all."

Dad blinked three times in a row.

I never heard his name mentioned again.

23

"Good Afternoon."

"Is Joe in?" The cold as ice voice asked. Carol had surfaced.

I rolled my chair over three inches, and peeked into my father's office. He looked up from his paperwork and smiled at me. I waved.

"No, he's not in, may I take a message?" I was almost whispering.

"It's Carol, and I'm calling long distance."

Sounds like a personal problem to me, bitch. "Uh huh, and would you like me to take a message on that?"

"I need to talk to him immediately."

I bet you do. "Does he know what this is regarding?" Sugar was dripping from my voice.

"Just tell him to call me as soon as he gets in. My number here is..."

By this point, there was no pen in hand, or "while you were out" pad in front of me. "Great, have a great day."

That was the last time I ever had the misfortune of hearing her disgusting, repulsive voice, but I knew it was only a matter of time before she reached him.

The following month, Dad and I were driving.

"I spoke to Carol last night."

I froze at the mention of her name, staring at the red light in front of me.

He continued, "You didn't tell Daddy that she called last month."

"Oh Dad, she's no good for us. She only calls if she wants something. Carol is a user." I'm sure Carol was sniffing around for money. We had just finished up tax season, the most profitable time of the year. Surely he wouldn't subject me to Carol, or would he?

"Well, as you know, tax season is over, and we will be gearing up for tree season very soon."

Let's cut to the chase. "What does she want?" I demanded.

"It seems she's moving back to Los Angeles, and has offered to run our tree decorating department."

She offered, yeah, for a steep price I'm sure. "What happened to her boyfriend in Norway?"

My eyes were straight ahead, focusing on the road, but I caught Dad glancing at me.

"Oh, I don't know if I would categorize him as her boyfriend."

"She was living with him for the past two years. What do you call that?" God, how could he be in such denial?

"She is very good at decorating. You have to admit that."

"Dad, we did just fine decorating trees for the past three years without her."

"She also wants to take on some large tree accounts. Go after theme parks, like Disneyland and Magic Mountain."

She was so dumb, she couldn't sell heroin to a junkie.

"I am grooming you to take over one day. Carol will be a pawn in the office, who will take orders from you."

The freeway lane in front of me was becoming blurry with the rage I felt.

"I am not a poodle, you can't groom me." I was steaming by now. "I don't want to give her orders, I never want to see her face for as long as I live. Did you forget how mean she was to me when I lived with you?" I had just opened up Pandora's box.

Dad shifted uncomfortably in my passenger seat. "Well honey, it was a difficult time for all of us."

"Carol made it more difficult. All she had to do was be nice to me for four more months until I turned eighteen. I would have moved out then." Instead, I left home four months shy of my birthday.

* * * *

December 1983

The clock in my bedroom read ten-fifteen. I had never slept in so late on Christmas morning. Until this morning, Christmas was my favorite day of the year. So much to celebrate, so much to be grateful for. Today, I just wanted it to be over.

Every year, bright foils, colorful ribbons and holiday theme paper spilled from under our tree. Our stockings above the fireplace were stuffed with little gifts from Mom.

Mom would never spoil us with expensive gifts, but took great care in each one she bought for Clair and me: - The exact T-shirt I wanted; the new Rolling Stones cassette for Clair; A telephone answering machine for our joint gift. The gifts from Santa were four books I wanted. The gift from Rudolph was a new set of nail polish colors I had been dying for. Mom always put such thought into each present.

This was the first time I woke up at Dad and Carol's house on Christmas. And the very last I had decided.

I lay in bed for fifteen minutes, and looked around at my manufactured room/guestroom. Cobwebs covered every leaf of the fake plant on the shelf. The photo that hung above the second bed was a drawing of a lady from the roaring twenties era. Certainly not something a seventeen-year-old girl would choose. The pale yellow plantation shutters

200

were covered in an inch of dust. Three old issues of Life sat on the coffee table in front of the window. The closet was half occupied with Carol's summer wardrobe. I wondered if Carol had told the housekeeper to avoid cleaning my room altogether.

I finally got out of the single bed, and the wafer thin rayon comforter slid to the floor, as it always did. I put on my white slippers and robe and opened my bedroom door. I could hear voices in the kitchen one flight down. I crept down the flight of stairs into the living room. Above the mantel there were two stockings. Eve's was overflowing, mine was as flat as a pancake.

I took three steps towards the Christmas tree, and looked at all of the beautifully wrapped packages that materialized overnight. All but two had Eve's name handwritten on the tags in beautiful calligraphy, Carol's work. Out of the remaining two, one had Clair's name, the last one, dented on one side, had my name. Only my nametag was written in regular penmanship with no, love Dad, Carol or even Santa. It just had my name, alone. Just like me, alone.

"Good morning sweetheart." Dad's voice was behind me. "Merry Christmas."

I wasn't sure what was so merry about it, but I pulled my eyes from the packages, and turned to face Dad. "Merry Christmas to you too." I wondered what Clair was opening up at Mom's right now.

"Carol picked out a beautiful gift for you." He said, so proud of "The Bitch".

"And gifts for Eve." I drew out the "S" in gifts.

Dad looked at me, unsure of what I meant.

I stood still in front of the tree, and Dad joined me.

Dad bent down to look at all of the gifts. "Carol didn't tell me she was going to buy so much for Eve. I'm sure some of these are for you." He began looking at each tag.

"No Dad, just the one in the corner with the big dent in it is for me."

Dad got up off of his knees and stared at me, looking perplexed.

Carol's voice boomed from the kitchen, "Oh Eve, that new holiday outfit is so beautiful on you. Joe, come in and see the new outfit we got for Eve to wear today."

Dad kept his eyes glued to me and shouted, "I'll be right in." His eyes dropped back down to the gifts, then back to me. "I'm so sorry."

You should be, is what I felt like saying. "It's okay," is what I said. One day I'll be so rich, I can buy anything I want, is what I was thinking.

Clair came by at one, sporting her new holiday outfit.

"That's a really cute outfit Clair."

"Thanks. It's all I really got today."

I didn't believe her for a second. I just knew her well enough to know that she didn't want to hurt my feelings.

By four that afternoon, it was time to open our gifts. Clair had spent so much time picking out a variety of things for me, knowing it was on her shoulders this year. T-shirts, makeup, books and a pair of gold hoop earrings.

I opened up my box from Dad and Carol. I ripped the silver wrapping paper off, balled it up, and chucked it over my shoulder. I tore it off not out of excitement to see what was in the thoughtless box, but because I knew it would piss Carol off, to be so obnoxious about it. She acted so prim and proper, yet no amount of money could, or would ever buy her class. You could dress a sow in designer clothing, but it would still be a pig underneath.

I unfolded the white tissue paper, and pulled out the ugliest down jacket I had ever seen. Clair and Eve got a similar version of mine, only nicer. Theirs were ankle length in black, with a fur-lined hood. Mine was cut above the waistline in a lime green color, minus a hood. I looked across the room at Carol, who was intently watching me for my reaction to this gift. A smirk was spread across her face.

"Oh Daddy, how did you know this was my favorite color?" I put my arms around his neck.

Having no idea what I was talking about, he just hugged me back, thankful that I was happy. "You're welcome honey."

It was the end of the evening, and everybody had gone home. Carol and I said our fake goodnight's, thank you's etc, and I went into my cave of a bedroom.

Thirty minutes later, when all was quiet, I crept down the stairs, and into the kitchen. I opened the refrigerator door and took out the remainder of the cake. I tiptoed into the living room with it, and smashed the icy goo under the couch cushion.

The following morning, I woke up to Carol screaming from down stairs. I cracked my door open.

"Somebody must have left their piece out." Dad's voice said.

"But I know I cleaned up perfectly last night." Carol sounded near tears.

I walked down the stairs and saw the green velvet cushion torn to pieces, shredded fabric and foam stuffing covered the living room floor. Shoon, the dog, had icing and green threads all over his snout.

"Oh no, what happened?" I asked with as much fake concern as I could muster up.

"It seems like somebody accidentally left their cake out." Dad said.

"Or on purpose," Carol's chilled voice said.

"Oh, what I shame. Will Shoon be okay?" But I knew he would be.

Fuck you bitch, thanks for the shitty present.

The following morning I woke up and went downstairs. Carol was bent over, on all fours in the living room, cleaning Shoon's diarrhea up from the carpet.

"Bye!" I yelled, startling Carol. She was saying something as I slammed the door and headed out to return the jacket.

"Oh my, look at this color." The saleslady took the jacket out of the box. "You wouldn't need your headlights on at night if you were wearing this."

She punched in a few keys on her register, and informed me that I had a $52.84 credit.

"May I just have the cash?" I asked.

"How would you like it?"

"It doesn't matter." It was all going in my savings account. I realized that money was power, and right about now, I didn't have much power. But I knew I would.

Six weeks after Christmas, I had to move out. Things were getting so bad at home; I didn't know how much longer I could take it. First, I had to plan my escape. With my paychecks from work, any school money I got from Dad, along with the twenty-dollar bill I pinched from Carol's wallet every week, I had managed to save over $2000.00.

My first priority was getting my own car. As soon as I left, they would take back the rusted out El Camino that I had been driving. On my way home from school the following day, I noticed a for sale sign on a British green MG midget, and wrote down the number.

I pulled my best friend aside the next day at school. "Hey Nicole, will you follow me home one day this week, and drive the El Camino?"

"Sure, but I don't have a license yet."

"It doesn't matter, it's not very far. Just tail me." I filled her in on my plan.

"Hey Patrick, is that offer to live with you and your mom still available?"

"Yeah, for sure. Has it gotten to the breaking point finally?"

"Totally." I started to cry on the shoulder of my friend.

"Whenever you want, just say the word."

"This week. I'll call you before I come over."

I was sure my dad had bugged the home phone, so I called from a payphone. "How much is the midget?"

"$1500.00. Runs like a charm, my friend." He said in broken English. Calling me his friend when he didn't even know my name should have been my first clue that he was untrustworthy.

"Where can I meet you to take a look at it?" Like I knew how to find problems. I still went to full service at the gas station. We set up a time and place the following day.

I went home after school, and went directly up to my room, as always. I left my room for dinner, washed the dishes, and headed back to my room. Dad brought home a TV from his office last month, so at least I had something to watch. It was all just a routine by now. See each other as little as possible.

Like clockwork, the screaming began at nine-thirty sharp.

"I don't know how much longer I will put up with her!" Carols voice cut right through my door and into my soul.

"But we hardly even see her. She stays holed up in her room all of the time."

"It's just the point, I know she's here!" She yelled even louder. "She's Jane's daughter, and should be living with her, not us. I don't want her here, send her back to her mom's."

"Her mom doesn't want her Carol." Dad was stuck between his wife and his seventeen year-old daughter.

"WELL I DON'T EITHER. It's her or me." Her always-composed voice now shrieked the ultimatum.

The following day, Nicole and I went to see the man with the MG in a parking lot. The engine started up and it was sold, to the desperate young girl - Me. We made arrangements to meet at my bank. I handed him the cashiers check, and he handed me the keys. My remaining balance was $400.00. Nicole followed me to my fathers in the El Camino, and I parked the MG down the block. She didn't drive too badly for a girl who never went to driver's ed. class. I took Nicole home, and found a note taped to my bedroom door.

"Carol, Eve and I went to dinner and a movie. We'll see you in the morning. Dad."

I knew I had a few hours before they got home. I gathered what little possessions I owned, as well as a few of Carols, and filled my MG with clothing, books, my alarm clock, TV, bedding and even the dusty plant from the shelf.

The following morning I left for school in my new car, and never returned.

I spent the next two months at Patrick's house with the nicest woman in the world, his mother Martha. To this day, I don't know what I would have done if she hadn't allowed me to move in.

I pretty much stayed to myself, but enjoyed watching TV in the den with his mom. She never asked questions, she just talked to me like I was a human being. I had forgotten what that felt like.

Three weeks before graduation, Martha got engaged. She put her house on the market, and it sold within a week.

"You can move in with James and me," she said over dinner one night.

"I would love to, but I can't. My dad said I had to move back in with him." I lied. I couldn't freeload off her anymore. She was beginning a whole new life, I was just grateful for the time she let me to stay with her. It had allowed me the chance to save up several hundred dollars.

I left the following morning to search for my own apartment. Hollywood was what I could afford. Survival was first and foremost and unfortunately school was secondary.

The following day I found what I could afford, and with my fake I.D., I was able to sweet-talk the manager into renting it out to me without all of the money up front.

"I'll give you one week to come up with the balance of $200.00."

"Thank you, I promise I will. I'm just waiting for a check to come in."

"Sure. Just have it to me within seven days, before the owner finds out."

I moved in that night, and made the most humiliating phone call in my life. "Toy, it's me." I hadn't spoken to my ex-boyfriend in over six months.

"Hi. How are you?"

"I'm okay, but I need to ask you a huge favor."

"Anything you want." And I knew he meant it.

"I need to borrow $200.00."

"You got it. When and where can I meet you?"

That was the last time in my life I ever asked anybody for a cent.

I got Arman to give me ten more hours a week at the dress shop and I found a second job at night as a hostess just to stay afloat.

One week before graduation, I dropped out of school. Nobody would be there for me anyway.

* * * *

"We'll see what happens sweetheart." Dad patted my kneecap.

Oh no we won't, I thought. The wheels in my head were already turning. If Carol was coming back, it was time to move on.

Three weeks later, I went with Tina to pick up her new car. An electric blue convertible Corvette, her dream car. Certainly not my first choice.

We pulled up in my midnight blue convertible Rabbit, and there it sat on the lot, my dream car. A red convertible Porsche. "Take me home." The sign on the window read. Below that, a second sign read, $28,000.00.

It didn't seem like a lot of money, but it was more than the $15,000.00 I had in my savings account.

Tina and I walked into the dealership, so she could sign some paperwork.

"I like that Porsche outside." I told the eager beaver salesman casually, while Tina was signing away.

His squat, chubby face lit up. The possibility of two sales excited him beyond belief.

A low whistle escaped his lips. "Oh yeah, she's a real beauty. Rock bottom price on her too. The owner just wants to blow her out. Best deal you'll find out there on a five year old car like that. It will be gone like that." He tried to snap his fingers in the air, but the fleshy fingers missed each other by a quarter of in inch.

I was sure he had that paragraph, snap and all, memorized by heart for whichever car was asked about.

"May I refill your coffee Miss," He rubbed his hung-over forehead, "I'm sorry, I don't seem to know your name."

Like he gave a hoot two minutes ago.

"We would love some more coffee." Tina shoved our empty mugs at him. "Don't forget, extra, extra cream." She shouted to his disappearing frame.

"Here you two lovely ladies go." There was a new spring in his step.

"Am I done signing? Can you give me the keys to my new car now?"

I stood up and walked over to the floor to the ceiling glass window to look at the Porsche.

"Just three more forms to put your John Hancock." He slid the forms in front of her, keeping one bloodshot eye on me. He wanted to make sure he didn't lose me to his competition one desk over.

Staring at the car, I heard the voice. The imaginary voice over my right shoulder sang into my ear, "You can cash in on that name you made for yourself four years ago."

"I guess I could."

"What could you do?" Tina asked from my left. Her new set of keys dangling from her finger.

"Nothing really. I was just thinking." And boy-oh-boy was I thinking. The idea was forming. A comeback. Tina was always telling me that my old videos were still top sellers at Video Exclusives. Wanda was always saying how my photo sets were constantly being resold and reprinted, not that I ever saw an extra dime. Oh no, we, the actors and models, had gleefully signed away all of our rights, once the check was in hand.

Who cared, I thought. That was the past. That innocent way of thinking would be long gone the second time around.

If I were to make a comeback, it would be different than the first time around. I wanted a piece of the pie this time.

I vaguely remembered a story Wanda had told me after I had quit the business four years ago. Ginger Lynn had set a new standard for actresses with a brand new company, Vivid Video. Wanda said that Ginger not only got her day rate, but, a percentage of each video sold, a royalty I believe it was called. I made a mental note to call Wanda when I got home.

"What are you thinking Christy?" Tina's voice interrupted my thoughts.

I tore my eyes away from the Porsche. "My dad's ex-wife is going to start working at the office with us."

"The lady who basically threw you out of her house when you were seventeen?"

"Yeah." I looked at the Porsche again. "Wouldn't that be funny if I made a comeback?"

Tina stared at me. "Let's go to lunch, my treat."

I followed Tina to the hotel she and Mark stayed at when they were in town. We walked into the hotel's restaurant, and surprise, surprise, there was her husband sitting in a booth, his eyes on the door. He had a big ole smile on his face, a rarity, and was waving at us. I had never seen Mark so animated.

"Hey girls, how's it going?" He actually stood up for us.

I thought I saw Tina on her cell phone on the way over.

Before I could open my menu, the words bubbled out of his mouth. "So, Tina mentioned that you were thinking of a comeback." He smiled and actually showed teeth for a change.

"I was thinking of it." With Mark on one side of me and Tina on the other, I suddenly felt like a new, unique animal that had just arrived at a zoo and was under observation in a cage.

"What companies were you thinking of going to see?" Mark asked.

"Oh, the high end ones." I wasn't even sure who was still around after my four years off, but I was playing their game.

"Just do us one favor, give us a chance too." Tina said, suddenly all business.

"Yours is included of course."

24

The following week, I went to work at Dad's. The idea now forming in my head about a comeback into the business, kept me from flying off the handle when ever I heard rumblings of Carol coming back to work at the office.

Lois' voice kept ringing in my head. "You can do whatever you want to do. You're an adult, and can make decisions on your own, just like your father can. You do not need to subject yourself to anybody that was ever mean to you." And Carol went above and beyond the word mean.

MONDAY:

Dad was on the phone. He was leaning back in his chair, and his feet were propped up on his desk. It looked as if the wheels would snap off at any given moment under the weight of his body.

"Yeah, it seems like she needs the old man after all. She finally figured out what a dog-eat-dog world it is out there." Dad thrust his empty coffee cup at me when I walked by his office to get a better listening spot. I had to know what was happening before I made my next move.

I stood at the coffee station, pretending to search the two-by-two refrigerator for the carton of milk right in front of my eyes.

"You know Popkin,"

Now I knew he was unloading on his older brother.

"I wasn't such a bad son of a bitch to live with after all." Dad was twisting and untwisting a paperclip, with a smile on his face from ear to ear.

Live with? I thought she was just going to work here. I made a big production out of putting the exact amount of sugar in his cup. In reality, I could do it blindfolded.

"I guess Carol realized that life is not a bowl of cherries." He let out a hearty laugh at his own joke. I poured his cup of Java, wiping off the imaginary spillage, buying as much time as I could to listen in on his conversation.

"She's been living with her mother for the last month. Wait until she sees my abode tomorrow night. I told her I've got an extra bedroom with it's own entrance and bathroom. We would hardly ever see each other."

That sure sounded familiar.

"They all come back to Daddy," he boasted.

Except for Mommy, I thought. "Here's your coffee Daddy." I was going to miss him.

Dad pounded his fist on the glass desktop; "I was her rock of Gibraltar." His coffee sloshed over onto some paperwork.

TUESDAY:

"Honey?" I could hear Dad's voice from the back office when I stepped in the front door at nine sharp.

"Yes."

"Come in here a moment please."

But Daddy wasn't in his office; he was boxing stuff up in the back office. "Will you help me clean out this back room today?"

"Sure. What's going on?" But I already knew.

"Well, I figured this is where we will put Carol when she comes to work next week."

She's welcome to use my office I thought. I'll be long gone.

Dad leaned against a broom, the top of the stick making an indentation in his belly. "You know honey, Carol is very excited about seeing you."

Yeah, but not as excited as I would be to see her hit by a car.

"Somehow, I find that hard to imagine Dad."

"No, she really is."

Who's he kidding?

WEDNESDAY:

"Honey, will you come into my office for a moment?"

"Sure Dad."

"I want you to go to the printer's, and have them make up some business cards." He handed me the artwork. It was our tree logo on the card, with Carol's name as sales representative. I stood in his doorway and just stared at what he handed me, my walking papers.

THURSDAY:

Dad wasn't scheduled to be in the office that morning until noon. That gave me the next three hours to strategize. I began my list of phone calls.

"Hi Lois, can I come in today?" It was one week before my scheduled appointment.

"Of course you can. I have a six-thirty available this evening."

"I'll take it."

Dad called in at nine forty-five sounding jovial. "How's the fort?"

"Perfect." I gave him a short list of calls that he needed to return.

"Oh, just put them on my desk. I'll be in around one. I'm showing Carol a warehouse I'm thinking of renting this year for the trees, then I'm taking her to lunch."

"I didn't know you found a potential warehouse."

"It just came up last night."

I was hurt that he was taking her to see it before me. I was the one who worked here for the last four years. Being in his gay mood, I saw an opportunity, and I took it. "Dad, can I leave an hour early today? I have a dental appointment."

"Sure honey, you've got to take care of those teeth. Daddy spent a fortune on those braces."

"So true Dad." Mom did, but I let it slide this time. "I'll see you when you get in."

Did he honestly think I was going to sit by and let Carol back into my life? Not a chance.

The next call on my list was to information.

"What number please?" The robotic voice asked.

"I actually need three numbers. I think they're all in Chatsworth, or the Van Nuys area."

"The names?"

I hesitated for a brief second. "Caballero, Vivid Video, and VCA." I wondered if she knew what sort of companies these were. Before I could cringe at that thought, she spat off the first two numbers, and hooked me up to the automated voice for the third.

Ten-thirty. I picked up the phone and punched in Caballero's number.

A chipper voice answered, "Good morning, Caballero."

"Hi, is Howie in?"

"He's in a meeting, may I ask who's calling?"

This meant that he was not in a meeting, and was screening his calls. "Tell him Christy Canyon is calling. I don't have a return number, so I guess I can just call back." I felt a surge through my body. I knew his meeting had just finished.

"Please hold."

While I was on hold, I listened to an ad for their company. "We carry over one thousand titles in our catalogue, starring every major star. Our toy department has dildos in every size imaginable. For some hot, wet phone sex, dial," It was a very short hold.

"Yes, this is Howie. Is this the one and only Miss Canyon?"

Suddenly, I realized that I wasn't prepared. "Yes, it is."

"Let me say, that it is an honor to be speaking with you. I don't know if you remember, but I met you over four years ago at the CES show."

"Yes, I remember. I was signing for Paradise Visuals." I couldn't muster up his face to save my life. Wanda had told me last night who was in charge there.

"That's right."

I didn't know how to start.

"Uh, what can I do for you Christy?"

I thought of Carol's face one room over and kicked into high gear. "I was thinking about a comeback, and I thought of you for one of the companies I would consider signing with."

"We would definitely be interested in seeing you. When can you come in?"

"Today at four-fifteen is the only time I have."

"That's a little soon, but I think I can arrange it with my partner. We're in the middle of casting for a new big budget production "Night Trips", so it may be a little crazed around here, so just bear with us."

I got the directions, hung up and made call number two.

"Vivid Video, this is Yvonne speaking."

"Hi Yvonne, my name is Christy Canyon, is the owner Steve available."

"Hi Christy! Wow, I haven't heard about you in a long time. What have you been up to?"

The second line in the office rang. "Uh, can you hold on one second?" I punched the hold button. "Good afternoon, may I help you?" I stared at the flashing light on line one. "Hello, is anybody there?"

"Yes, is Joe in?" A feeble older mans voice asked.

"No, he won't be in 'til after one, call back then. Have a nice day" I could hear him asking if he could leave a message as I was hanging up.

"Sorry about that Yvonne."

"Steve just walked by, let me tell him you're on. I'll talk to you later."

I took a big gulp of coffee.

"This is Steve, can I help you?"

"Hi, I'm Christy Canyon, I worked for you in 1985 before I quit."

"Yes, I know who you are. What's going on?" He was so casual about it. Not all kiss-ass like Howie.

"Well, I was thinking of making a comeback, and I know you have girls under contract, so I was wondering if you would be interested in me."

"Absolutely. What kind of money were you thinking about?"

Sheesh! he sure got right to the point.

I told him my price per film, along with a royalty amount.

"I stopped paying royalties when Ginger Lynn quit. But I would be interested in working on your price with you."

There was no working on it. It was non-negotiable.

"No, I really want a royalty. I think I'll see a few other companies then."

"Okay, let me know. I would be very interested in seeing you. I hope you understand that we just don't do royalties anymore."

"Oh, I do. Thanks, I'll call you and let you know." I hung up and wondered if he understood who I was. I thought of Tina and Mark, my trump card. I knew that they would agree to almost anything within reason. I had been toying with an idea to toss into the contract that would definitely fall into that within reason area.

I crossed off Vivid's number, and didn't bother with VCA. I would go see Caballero. If their offer wasn't decent, it was straight to Video Exclusives. I didn't have time to pussyfoot around. I had to survive.

By two that afternoon, Dad finally surfaced in the office. As soon as I heard the squeak of the door, I shoved my list of numbers and directions to Caballero into the top drawer, and pretended to be busy on the computer. A flick of the switch, and my computer game of Tetris became the accounts payable screen.

"Hi Dad. I put all of your messages on your desk. It's been pretty quiet in here."

"Carol thinks that warehouse will be perfect for us.

In that case, I knew it was going to be all wrong. "What does she know?"

"She is really a changed lady since the last time you saw her. Carol and I were fighting a lot when you moved in, and she admits that she threw the blame on you. She feels horrible about it too sweetheart."

Over fifty videos and forty magazine layouts later, it was a bit too late for her pathetic apologies. "I'll never forgive her."

"In life sometimes, you need to learn to forgive. It's known as water under the bridge."

"Carol took her problems out on a seventeen year old girl. I wasn't a bad kid Dad, I just needed some love and attention. Her own daughter stole credit cards, tore shutters and doors off their hinges in the house, crashed two cars and always told the two of you to fuck off. Carol never reprimanded her. I just tried to make myself invisible in that house, and look where it got me."

Dad sat on the edge of my desk. "I know how you feel honey, but it will be different this time."

"Are you two getting back together?"

"Well, we haven't talked about it, but my personal feeling is that Carol needs me."

"Why would you want somebody who just needs you because they are flat broke, need a job, and a place to stay? Don't you want somebody who wants you for you, and not what you can provide for them? What about Eve? Can't she help her mom out?"

Dad looked at me, unsure of where that came from. "Well, it seems that Eve isn't talking to her mom these days."

"How can Eve have respect for a mom who never gave her guidance? She let Eve walk all over her."

"She meant to be a good mother."

"She's a piece of shit."

"Watch your language." Dad was getting uncomfortable. "Is this what you learned in therapy? To call people names?"

"She's not a person, she's a monster. Don't ever knock my therapy again. You should be grateful Lois has helped me work through things."

"It seems she hasn't helped you work through your anger with Carol." Dad took a defensive stance, protecting Carol over me, again.

"There's no redeeming quality in Carol. She is what she is, a piece of shit. There's nothing Lois or any panel of therapists could do to change my mind. To treat a defenseless, heart broken teenager like she did was unforgivable."

Dad pushed up on the bridge of his glasses, which were already in place. "Well, she's coming to work here, so you better go see Lois and figure it out."

"I am, today at six-thirty." But not for the reasons you seem to be thinking.

"Listen honey," Dad was calming down, "The past is the past and we can't change it."

No, but I'll be damned if I repeat it. "You do what you have to do, and I'll do what I have to."

"What does that mean?"

"Just what I said." Shit, I said too much. "One way or another, I'll figure it out." What I said didn't make much sense, and was very vague, but it seemed to appease Dad, who I'm sure just wanted the conversation to end.

Dad got up from the corner of my desk. "That's my girl."

One hour later, at three-thirty, I poked my head in his office. "I'm going to head out for my dental appointment now."

Dad glanced at his watch. "Okay, I'll see you tomorrow morning." After our confrontation earlier, I didn't think he would argue with me about leaving thirty minutes earlier than I had asked.

I drove home to change for my meeting with Caballero. I chose a black Lycra dress that hugged every curve, and a pair of black heels. I stood in front of my full-length mirror, and thought about what I was getting back into.

Mom and I hardly spoke. A monthly dinner with Clair was about the most I saw her. I realized through my sessions with Lois, that it wasn't about me, it was about her. About six months after working for my father, M om told Clair that she was ready to see me. The three of us went to dinner, and a half-assed relationship was started. Eventually, we worked

213

Marv into the equation. He was still an unemployed idiot. Surprisingly, he never once brought up my past. She, for whatever her reasons were, kept me at arms length.

I got in my car, and headed out to Caballero's headquarters.

25

I found Caballero's address among a row of industrial buildings. Their building sat back about twenty feet from the sidewalk, and had a large gate surrounding the entire property. Barbed wire was looped along the entire top of this fifteen-foot barricade. Security cameras placed every three feet panned the entire area continuously.

I parked my car out on the street and turned off the engine. I sat for a minute, wondering if I were doing the right thing. I checked my sparse makeup job in the rearview mirror, and decided that I was. I wiped off some traces of mascara from under my left eye, applied another layer of my ice pink lipstick, rubbed my lips together, and got out of the car.

I walked across the street, straightening my already perfect dress. Lycra never wrinkled, it was just out of nerves. I was nervous in an excited way. I knew I was a valuable commodity in this business, even if Steve at Vivid didn't want to give me a royalty. I was sure Caballero would. And after all, Howie seemed so happy to hear from me.

I stepped through the open gate and was met by an extra large Samoan security guard, clipboard in hand. His dark brown hooded eyes checked out my entire body, starting at my black pumps. He stopped at my chest and cocked his boulder shaped head.

"What's your name?" He asked while scratching the back of his left ear with the antenna of his walkie-talkie. There was no enthusiasm in his voice, as he scanned his list of visitors due with his sizable index finger.

"Christy Canyon, and I'm here to see Howie."

His finger stopped midway down the list, and his head jerked up. He attached his clipboard and walkie-talkie on a hook near his left side and squinted at my face for the first time.

"You're Christy?" His hand went up to his forehead, creating a make shift visor against the June sun beating down. He looked down at his size fifteen feet and giggled. "I use to watch my father's videos of you when he wasn't home."

His father's videos? I was only twenty-two. Amused at this, I asked, "How old are you?"

"I just turned nineteen last month. Hey, what was Traci Lords like? My buddy loved her, and I loved you."

"She was pretty cool I guess." For a fifteen-year-old, I thought.

"So what are you doing here? You've been gone for a while haven't you?"

"For four years, but I was thinking of making a comeback, so I'm here to see Howie."

He looked off to the right, in a far away stare, deep in thought about something. "A comeback, huh? My friends won't believe this." He looked from right to left, and let out a low whistle. "Is there any way I can have your autograph?"

"Sure." I was flattered, but getting bored quickly. I was already five minutes late for my meeting.

I signed a blank piece of paper. "There you go, I'll see you when I leave."

"Goodbye Miss Canyon." I heard him say as I headed to the front doors.

His father's videos? Now that was a first.

I passed a man hand washing a brand new Porsche in the front parking spot under a sign that read Howie, and pressed the intercom button.

"Name please?" Came out of a speaker.

"Christy Canyon for Howie." I looked at my reflection in the tinted glass.

The door buzzed, and I stepped in. Directly in front of me was a circular reception desk. Sign in and out sheets on top, along with a row of badges that read visitor. Behind the desk was a gigantic waterfall from the ceiling to the ground. I remembered Tina telling me that Caballero was leasing their offices for $28,000.00 a month. What a waste of money.

The no-nonsense lady behind the desk gave me a tight smile and told me to sign in. She picked up her phone and punched in some numbers. "Howie, there's a Christy Canyon here to see you." She eyed me, said "okay" into the phone and hung up. "You need to attach this badge on your dress before you enter." I attached the stupid necessary I.D., thanked her out of courtesy, and walked to the door. She pushed a hidden buzzer and I opened the wooden passage into the next step of seeing Howie.

"Hello Miss Canyon, I will show you the way to Howie's office." A male voice said to my left. A man in a security outfit stepped in front of me. "Would you please follow me?"

Oh brother, they act like they're Fort Knox.

We passed rows of desks with busy bees behind them, and up a flight of stairs.

"Christy!" I heard at the top and turned around.

"I'm Nancy, do you remember me?" A woman with brown curly hair and large round glasses reached out to greet me. "We met at the VSDA show in Chicago in 1985. How have you been? What have you been up to? Is it true you're making a comeback? Well, I guess it is if you're here to see Howie. He's an idiot."

The questions came in rapid fire at me. I think she was on a caffeine overload.

I didn't recognize her. "How are you?"

"Good, good, listen, about your comeback," she was holding onto my forearm by now, bent over her messy desk. "I think you should know that you are still our top seller here." The bottom of her blouse was dipped in her cup of coffee and the liquid was spreading at a rapid pace on the fabric.

"NANCY!" Someone screamed from across the hall.

Nancy's head jerked up and a nervous smile spread across her face. "Yes boss. I was just saying hi to my old friend here!" She let go of my arm. "Don't settle for anything less." She whispered from the side of her mouth.

"Thanks, I'll see you later." I took that bit of information into Howie's office with me.

"So nice to see you again. Would you like anything to drink?"

I guessed this was Howie.

"No, I'm fine."

We stepped into his large corner office. Two sides of his office had floor to ceiling windows. One window overlooked the full parking lot giving him a perfect view of his employee's cars, the second overlooked the industrial street lined with gates, barred windows and the occasional drug deal. Not a great view at all.

He had a massive rectangular black lacquer desk in one corner, with a comfortable looking overstuffed black high-back leather chair behind it. Two stiff black leather chairs were in front of his desk for his guests. A full service bar was along the opposite wall, and a black leather couch took the third wall. This was eighties decorating at it's best.

"Please take a seat." He gestured with his hand, a gold and diamond Rolex peeking through the sleeve of his charcoal gray suit jacket.

I sat down opposite him as he began to speak. "I've been giving this a lot of thought since your call." He paused. "We're in production right now on a big budget film by Andrew Blake called 'Night Trips'." He paused again for my reaction. It was all Greek to me. I had no idea who this guy Blake was.

"We have Tori Welles as the star, and I figured you could play the nurse in this film. It was originally cast with Porsche Lynn, but I would rather see you in that role." He picked a piece of lint off his jacket and smiled at me, settling back even deeper into his chair. I on the other hand, could not believe what I was hearing. After a four-year hiatus, I was being offered a minor bit role that was given to Porscha Lynn? I just stared in disbelief.

He was oblivious and went on with his ridiculous brainstorm. "Now, we were going to give Porscha five hundred for the scene, but my partner and I spoke about this after your call. By the way, I'm sorry Mr. Bloom can't be here with us today, but he could not get out of a prior commitment on such short notice." He stopped talking, trying to remember what he was saying before he diverted. "Oh yes, we decided that with your name, we are willing to give you two thousand for the scene, and of course second billing after Tori."

This was worse than I could have imagined. This pompous little turd behind his desk was insane. Me, a co-star? Tina and Mark were looking better by the second. I was speechless.

"How does that sound to you?" He asked, proud of his insane offer.

"Actually, I don't think it's what I'm looking for, at all. I want to be the star, and it is about one fifth of the price I'm looking for." No need to even bring up a royalty figure.

He flinched. "A fifth?" We both knew this meeting was over. "Well, I think that may be a bit much. Tori is under contract with our company right now." The uncomfortable silence was broken by his office doors being flung open. I turned around and saw the most beautiful brunette entering his office like she owned the place.

"I heard Christy Canyon was here." She smiled, showing off a perfect set of straight, white teeth. She was in skintight black pants, five inch black pumps, and a cropped, white halter-top. Her six-pack abs showed on her deep dark skin. She had wavy brunette hair and chocolate brown eyes that sucked you in. She strutted towards me, and stuck out her hand. "Hi, I'm Tori Wells."

She was so exotic, and breathtaking I suddenly felt frumpy.

"Hi, I'm Christy."

She plopped down in the seat next to me. "Hey Howie, when am I going to get a new car?"

"Well, since you totaled the last one, my insurance is giving me a problem about insuring a new one for you."

"I don't give a shit, go through a new company then. Our deal was that you lease me a Camaro, and I want a new one by Monday."

She smiled and looked at me. "I guess I had one too many beers that night. So, Howie told me that you are going to be in my next movie! I'm so excited. It's because of you that I got into this business. My ex and I use to always watch your movies. He would start fucking me the same way you were being fucked on film. Then one night he dared me to make a movie, and I never lose a dare. So, the next day, I went to see Jim South, and five months later, here I am! Now I'm going to make a movie with you. I dumped the guy, but he'll be so jealous when he finds out."

She looked around the office. "Hey, where's Randy? I want you to meet my boyfriend, he said he never worked with you before."

"Who's your boyfriend?" What a trip she was.

"Randy West. So Howie, did you work Christy and I in a sex scene together yet?" She eyed me and I felt naked. "There he is. Where were you? Hey, meet Christy, she's going to be in my movie with me. I'm going to have sex with her."

Randy stuck out his hand. "It's very nice to meet you." I extended my hand out, and thought of how good looking this guy was.

Tori wet her lips, "Christy, you look great. I love your body and your real tits. I can't wait to bury my face in those famous tits. Isn't she sexy honey?" She ran her fingernails up and down Randy's arm.

"Yeah, she sure is baby." He was bent over her, licking her ear.

Tori's eyes were becoming hypnotic. "You know, before I started making films, I was a striper at a club in Van Nuys called the Odd Ball. When I decided to make pornos, I lost over fifty pounds in a month."

Somehow I didn't think she went on the Jenny Craig diet.

"Did you cover up that hole on the couch yet?" Tori asked.

"No honey, I think it's ruined."

"FUCK! That was my favorite couch."

I had to know what happened to this wild woman's couch. "What happened?"

"Last night I dropped a lit pipe on it. It was the first piece of furniture I ever bought too, it had such memories."

I wanted to know more, so like a geek I asked, "What did it look like?"

"It was a black leather sofa in the shape of lips. Oh well, fuck the stupid couch, let's talk about my movie with you." She turned to face me and put her hands on my legs. I froze. Outside of making films, I had never been with a woman before, and felt nervous at her blatant flirting with me.

"Maybe we should practice, Randy can watch and play with himself in a corner." Her voice was almost a whisper, and her hands were getting closer to my crotch area.

Randy rubbed Tori's shoulders, "Mmmm, I'd love to see that baby."

Now I'm no prude, or maybe I am, but I suddenly had to get out of there. Her red fingernails were getting dangerously close to my white cotton underwear.

Howie broke the tension, "Come on guys, as much as I would love to see you two getting it on, I have a meeting with the bank manager in five minutes."

"You prude." Tori shot Howie a disgusted look. "Here's my number Christy, lets go party soon." Tori wrote her number on the back of one of Howie's business cards. "I can't wait to fuck you." She got up and headed to the door. "Hey Howie," she said when she reached the door, "Don't forget, a new car by Monday or I'm going to Vivid." She jerked the door open and strutted back out, Randy tailing her.

"Well," Howie looked uncomfortable, "Why don't you think about our offer, and get back to me." He picked another piece of invisible lint off his jacket.

"Oh sure. I'm just going to talk to another company first."

We both knew that we would never work together.

I left Caballero's office and realized that I had just met a girl with the biggest set of brass balls, and a company owner with no balls.

One week after shooting "Night Trips", with Porscha as the nurse, Tori left Caballero and signed with Vivid Video. Howie was left holding a bag of shit.

I walked back into my car, saying goodbye to the security guard and headed to my next appointment.

I sat down in my familiar chair in Lois office. "I'm thinking of getting back into the adult business."

"What brought this on?"

I filled her in on the latest developments with Carol coming to work for my dad. "I never want to have to see her again Lois, let alone work with her."

"Then you don't have to. What about your mom and dad? How do you think they'll react to this?"

"It doesn't really matter, I'm still the same person. Dad is putting Carol before my feelings, and my mom and I have a strained relationship anyway. Mom and I have never talked about the past. I think she wants to pretend it doesn't exist. I just have to do what I need to do, and you know what Lois? I'm actually kinda excited about it."

"What excites you about it?"

I thought for a minute. "I'm ready for some attention. I feel like I'm invisible, left out. Mom favors Clair and Dad favors Carol. I know this sounds stupid, but the business favors me. I haven't finished with that path in life yet."

"What path would that be?"

"I think a very rebellious path."

"What are you rebelling against?"

"Trying to please my mom and dad, which doesn't get me anywhere. I told my dad I wanted to go to college, and his answer was that I was in his college, the school of hard knocks, the best kind to be in."

"Did you tell your mom you wanted to go to college?"

"Yeah, she said that after five years of paying for Clair's tuition, and Marv still not working, that I should apply for a student loan."

"How did this make you feel?"

"Left out of course. Clair got it all. I feel like a trapped rat running and running on one of those wheels but going nowhere.

"What do you want to study?"

"Something in fashion. I don't want to stay at my dad's office any longer and I know that I can make enough money in the adult business to do whatever I want."

Lois just looked at me.

"It's what I'm going to do and nobody can stop me."

"I wasn't trying to. I just want you to be prepared for your parents cutting you off again."

"If I survived it at eighteen, I know I can survive it at twenty two. I can't live my life in fear of them cutting me off every time I do something they don't like." The thought of not speaking to my parents again made me feel sad, but the thought of being free again was intoxicating.

Our hour was up and Lois had one parting statement. "Be sure you know what you're getting into."

I stood in her doorway. "I do." And I really felt that I did. "I'll see you next week."

Driving home, I thought about Lois' last words. I had no idea what I was getting into, but I was going to do it, my mind was made up, and there was no stopping me. Whatever happened after with my parents, had already happened when I was seventeen. I learned at seventeen that anybody at anytime could let you down and cut you out. I only had myself in the world.

I got home and called Tina.

"Hi Tina!"

"Hi Honey! How did your meeting go with Howie today?"

"It went really well actually." I couldn't tell her the truth; I had to pretend like this would be a battle between companies over my comeback. "Steve at Vivid is so adorable." Of what little I could remember of him four years ago. "And that Howie! What a great guy." For a total loser. "I met Tori Wells today at Caballero. She's so beautiful." My first true statement in the conversation.

"What about Mark and me?" I could hear a tinge of worry in her voice.

"Well, if you guys still want to talk to me." It came out so casual, yet inside I was anxious. I was worried that maybe I wasn't as popular as I thought I was. What else could I do if no company was willing to pay the price I was asking? If I was going to make a comeback, I had to get as much as I could. No way was I going to earn what I earned four years ago. I realized now that Video Exclusives was my best shot at getting everything I wanted.

"When can we meet?"

"Well, I have to work for my dad tomorrow and then a half day on Saturday."

"What time do you think you can get to our office on Saturday?"

"Four thirty."

"We're really excited about it. Hey, want to go to dinner after? No matter what company you end up with, we're always going to be best friends. I know you have to do what's best for you, but I think Mark will match anybody's offer."

That wouldn't be hard to do.

"Yeah, let's go to dinner after! That sounds great. Hopefully it will be a celebration dinner." I threw in for good measure.

"I'm sure it will."

We hung up and I crawled into bed with a pad of paper. I wrote down a list of what I wanted for my comeback. The last item on the list was the only one I would negotiate, it was a long shot.

FRIDAY:

Friday morning I was at the office at nine o'clock sharp. I walked in and felt a wave of nostalgia. I was alone, and went about my daily routine. I turned on the coffeepot, Xerox machine, lights, and the ten-year-old computer. While the relic was warming up, this gave me plenty of time to check the messages, pour myself a cup of coffee and water the plants.

Nine fifteen and Dad called. "Hi honey. How's the office?"

"Good Dad. No urgent messages. When are you coming in?"

"Well, Carol and I are going to take a drive down to Irvine to check out some Christmas tree decorations at a warehouse. Carol found a company that is going out of business, and I think we can get a real steal on them. I should be in around two."

The computer finally booted itself up. "So, she really is coming to work here?"

"Yes, it's official. She got an advance on her first paycheck. I want you to welcome her back on Monday morning. This is a family business, and we need to all get along and work together. Carol told me to tell you hello."

"How nice."

"Honey, don't give Daddy any problems."

"Oh, believe me I won't."

"That's my girl. I've got to go, but I'll see you in a few hours."

After we hung up, I went into Dad's office and opened up his checkbook. The record information for the last check written was made out to Carol in the amount of $300.00 for twenty hours of work. Carol was making five dollars an hour more than I, and she hadn't even stepped into the office. I was livid.

I went about my boring daily routine of answering the phone, going through the mail, making out the bank deposit and filing tax returns.

At twelve thirty, I went to get lunch and made the bank deposit. After eating a sandwich at my desk, I decided to file away Dad's personal credit

222

card receipts in the bottom drawer.

I sat down on the ground near the black metal filing cabinet and began to file. The last one in the pile was from three days ago at the department store I. Magnin. He was with Carol that day. I leaned back against the wall, and read the American Express receipt. It was from the "Studio Dresses" department, in the amount of $453.00. Since I knew my father was not a cross-dresser, I realized that he must have bought Carol new clothes.

By two-thirty, Dad came to work.

"Hello darling. Wait until you see the beautiful decorations Carol picked out for us."

"Yeah, I can hardly wait." You've seen one glass ball, you've seen them all. "Hey Dad, how much is Carol getting paid?"

Dad stopped walking and stood in the hallway between my office and his. "Well." Dad paused and turned to me. "Why don't you come in my office."

I followed Dad in, and sat down opposite him. Oh shit, this was it, the final showdown.

Dad started. "Well, since Carol returned from Norway, she has had some financial troubles. I am going to be paying her fifteen dollars an hour until she can get back on her feet, then I will be cutting her pay back to what I pay you. She just needs a little help right now."

"I could have used a little help when I bought my new car last year, but I didn't ask you. Why is it that she's in her fifties, I'm in my twenties, and you're helping her out over me? What happened to all of the money that she made from selling the house you two had together after the divorce?"

"Well, it seems that Carol isn't good at budgeting, and went through it in two years."

"She blew over two hundred thousand in two years?" What an idiot.

"That's why she needs me." Dad was getting defensive.

"So I get the short end of the stick, because I can budget myself every month?" Somehow it wasn't fair just because she chose to blow every dime as fast as it came in.

"Don't you see how unfair that is Dad?"

Dad slammed his fist down on his desk. "I can spend my money however I want to."

"Oh, I know you can. It just doesn't seem fair. Besides my paycheck, I have never asked you for a dime, and yet she's making more money than me now, and, you took her shopping the other day for clothes because she can't budget her money."

Dad was about to say something, then stopped himself to regroup. He sat back in his chair, crossed his arms, and looked over my left shoulder, his eyes focusing in on the blank wall. I sat still, waiting for him. The sound of the clock ticking away was louder than ever in the quiet office. I looked behind Dad at the photo of Clair and me as kids on the second shelf. We were in matching yellow dresses with a white ribbon in our hair. My eye caught sight of a photo on the shelf above that I had not noticed before. It was a photo of Carol and Dad, taken at their old house. Carol was sitting on their green couch, Dad bending over her from above. The photo was propped up and blocking another photo of Clair and me.

Dad finally broke the uncomfortable silence. "Until Carol can get back in the black, I am going to help her. It doesn't mean that I love you any less if I take her to buy a few dresses, or pay her a little more for now."

"I know it doesn't mean you love me less, that's not the point. Don't you see that Carol will never learn how to budget? If you give her $300.00, she will spend $400.00 and just ask you for more."

"That's where you're wrong. We had a long talk about her finances the other day, and she wants me to help her with her budget every month. She realizes what a mistake she made spending all the income from the sale of our house. I'm telling you Christy, she is a changed woman."

What a crock of shit. She knew just how to play him. "Well Dad," oh God, this was hard to say, "I've been thinking about this all week, and I've come to the conclusion that I can't work here if Carol's going to be here."

Dad and I locked eyes from across his desk. "I cannot believe my ears. You are going to cut your nose off to spite your face."

"That's not it at all. I don't know how to make you understand how much I loathe Carol. If you want her to work here, pay her more than me, and take her shopping, that's fine. Like you said, it's your money and your business, I can't stop you, nor do I want to, but there's no way in hell that I'm sticking around. So, you do what you need to do, and I'll do what I have to."

Dad leaned forward on his desk. "And what is it that you are going to do?"

"I'm not sure, but I'll survive."

"You listen to me." He was angry now. "If you ever get back into the adult business, I'll cut you off, and never speak to you again."

"Why do you think I would get back into adult?" How did he figure that one out so fast?

"I just have a hunch. You've never said one bad word about it, and I know you still speak to Wanda and that Tina girl. She's trouble that Tina, a real wild child. You be careful with her."

"You be careful with Carol. She's a real idiot." And somehow, it didn't matter anymore. I just told my dad that I was quitting, and he again chose Carol over me. Dad wanted people around him that were needy, like

Carol.

"Don't talk about Carol that way."

"Don't talk about Tina that way. She's nicer to me than Carol ever could be."

We were back to the staring contest.

Dad broke the silence. "I want you to be honest with me. Are you thinking of getting back into porno?"

I kept my eyes locked into his. Should I be honest and get it over with? No, I just wanted to leave. "No Dad."

"Do you know the humiliation I went through four years ago trying to explain to my friends why you were doing what you were doing?" He twisted his head from side to side, cracking it in the process, then straightened his glasses with a push of the right index finger.

I froze in my seat. This was a topic that had never come up before. I still had never asked how he found out, although I assumed he saw my photo on a magazine cover at his neighborhood liquor store. "I wasn't concerned with your friends Dad, I was concerned about surviving after being thrown out on the street."

This really riled him up. "You were not thrown out on the streets! You left for school one day, and never came home. That is what happened. I was worried sick about you."

"Did you ever come by my school and ask the principal to find me in class?" But I knew he hadn't, I just wanted to watch him squirm.

"No, I figured that you would come to your senses and come back home soon."

"After the first month, didn't you wonder about it? Or was Carol not really pushing you to find out? Do you honestly believe that I didn't hear her through your door telling you every night how much she hated having me there? I guess I could have stayed and gone insane from her abuse." It was finally being talked, actually yelled about. I realized I was screaming by now. Screaming from frustration. Frustrated that Carol had treated me so poorly, and he was defending her, bringing her back, and worst of all, questioning why I got into pornography. Why did he think his eighteen-year-old daughter decided to basically sell her body? For kicks? For the fuck of it? "Don't you have any clue what I went through when I was seventeen, Dad? And yet, I take full responsibility for getting into the business. I have never blamed you, Mom, Marv or Carol for me making the decision to do what I did, but don't act like it never happened, because it did."

"What? Don't act like what never happened?"

"All of it, Goddamnit." I began to cry out of frustration and pent up anger that things were never talked about. They were always brushed under the carpet. I was hurt that once again, Dad was choosing Carol's

225

feelings, needs and wants over mine. I was sad that Mom and I had never patched up our relationship. I was concerned about how I would survive another round of being shut out by my parents. And most of all, I was worried that if Video Exclusives didn't want me, who would? Insecurity crept in, clouding my feelings and judgment even more than they were before my pathetic meeting with Caballero.

The phone rang, breaking the tension, the sadness, and the self-pity that I was allowing myself to feel. "I'll get it." I heard myself say. Dad began shuffling through some paperwork, relieved that he was let off the hook from a confrontation.

"Hold on a minute." I pressed the hold button and told Dad his brother Popkin was on the line. Normally Dad would tell me to take a message. A call from Popkin was usually trouble. Popkin only called when he needed something, or just to unload on my father about what a shitty hand God had dealt him. But today, he picked up his extension before the sentence was even out of my mouth.

I sat down at my desk and stared at the blank computer screen. This was the hand that I was dealt. Use it, I told myself. Make the best of what you've got. You're a survivor, so enjoy the adventures that lie ahead. If Dad wants Carol, he could have Carol. If Mom chose that decrepit Marv's feelings over mine, so be it. Don't look back baby, just keep on going.

I made out another bank deposit and poked my head into Dad's office. "I'm going to the bank, then I'm going to call it a day."

He cradled the phone between his ear and shoulder to glance at his watch. It was four-ten. He pulled the receiver one-inch from his mouth as Popkin rambled on. "Okay, I'll see you tomorrow."

I grabbed my purse and headed out the door.

26

If all went well with Tina and Mark tonight, this would be the last time I walked up the flight of stairs to Dad's office. It would be Dad and Carol's office now. Walking towards the front door, it dawned on me how excited I was at the thought of never having to work here again. My time here was long gone. I thought about Carol's return as a blessing in disguise. I opened the front door, and heard the familiar squeak. God I hated that sound. After four years of hearing that sound, I realized that I wouldn't miss anything about this job - the flight of stairs, sneaking off to smoke a cigarette downstairs, fighting for a parking space, and most of all being under Dad's watchful eye. I was done. No matter what happened tonight, it was time to move on.

Dad was in Carol's office arranging two new potted trees. "Good morning." Dad said as one of the trees toppled over, leaving a pile of wet dirt on the carpet. "Fuck." He screamed.

"Good morning Dad." I walked into my office and booted up the computer. I filled my coffee cup and tried to avoid Dad whom I could hear grunting in the other room.

"Do you think you could give me a hand in here?" He asked.

I felt so peaceful. "Sure thing Dad."

"Is that a new dress you're wearing?" He asked, with accusation in his voice.

Like it was any of his business, I replied, "No, Mom gave it to me three years ago."

"It looks new to me, and pretty expensive."

"Well, you know Mom."

Dad glared at me for a minute as I sipped my coffee. "Will you vacuum this pile of dirt up?"

"No problem." I left the room to get the Hoover. I plugged it in and Dad asked, "You seem pretty subdued today, did you stay out late last night? You look tired."

Tired of this shit I thought. I couldn't stand it when people told me I looked tired. "No, I was at home." I turned on the vacuum to drown out his next question. I cleaned the entire office while I was at it, anything to make the day go by without having to talk to him. Dad was in one of his dark moods, and I was sick of being his punching bag.

"Those trees really brighten up that room Dad. I'm sure Carol will love them." I looked over at the dying plant in my office. "What time does she start on Monday?"

"Well," Dad paused and I sensed trouble in paradise. "It seems she needs to take her mom to see a doctor on Monday, so she won't be starting until Tuesday."

There was the answer to his crabby mood. His star employee already backed out of day one. Just to twist the knife I asked innocently, "Her doctor's appointment takes all day? How weird, I hope the old goat's okay." Actually, I couldn't believe Carol's mom was still alive, ornery as ever I bet. It didn't matter when she started, I was done today, and three o'clock couldn't roll around soon enough.

"Well, she's really old you know." Dad growled.

"You're right Daddy. How old is Carol now? Sixty? Seventy?"

"Not Carol! Her mother Goddamn it!"

"Oh yes. She must be nearing that century mark by now."

"We will welcome Carol with open arms on Tuesday young lady. I don't know what's gotten into you today, but there will be no attitude come her first day here, little Missy."

"Oh no Daddy, not from me." I'll be long gone, just like I said I would be.

He eyed me suspiciously before stomping into his own office.

I was bored silly.

I went through the same routine as I had for the last four years, praising the lord that it was the last time.

At one-thirty, Dad came in and gave me my paycheck. My last one, unbeknownst to him. "I'm leaving now, but I want you to stay 'til three sharp." He had calmed down throughout the day, but was still a nervous Nellie about something.

"Oh I will Daddy. Goodbye."

He followed through with his promise to cut me out of his life if I ever returned to the adult business.

Clair told me that Carol never showed up on Tuesday morning for work, or ever. One week after my final day, she reunited with her boyfriend and moved back to Norway.

27

The deal was going down. I didn't have a piece of paper with my requests; it was all memorized. Six points met, and we would have a deal. A deal that would bring me out of my four-year retirement.

I followed Tina into Mark's office.

Video cameras were placed in every office, storage room and the large warehouse in back, transmitting real time images on fifteen televisions mounted on Mark's back wall. The only window, behind Mark's black leather seat, was bulletproof. Two light tables, side by side, to the right of his desk, were covered with chromes of movies in the making. Box cover shots, three-way sex scenes, all girl orgies, and close up shots of male and female body parts. Three loops were scattered around the chromes, to give the viewer a closer, clearer image. In a pile to the left of Mark's desk, waiting for his approval, was a stack of artwork waiting to go to the printer. A box filled with posters and movie slicks, that had just come back from the printer was by the front door.

This was the office of a porn lord.

Tina and I sat down on one side of Mark's mahogany desk in his hi-tech office.

Mark, sitting opposite us, folded his arms behind his head, leaned back in his chair, and propped his black ostrich boot on the desk corner. "So, you're ready to come out of retirement."

"I want cast and script approval."

"What?"

"I also want to fly first class and stay in four-star hotels." So much for a warm up. There was so much in my head, it just tumbled out.

"Jumping the gun here. Let me at least write this down." He swung his boot off the desk, found a yellow legal pad of paper and his Mont Blanc pen. Mark began writing while I continued.

"One thousand dollars a day for any personal appearances at stores or conventions." There, that got the easy ones out of the way. The next few deal points were the make it or break it ones. I looked over to Tina for support and encouragement, but she was too busy admiring her new three-carat diamond ring Mark had bought her. It wasn't until later that I found out Mark bought it for her for bringing me to him on a silver platter. So there I sat on my own in a cheap, tight, white dress that I bought at The Limited. The chintzy label sewn in was itching my neck. I made a mental note to cut it out when I got home.

Trying my best to cough out the next demand, I could hear Tina's gold cigarette case open, the flick of her lighter, and a deep inhale. I wished she would hand me a lit cigarette. "Ten thousand a movie for three sex scenes."

Mark's pen found its way to his mouth, not to the pad of paper.

"Plus, a royalty of one dollar per tape sold."

"Our little girl here is a business woman Mark." Tina smiled at me, Mark just stared, mouth partially open, and I went in for the kill with my final request. "And a convertible Porsche no older than 1987." My eyes never left Mark's face. "And I don't like red or black."

Tina giggled and threw in. "We want to go to Hawaii too."

Two weeks later, Tina and I were flying to Hawaii for six nights. First class of course.

28

It was eleven o'clock on Monday morning and I was lounging around, yakking on the phone with Wanda.

"Wanda, you have no idea how great it feels to be free and never have to work at my dad's office again." I crawled back in bed with a cup of coffee. "I think Carol's threat to return was a blessing in disguise."

"I think you just outgrew your dad's office and it was only a matter of time."

"Yeah, I should have left a year ago." I turned on the TV "Oh! 'Charlie's Angels' is on!" When I was a kid, my best friends and I use to pretend that we were the Angels, and I was always Kelly."

"Have you talked to your dad?"

"No, I think he knows I'm getting back into the business." I looked out of my window and saw the sun shining. God I loved the summer. "He told me that if I ever got back into it, he would never speak to me again." Oh well, it wouldn't be the first time and I'm sure it would be easier now at twenty-three than at eighteen.

"How do you feel about that?"

"It's his choice, not mine." I couldn't believe how alive I felt. "You know Wanda, I can't stand people trying to control me, telling me what to do and what not to do. I'm sorry to say this but I think my dad is more upset about losing his control over me, than me having sex on film." I stretched out in bed, pointing my toes and fingers out as far as I could. Right about now, sex sounded great. I tried to think back to the last time I had even had it.

"And who's your dad to make any judgments about casual sex? Remember that time at your condo last year? He practically dry humped me. I had to push him off."

My God, I couldn't even remember the last time I had gotten laid. "Don't remind me, I'm so embarrassed about that." He also tried to screw another friend of mine, but I never told Wanda. "Didn't he say he wanted to give you a back rub?" I also never bothered to tell Wanda that after she rejected him, he hated her and always put her down when I brought her name up.

"It was more like he wanted to massage my pussy with his cock."

I cringed at the thought of my dad wanting to screw my best friend. Her father Ron, who had shot me hundreds of times stark ass naked, never once even flirted with me. The first night my dad met Wanda, he wanted to jump her bones. How ironic is that? I got out of bed, opened my sliding glass door and stepped out on my patio. "He's always having casual sex." I could hear birds chirping in the tree outside my window. "He's screwed every secretary we've hired in the last four years."

"That's my point Christy. I was pretty much a stranger, and yet he was willing to fuck me right on your living room floor with you in the next room. So, what's the difference if it's on film or in somebody's living room? Sex is sex, do you see my point?"

I heard her loud and clear. I believe the word is hypocrite. How dare anybody judge me, be it family, friends or strangers. I tried to remember a saying I had on a poster in my room when I was ten. Something about not judging others until you had walked a mile in their shoes. I could still see the silhouette of an Indian wearing moccasins on the poster, with the sun setting in the background. Mom had bought me the corny, seventies-style poster one day at the mall instead of a puppy I had wanted, and I had cried all the way home.

I wonder what happened to that poster.

I suddenly got bored with talking about my father. "What set are you on today?"

"Oh, a movie that's being shot by the Pink Ladies."

"Aren't they that group of girls that formed a club for women's rights in the business?"

"Yeah, are you going to join them?"

"No. I'm getting everything I want with Video Exclusives. I have nothing to complain about." Friday I was going with Tina to pick up my new Porsche. "I couldn't be happier."

"You know Christy, there's this really cute guy on the set named Shadow."

"No way Wanda, you know I would never date a porn star."

"He's not a porn star, he's a caterer. He cooks all of the meals for the high budget movies. Listen, I'm not trying to set you up, I just thought it might be fun for you to go out with him. You know, catch up on the business now that you're making your comeback after four years off.

She had a point. "Does he always have good dirt on the girls?" It would be fun to catch up on all of the industry gossip.

"Oh yeah. He's cute too. Hold on." I heard Wanda yell, "Tell her the Today Sponges are in here." "Sorry about that, Nina Hartley's on her period."

The Today Sponge is the perfect remedy for a girl to use in a sex scene when it's that time of the month. It stops the girl's monthly visitor from making a camera debut, which would turn the movie into a European only release.

"Tell Nina I said hi. I haven't seen her since we shot 'Battle Of The Stars' in 1985." I suddenly felt a wave of nostalgia for those days. As screwed up as I had been in the self-esteem department, I had such good

232

memories of the business. Were they real, or did my brain have selective memory? "So, you were saying he's cute?" Suddenly I wanted to meet Shadow.

"Hell yeah, if I wasn't married, I would fuck him in a heartbeat."

I filled up Ninja's food dish. "What does he look like?" My big black kitty came running into the kitchen at the sound of the food hitting the ceramic bowl.

"He's got the most amazing long brown curly hair, sexy brown eyes and he's such a cool dresser."

"Does he know who I am?" Although I knew he did.

"Know who you are? Oh please, who doesn't?"

"Do you think he would want to go out with me?" But I knew he would.

"Want to go out? Oh my God Christy, as soon as I told him you were my best friend, he got an instant boner."

"Does he have a car?"

"I don't know what kind, but I know he has something. He's always picking up and dropping off girls from the sets. They all seem to love him."

Okay, he had the two necessities, a car and a job. That wasn't asking for much was it? "Okay, give him my phone number."

Three nights later, Shadow was knocking on my door. I didn't know what to expect when I opened it, I just knew that I was excited. Excited to be breaking free from my father and taking control of my life again. I seemed to have lost myself somewhere along the way.

* * * *

1988

I came back to the office after getting Dad's lunch, lost in thought about my latest dilemma.

"Here's your sandwich Dad." I absent-mindedly put it on his desk. "I'm going to finish that filing now." I began to leave his office.

"Christy, I think it's wonderful that Alan asked you to marry him last week."

I didn't think it was so wonderful. "But I don't know if I'm ready for that Dad." I stopped in his doorway. "I'm only twenty two." Maybe he would finally understand where I was coming from.

"Twenty two? You're not getting any younger. In a handful of years, you will be a quarter of a century old. You need to settle down and pop out a few kids."

That's funny, that's exactly what Alan had said on the night he proposed to me. "But I'm still a kid myself."

"Oh Christy, Alan is a good stable man for you. A young lady such as yourself can't boogie-woogie every night. It gets old my friend. You can dance all night, but eventually you must pay the fiddler."

What was he talking about? I hated it when my dad flew off on tangents that made no sense in a conversation. The thought of being tied down to my father's partner scared the shit out of me.

"Alan said he wanted a home-cooked meal every night."

"And what's so wrong with that? Is it too much for a man to ask his wife to have a hot meal on the table after work?"

Not if he's content with tuna melts or scrambled eggs, which was all I knew how to make. "I've never cooked a meal in my life." Suddenly I realized I never wanted to cook for Alan or anybody. Just because I was a girl, was I expected to cook?

"Well that's your mother's fault. She should have taught you and your sister how to cook." Dad pointed his finger at me. "Among many other things."

"This isn't about Mom teaching us how to cook. It's about me not wanting to get married to anybody right now."

"You're a damn fool if you let him get away."

"If he's so great, you can marry him." My dad knew just how to rile me up. He never seemed to listen, or be on my side. "Don't you care that I'm not in love with him?"

"Love." Dad got that far away look in his eyes. "You learn to love people and things in so many different ways. I love my dog, I love my house," Dad threw his arms up in the air, "I even love my car."

"Alan is not a dog or a thing that I will grow to love." And I'm not ready to get married. Didn't he hear me? "You two want to train me like one, but I won't have it. I will not have my life run by the two of you."

"We don't want to run your life. Why are you acting like there's a conspiracy between Alan and me?"

Dad smirked and I saw red.

Then I saw the red vacuum cleaner sitting in the middle of the floor.

Dad unwrapped his sandwich. "You will marry Alan, and then the two of you will eventually take over this business." Dad bit into his ham sandwich. "It's a perfect partnership."

"I will not get married!" The vacuum cleaner flew across the office, wiping out three lamps on its way towards him.

Dad stopped mid-bite, a few strands of coleslaw clung to his chin before they fell on his desk.

"I quit!" I could hear the splintering of wood before I slammed the office door.

Five minutes later I got home fuming at my father. Why was it that he

234

wanted me to marry a man that I didn't love? I pushed the play button on my answering machine. "Hi honey, it's Mama! I can't wait to see you and Alan tonight and go over the wedding details. Come by at six. I love you."

I pushed erase, took the phone off the hook and climbed into bed. By four-thirty, I was fast asleep.

The following week, with Dad promising Clair the marriage would never be brought up again, I went back to the office.

Three brand new lamps sat on the end tables. A new vacuum was propped up in the closet. That will teach him. The marriage to Alan was never brought up again.

* * * *

I checked myself out one last time in the hallway mirror. I was wearing torn jeans, a tight red tank top and red Reebok tennis shoes.

Perfect.

I opened the front door, and didn't know what to think of this comic book character standing in my doorway.

"Hi. I'm Shadow"

"Hi, I'm Christy. Do you want to come in?" It wasn't so much that I wanted a stranger in my place, but God forbid the old timers on my floor caught a look at this. They would really have something to gossip about at the next Homeowners Association meeting.

I pulled him in, took a quick look to the right and left of the common hallway, and closed my door. "Wanda has told me so many great things about you Shadow." This 6'1" man stood in my living room, and I wasn't sure what to make of him. Okay, so Wanda left out a couple of details. His disheveled head of hair fell to his mid back. He flipped his head over, shook out his ringlets with his fingertips, then flipped his head back up. His long head of hair fluttered back to the exact same spot. "She did huh? Well, I hope it was all good stuff." He winked at me.

"Your hair is so beautiful." He obviously took great pride in it.

He made a gesture with his lips, that I think was supposed to resemble a roar. "Thanks, I think it's the Leo in me." He took a strand of his hair in between his right index finger and thumb and stared at it for a few seconds. "I've been told I resemble a lion." He released the hair. "I think it's time for a trim."

He wore a tight black spandex tank top, with two white lightening bolts down each side. The black fabric was so taut across his chest, that I could see the outline of his chest hairs, and erect nipples underneath. "Oh yes! She told me all of the good parts." Just not all of the parts in general.

"She told me some great things about you too Christy."

My eyes settled on his crotch for just a second. That had to be a banana he stuffed inside. Inside his what, I wasn't quite sure. He wasn't wearing pants, and they weren't leggings. Dare I say my date was wearing a pair of tights? Zebra print to boot.

He smiled. "I love that Wanda. She's good people."

Wanda was a person, not people. "Yes, she's the best." My eyes settled on his feet. I hadn't seen shoes like that since the sixth grade. I begged and pleaded with my mom for a pair just like them.

"I will not buy you a pair of platform tennis shoes. You're only twelve years old Christy!"

"But Mommy! I want a pair."

But it was a no-go. Mom bought me a sensible pair of sneakers the following week.

Shadow had my dream shoes on eleven years later, only in black. I had wanted red.

"I hope you're hungry. I made reservations at a French restaurant in Encino."

"I'm starving!" I grabbed my denim jacket and Shadow helped me into it.

He smiled, and I realized that there was something cute about this quirky, wanna-be rocker.

We went outside of my complex, and I was blinded by the sun's reflection off the hood of a burnt orange truck. I held up my forearm to shield out the intrusive light and color of the paint. "Why would anybody buy a car in that...?"

"Your chariot awaits my fair lady." He held out his arm and pointed a remote directly at the burnt orange truck. The headlights and taillights flashed twice.

Like he needed an alarm on that thing. Who would steal scrap metal?

"Let me get the door for you." He pulled up on a piece of rope that acted as a door handle, and hit the left side of the window twice. Presto, the door moaned and groaned but it finally opened. Partially that is. "You have to kind of go in sideways."

"Oh that's no problem." I took a deep breath, and sucked in my tummy.

Shadow hopped in on his side, and fired up the engine. I could hear two car alarms go off down my street. "I've got a real tricked out engine in this baby." He pulled away from my street and popped in a cassette.

I was surprised it even had an engine. "Do you drag race in it?" But I knew he didn't. Or should I say couldn't. Driving down Ventura Blvd., it could barely hit the fifteen miles per hour range. "What tape is this?" It was awful. I didn't know what gave me a headache first, the loud metal

236

music, or the loud metal sound of his muffler dragging on the road.

"Twisted Sister. I've been told by numerous people that I resemble the lead singer Dee Snyder." He checked out his image in the rear view mirror. All one-half that was left of it. "Only with brown hair."

I had no idea what the singer looked like, but unfortunately, I now knew what he sounded like. "Yeah, I can see that."

"You can check out my glove compartment for other rockin' cassettes I have."

"Cool." I stared at the button, or what should have been a button to the compartment. "Uh, how do I open it?" Was that a penny stuck in the slot?

Shadow stopped at a red light. "Oops, forgot about that. It broke last week." He reached under his seat and pulled out a screwdriver. "Just stick the tip of this against the penny and hit it twice."

It popped open on the third whack, and out came the door handle, right on my baby toe. It was a heavy little sucker too. I could already feel my toe smarting.

"Oh, I'm so sorry about that. I've been meaning to get it fixed." Shadow smiled, "Are you okay?"

"Yes, but it was pretty heavy."

"It's such a solid car, they sure don't make them like they use to."

Thank God. "How did it fall off?"

Shadow got a dark look in his eyes. "That girl Victoria Paris yanked on it so hard one day, it just fell right off. I don't think she had any respect for Lady."

I assumed he actually gave this pile of shit a name. "I haven't met her yet, but I hear she's really nice." I could hear the sound of my stomach growling.

"Nice?" He changed lanes a bit too fast and cut off another driver who honked. "She's an ice queen if you ask me."

How odd, I had heard such great things about her. Wanda and Ron raved about what a sweet girl she was. They couldn't say enough nice things about her actually. "So, tell me about the Pink Ladies." I wanted dirt.

We pulled up to the restaurant and parked three blocks away. "I don't trust the valet with Lady." He slid his hand across the dashboard. "Don't you dare move, I'll get the door for you."

That was a good thing because I couldn't find a door handle from the inside. Just a big hole where I think there used to be one.

During our three-hour dinner, he filled me in on all of the latest gossip in the world of adult, the world that I was about to reenter. With the exception of a dozen actors, there was a whole new slew of talent. Several of the major companies went belly up, but plenty of new ones replaced them.

I told him about my meeting with Caballero, my phone call to Vivid, and my final meeting with Video Exclusives, whom I ended up signing with.

"Tina is one of my best friends, and she'll be directing all of my films." I stopped to take a bite of dessert. "I feel so comfortable with her." Shadow looked so sexy across the table. I felt comfortable talking to him; and since we were both in the same business, I felt that we had a bond.

Our fingertips touched across the table. "You deserve the best Christy."

I felt my heart skip a beat. Maybe a boyfriend in the business is the best thing. He would understand my lifestyle. I took another bite of dessert and casually asked, "Do you date a lot of the girls in the business?" I didn't want him to think I was fishing, which I was. I never wanted to be with the playboy type. I seemed to opt for the shy, reserved men.

"No, I've never been with a girl in the business. I don't believe in mixing business with pleasure." The palms of our hands were now touching. "It's a strict rule that I enforce. I have never once made a pass at a star."

"But you're so cute, I'm sure they have made passes at you before." I felt relieved that he had never slept with a porn-star. There was something so pure about that.

"Well," He flipped his hair back. "A few have made passes, but I have always stopped it at that."

"Like who?" I smiled to mask my twinge of jealousy.

"Well, I don't want to start any gossip." He smiled back.

What was he talking about? Didn't he just gossip about everybody in the business for the past three hours? "Oh come on, you can tell me. I promise I won't tell anybody." But my head was already bursting with gossip that I couldn't wait to relate to Tina and Wanda.

"Well," He signaled to the waiter for our check. "Not too long ago, I had to take Victoria home, and she kept trying to get me into her apartment. She was all over me in the truck." The check was placed in front of him. "I actually felt sorry for her."

That hussy. "Oh Shadow, what do I owe you for dinner?"

"Nothing honey, it's on me." He pulled out a credit card. "So I had to tell Victoria that I wasn't interested." He shook his head. "She didn't take no very well either."

"Why? What did she do?"

"Well, she kept trying to get in my pants. I had to pull over at one point and set her straight. I had to tell her, 'sweetheart, this just isn't going to happen.' Then she sulked all the way home."

"So what happened the next time you had to pick her up?"

238

Shadow signed his credit card receipt, and tore off his copy. "I had to tell production that I just couldn't be her driver anymore." He kept his eyes on the table. "I have to keep everything one hundred percent professional."

"Of course you do." I wondered what he was like in bed. "Thanks for such a great dinner." I was sure he was excellent in the sack.

I sat close to him on the drive home. Our thighs touched, and his right arm was draped over my shoulders.

He walked me up to my door. "Thanks again. I really had fun tonight." I didn't care who saw him on my doorstep anymore.

"Me too sweetie. You're a real special lady."

We stood silent for a few seconds. "Can I see you again Christy?"

"Yes, I would love that."

He kissed me softly on the lips. "I have to work for the next two nights, but how does Sunday sound?"

His eyes were so intense; I could barely think, let alone talk. "That sounds perfect." He kissed me harder and deeper. Was that a Wild Cherry Chap Stick I tasted on his lips?

His hand was touching the back of my neck. "Come to my place and I'll cook dinner for you."

He even cooks. "Perfect." His warm hand felt wonderful.

"May I call you tomorrow?"

"Absolutely." I was in heaven.

He took his index finger and traced it along my jaw line. "I'm really starting to like you lady."

One more date and you'll be in love. "Bye."

I closed and locked my front door and ran to the phone. "Wanda, where are you? Oh he's so cute! I really like him." Where was she? "Call me when you get in."

I crawled into bed and thought about how my life had changed since Carol's call to the office last month. One call had altered the path of my life and there was no going back, not that I would ever want to. I was so ready to move on.

I hadn't yet finished my path of porno.

On Friday night, Mark and Tina came by at five to take me to Culver City. I was getting my dream car.

"I hope you like midnight blue Thumbelina." Thumbelina was a nickname Tina had given me when I had hair extensions sewn into my hair last year. She said I looked like a fairy tale princess with my hair falling just above my tush.

I didn't care what color a free Porsche was. "Are you kidding? I'm so excited you guys, I can't thank you enough."

Two months after having the extensions put in, Tina and I went horseback riding for two hours in the Hollywood Hills. We galloped our

239

horses through the mountains, feeling the rush of warm summer air blowing on our skin and through our hair.

"It was part of the deal, and you deserve it. What are you going to do with your Rabbit convertible?"

As if I would want to drive that over a Porsche. "Hold onto it for a few months and then probably sell it."

We got home from our day of riding and I looked in the mirror.

"Do you want to go and eat after we pick up your car?"

"Sure, anything sounds good to me."

My head of hair was one giant fur ball. As hard as Tina and I tried, we couldn't loosen up the tangled snarl and free my real hair from the fake hair. I was a mess.

We pulled into the showroom and I could see my beautiful new car sitting out front. A man was rubbing the back bumper with a cloth. He stood back and I gasped at the sight of this magnificent automobile. It was all mine and I could feel a tear of joy in my eye.

Mark spoke for the first time on the twenty-five minute drive. "They just finished detailing it for you."

The following morning, Tina and I went to our hair salon near Venice Beach. "Joy, look what happened to my hair after I went horseback riding!" I plopped down in her chair.

"Did you make two braids with it like I told you to?" Joy began trying to run a wide toothcomb through the unsightly mess.

I vaguely recalled her mentioning braids for something. "Was I supposed to?"

I could see Joy's bicep flex with each tug of the comb. "I gave you a list of do's and don'ts before you left. Did you read them?" A tooth in the comb snapped off.

"Oh, I think I forgot." Actually, I think that was the piece of paper that flew out of my car on the 405 freeway, while I was driving home.

Thirty minutes later, Tina and I left the salon. Last I saw, my five hundred dollar extensions were being swept up from the floor into a dustpan.

"That was a waste."

"Oh well Thumbelina, let's go and eat lunch. My treat."

I got out of Mark's car and ran to my new one. I was in love.

Mark and Tina went to look at the new arrivals of Aston Martins while I followed the goofy salesman with the bad fuzzy wig into his office. He handed me the title and the keys. "Say there, would you like to go out to dinner one night?" He sat his plump ass down on the corner of his desk, knocking over my cup of coffee.

I stopped dead in my tracks, one hand on the keys, the other on the title. Where did that come from? I looked around for Tina to get me out of this fine mess.

"I'm going to drive with you Christy, we'll follow Mark to the restaurant." Where did she come from? Tina hooked her arm through mine and we left his office.

I had my car and Tina. Life was beautiful.

Saturday afternoon I was lounging around when my phone rang. "Hello."

"Hi there sexy lady."

My heart skipped a beat. "Hi Shadow, how's work going?"

"We're going to wrap around six. Is there any chance of me seeing you after?"

God how I would love to, but I already had plans. "I can't. I'm going to see 'Beaches' with Tina tonight." There was nothing worse to me than a girl abandoning her friends for a guy. "But I can't wait to see you tomorrow."

"Alright, I'll be a good boy and wait until tomorrow." He gave me directions to his place. "I'll see you at seven."

Oh yes he will. I had already picked out what I was going to wear. A sexy black lace skirt and a matching top. I was overdue for some good sex. "I'll be there." Way overdue actually.

I left my house at six thirty the next night, feeling on top of the world. I cruised at sixty-five miles an hour on the 101 freeway towards Woodland Hills. No cop would stop me and give me a ticket, I wrote my own ticket. The world was my oyster. Was that one of Dad's sayings or was it Michael who said that? Well, for once, one of them got it right.

Dad and Michael. They both seemed like they were from a different life. They both loved me, they both controlled me, and they both mentally abused me to a degree. They were both out of my life. This would be the start of a new me. I am in control one hundred percent of the time. It's my way, or the highway. I looked up and saw that the exit I needed was three miles ahead. I looked down and saw that I had reached eighty-five miles an hour. I looked in my rear view mirror and saw the Highway Patrol behind me. I took my foot off the gas pedal as the cop pulled up on my left and looked at me. I smiled and blew him a kiss. He smiled and motioned for me to slowdown. I smiled again, waved and changed lanes.

I exited the off ramp, and the cop kept on trucking. I looked at my directions and made a right hand turn. That cop was cute. I found Shadow's apartment complex and parked in the guest section. Now I had to find the second door to the East entrance of building three, unit 209. What a maze this was.

Shadow opened his door, a tad more subdued in the clothing department. He wore a white T-shirt, two sizes too small, with a picture of Marilyn Monroe in silver glitter on the front. He was wearing faded jeans that were so tight I couldn't breathe for a moment just looking at them. My eyes, once again, were drawn to the general vicinity of his crotch, only to find no denim covering the area. This entire area of his jeans was torn to bits, tattered, shredded, gone. The only visible fabric covering his privates was a pair of skimpy undies in a cheetah print. Like I said, just a tad more subdued.

"Good evening angel face." He gave me a big hug. "Please, enter my humble abode."

A humble hovel was more like it. But it smelled delicious and felt inviting.

"I hope you're hungry. I'm making pasta with a garlic tomato sauce, garlic bread and a tomato and buffalo mozzarella salad." He stirred the sauce. "You sure look stunning tonight." He spoon-fed me a taste of the sauce. "I trust you like garlic being half Armenian and all."

"I love it. It reminds me of my granny," whom I hadn't gone to see in a while.

"Does she live around here?" He opened the oven and put the garlic bread in.

"She lives in a nursing home. She had her own house until about two years ago." I'll never forget how Dad and his two brothers couldn't wait to get her into that nursing home so they could sell her house and split the money. Dad had taken the first flight to Vegas the day they closed escrow.

"Were you close to her when you were growing up?" He seemed so genuinely interested in my life.

"Yes. My dad would drop me and my sister off at her house for the weekend if he wanted to get away with his wife."

"Did you grow up living with your dad?"

"No, he would see Clair and me every few weeks."

* * * *

1976
Ten years old

Six months after my Dad and Carol got married, Dad came to pick Clair and me up for his monthly visitation. He had to cancel last month, and I actually missed the old fart.

Waiting in our living room, I saw a car pull into our driveway at five-ten. It wasn't his big black Caddie, it was an even longer, wider Cadillac in canary yellow. The foghorn blasted three times from our driveway, which was our signal to meet him outside. Daddy used to haul his rear from the car, walk up the path to our front door, ring the doorbell, say hello to our mom and carry our bags to the car for us. One week after his marriage to

Carol, she banned Daddy from this ritual. I guess that ten years after Mom dumped his ass, Carol was worried that Mom would have a bout of insanity and want him back.

Everything was changing.

Clair and I kissed our mom goodbye and grabbed our overnight bags.

Daddy was standing outside of the car on the driver's side, with the larger than life door wide open. With his right hand on his hip, he asked, "How do you like Daddy's new car?" He shifted the toothpick in his mouth to the left with his tongue, and pushed his glasses over the bridge of his nose with his stubby right index finger simultaneously.

"It's real pretty. I like the color." Clair said.

I remained silent.

"It's fully loaded - Air conditioning, power windows, power seats, the works! Come here girls, listen to the stereo system."

The three of us, parked in Mom's driveway, climbed in the front seat. Dad popped in an 8-track of Mac Davis. Mac's pained country voice filled the cream interior of Daddy's new car.

Daddy put the boat in reverse, and we headed to his house for the next two nights.

"What are we going to do this weekend?" I asked.

"Well," Daddy paused and patted my left kneecap. "You're going to see your granny this weekend. She really misses you two. She said your mom hasn't taken you to see her in quite a while."

Daddy was always trying to get a jab in at our mom.

"But she's your mom, Daddy. Mommy takes us to see her own mom."

Clair asked, "Are we going there for dinner tonight?"

"Actually, I'm taking you there right now girls. You're going to spend the whole weekend with her." He said, trying to muster up some enthusiasm. "She can't wait to see you," he threw in for good measure.

Daddy looked over at Clair, her body between me and the passenger side door. "Don't you miss your granny honey? You haven't seen her in two months."

"We haven't even seen you in a month Daddy." I reminded him.

Daddy tried a new angle. "She's prepared all sorts of nice dishes for you. Grape leaves, lamb shanks, and your favorite, rice pilaf."

Granny's rice pilaf was delicious. It was white rice, with a whole stick of butter melted into it. She couldn't go wrong.

Her eyes never looking up from her Wallaby shoes, Clair said, "I guess it will be fun."

"Where are you going to be?" I asked. "We haven't seen you in a month."

Daddy stammered. "Uh, well, Carol and I are going to spend some time together in Palm Springs this weekend."

I sat still on the plush bench like seat, letting what he said fully absorb.

Mac Davis, playing softly now on the stereo, took a pause mid-word during a song, while the 8-track tape jumped from track three to four.

"Where's Eve going to be this weekend?" I demanded.

Mac's voice started singing where it left off.

"Well," Daddy paused, cocking his head to the right to look at me. "She's going to be coming with us," he answered softly. A pained smile across his face; he knew he was screwed.

"I WANT TO GO HOME TO MOMMY!" I screamed, drowning out any traces of Mac's sweet sounds. But I knew I couldn't go home. Mom made plans to go away this weekend. She was already on her way to San Diego with her girlfriends.

We cruised through the winding canyon, heading to Granny's house in the Miracle Mile district. Every so often, Dad would ask us a question. "How are your guitar lessons going Clair?"

"I play the piano Daddy. They're going fine."

"You've grown two inches since I saw you last Monkey," he said. His hand rubbed the top of my head.

I jerked my head away from his hand. "I don't want to go to Granny's. I want to go with you to Palm Springs." I began crying. Tears rolled down my face. Clair reached over and held my hand.

"We'll have fun. Maybe Granny will take us to the Farmer's Market Sunday morning."

"Of course she will Clair! You guys will have a great time." At least Daddy had one of us on his side.

He sure didn't have the little one on his side. The one that counted. The one that would make or break his trip to Palm Springs.

Stewing in the car on our twenty-minute drive to Granny's, my hurt feelings shifted into anger. Anger at the father who put this new family before us. Anger at the father who could afford this new car, yet never paid child support. Anger at the father who always knocked our mom, yet he was never there for us. Anger at the father who wasn't even sure what instruments we played at school. Anger at the father who began seeing less and less of us. Anger engulfed my seventy-pound body.

We pulled up to Granny's house. Dad walked us in, spoke a few words to his mom in Armenian, they both glanced my way, and Daddy was off to Palm Springs.

"I love you two. Daddy will pick you up in two days." He got down on his knees and drew us both into his arms for a big hug. He kissed our tiny cheeks and walked out the front door.

I didn't say a word.

I stood in front of the living room window and watched Daddy's new Cadillac pull out of the driveway and back in the direction we just came from.

I stood in front of that window as the sun was setting.

"Want to play chess?" Clair asked. She had already set up the game on the coffee table in front of the TV " You can be red this time."

Daddy called us two hours later at Granny's as promised, to give us his telephone and room number.

I picked up on the first ring. "When are you picking us up?"

"Sunday afternoon honey, then the five of us will go have a good dinner. Pick out any place you want to go, then, I'll take you home to your mother's."

"Pick us up now. This is your weekend with us."

"We just got here."

"It doesn't matter. This is your weekend with us."

There was a moment of silence on his end. "May I speak to your sister honey?"

"Hurry home." I said into the receiver, before handing the phone to Clair.

"Hi Daddy." Clair was silent.

"We really like seeing Granny, but we miss you too. We haven't really seen much of you since you got married."

"At all!" I piped in.

"Okay Daddy." Clair replaced the receiver.

"What did he say to you?"

"That he'll be here Sunday morning instead of Sunday afternoon."

I was fuming. How dare he take Carol and Eve and leave us behind.

"Lawrence Welk is on tonight girls." Granny came into the room with a tray full of shish kabobs and lama-june.

Lawrence Welk? I looked down at the black rotary phone sitting on the round, wooden end table.

Granny set the plate of food down on a metal TV tray and scurried back into the kitchen. The kitchen was her pride and joy.

"Thank you Granny." Clair and I said in unison.

I picked up the phone, dialed the area code and phone number and asked for room 211.

Carol's voice answered. "Hello."

"When are you guys leaving to pick us up?"

"Let me put your father on."

"Yes honey."

"When are you guys leaving to pick us up."?

Daddy paused before answering. "How about if we leave late tomorrow afternoon and pick you up by 8 p.m."

"No, I want you to pick us up now." I began sobbing in the phone. Why didn't he want to be with us? "Please Daddy, I miss you so much. I just want to be with you."

"I'll be there. Give me a few minutes and I'll leave. I'll pick you up. Don't cry honey."

Daddy's car pulled up at eleven-thirty that night. My bags still packed, sat where I left them in the living room four hours earlier.

"I'm sorry girls." Putting an arm around each of us, we walked to his car.

Clair and I climbed into the backseat with Eve and Daddy shut the door.

Carol, without turning her head asked, "Are you happy now?"

"Very. I just wanted to be with my daddy this weekend. This is our weekend with him."

Daddy got into the car, which made Carol shut up, and we drove home to our dad's for our weekend a month with him.

* * * *

"Wow, that must have been tough being shuffled back and forth like that." He took the garlic bread out of the oven. "My parents have been married for forty three years."

"It really wasn't that tough. All but one of my friends in school still had parents that were married. It must be an LA thing to get married and divorced so may times. I don't think it effected me."

Shadow dressed the salad with oil and balsamic vinegar. "So, when do you shoot your first film for Video Exclusives?"

Maybe six marriages between my mom and dad had had a little affect on me. "In two weeks."

"Dinner is ready."

We sat down at his card table and I dug into the scrumptious meal. I finished my glass of wine, or was it my second glass, with the last bite of my garlic bread. I could feel my head spinning just a little. I wasn't drunk, but I sure was tipsy. I felt so full, relaxed and horny as hell.

Shadow picked up the candle from the center of the table. "Follow me." He held out his hand and I grabbed it.

I followed him through a hallway until I saw paradise. His bedroom. He had a queen size bed with a black lacquer head and footboard that my eyes zeroed in on. Sex, how wonderful it would feel. I actually felt my juices flowing at the thought of him inside me.

He set the candle down on a night table and lit three more. How romantic it looked with the glow from the candles in the room. He began to kiss me deep and hard. I kissed him back with more hunger and lust. I wanted him deep inside me soon. I began to take off his shirt while he started to pull my skirt down. I traced his nipples with my tongue while he caressed my ass and pussy with his hands. My God his touch felt so good. He unbuttoned his jeans and they miraculously slid to the floor. I wasn't sure how those tight things could slide down so fast, but I couldn't care less, they were off. He slid my top over my head, unhooked my bra and flung both onto the ground.

He pulled my body into his and we stood there, chest-to-chest, skin on skin. I grabbed his ass trying to pull his body and skin even closer to mine and realized I was touching his bare buttocks. How funny, I had never seen a man in a g-string before. Oh well, it was off in two seconds anyway.

We fell onto his bed, and I could feel the tip of his hard cock against my clit. I pushed my hips closer to him. Fuck the foreplay, just get inside me before I come just thinking about it.

Shadow whispered in my ear. "Do you want to use the silver bullet?"

I reached down and began to guide him inside me. "The what?"

"My silver bullet. Should I get it?" I felt his cock get a bit bigger at the mention of the silver bullet.

Maybe it was like that thing people sniffed in the early eighties "Locker Room". It was supposed to intensify an orgasm.

"Sure, I guess so." Not that I would need any help with an overdue, major orgasm. It was right there, I could feel it filling up inside me. I just needed to feel him inside my body.

Shadow reached over and opened a drawer. "This is the ultimate for me." He held up a silver dildo shaped vibrator.

Hell, I didn't need that thing. I had the real thing millimeters away. I could use one of those at home. "I don't want that Shadow."

"You don't even need to lube it up, just put it inside me."

"But I prefer the real..." Wait a second, did he just say inside him? I looked over and saw Shadow with his legs spread apart and his finger caressing his asshole. Oh God, what a freak. "You want ME to use that on YOU?"

His eyes were in slits of ecstasy. "Yes, it feels so good." He now spoke in a baby voice, just like Tina used on Mark when she wanted something.

I sobered up in one second flat, my head now spinning from his bizarre request. Was it so odd, or was I just totally out of it in the sexual revolution? Were we even in a sexual revolution? With Shadow and his silver bullet, it was more like revulsion. I sat up in bed; my overdue orgasm went back into hiding.

"What's wrong?" As if he needed to ask. "Would Mistress Christy like me to dress up for her as well?"

247

Oh Lord. "What do you have to wear?" I envisioned him in a pink baby-doll style dress, with rosy, round cheeks from too much cheap rouge.

"I have a full bondage outfit in black leather. You can even hook me onto the wall with it." He pointed to a corner. "See, there are the hooks."

And sure enough, three silver hooks were screwed into the wall. I didn't even want to know.

I made a beeline for my clothes scattered around the floor. "Not tonight." I yanked my skirt up, and pulled my shirt over my head.

He sat up in bed, his dick shriveling before my eyes. "What's wrong?"

I grabbed my bra and underwear. "Wrong girl pal."

I trotted out of his bedroom and got my purse. I could hear him fumbling in the bedroom through the paper-thin wall.

My hand reached the doorknob and I twisted it to the right. The door opened partially but was caught on the chain and stopped. "Fuck."

"Did I do something wrong?"

Did I hear sarcasm in his voice? I turned around and saw him in a short, red kimono, leaning against the doorframe with his arms crossed. I closed the front door and un-slid the chain. "You know Shadow," I turned to look at him. "Call me nuts, but I think you should be inside me, not me inside you." The gall of wanting it in him. "I'm the girl, not you." With that, I flung open the door and stepped into the hallway.

Now, if I could just remember how to get to my car.

I heard his voice echo in the hallway. "It could have been great." For him maybe, but that just wasn't my bag.

I found my car in this despicable concrete jungle and got in. I fired up my engine and put my purse, bra and, that's funny, I didn't seem to have my undies anymore. I must have lost them on my way out.

I backed out of the parking spot and began to laugh at the evening. What an oddball he turned out to be.

I turned onto the freeway on ramp and thought about what he said on our first date. The ice princess he had called her. I shifted into fourth gear and knew that I would like that girl Victoria Paris.

29

I left the set, and headed home. Working for Suze was fun, but three long days of posing for High Society was exhausting. On my way, I decided to check out a hot, new trendy place in Hollywood called The China Club.

I walked to the front of the long line, and was let right in.

Leaning over the bar, I yelled to the bartender above the music, "I'll have a cranberry juice." I was never much of a drinker. I turned my head to the right, so I could hear the bartender above the noise tell me I owed him four-fifty. He had stinky breath. There, five feet away, was Grant among the sea of people. I stood on the stool, and cupped my hands around my mouth and yelled, "Grant!" above the smoky club.

Stinky yelled up at me, "Hey miss, get down from there."

I, of course ignored him, and saw Grant look up at me and smile.

I felt stinky pulling on my pant leg. I shook him loose with a swift kick, and jumped down to meet Grant, when I smelled Stinky's breath near me. "You're not allowed to get on these stools."

I plugged my nose. "I can't hear a word you're saying to me." With that I scooped up my two quarters, and ran over to Grant.

"God, I haven't seen you in three years, since we had lunch together when I worked for my dad." I yelled above the music.

Grant jerked his head away from me, and rubbed his ear canal.

"Do you still work for him?"

Eeks! I guess my return two months ago into the adult business hadn't hit the gossip vine yet.

"No." We walked outside.

"So what are you doing now?"

"Well, I kinda got back into the adult business." For some reason, I didn't feel ashamed of it anymore. This was the life I had chosen, and I liked it. Maybe I wasn't cut out for marriage, kids and the minivan sort of life. I loved my independence, the freedom to come and go as I pleased. I loved the experience I got from working at my dads, but after four years, it was time to move on. That and Carol surfaced. But that was okay. Working with Lois for the last few years made me understand that Carol was my dad's desire, and I could not change him, just as he could not change me.

The adult business was what I knew best at twenty-three years old. I felt comfortable, like putting on an old shoe. A very high-heeled stiletto shoe that is.

"Why did you go back? Didn't you like working for your dad?"

"Yeah, I did like working for him, but it was just time to move forward." I guess it was kinda going backwards in a way. "I got back in the business because it's the only thing I know how to do right now. I'm going to enroll in college next year."

I saw the look of disappointment on Grants face, so I kissed him smack dab on the mouth. A big wet kiss, tongues and all. The disappointment went away.

"I've got to go Grant."

"Yeah, it's good to see you."

We didn't even bother exchanging phone numbers this time.

The valet pulled up in my new Porsche, top down of course. I jumped in and waved goodbye.

I thought of Grant and shifted into fifth gear as I got on the freeway. He was even cuter than before

Maybe one day, but not now.

30

Tina and I were returning from a three-night stay in Palm Springs. Mark had gotten us a bungalow at the resort but couldn't make the trip. "Oh, there's so much work to be done at home but you girls enjoy." And at twelve hundred dollars a night, enjoy we did.

Funny enough, Tina never seemed to be able to reach him during our trip.

Driving home, Tina asked. "So, are you nervous about tomorrow?"

Tomorrow I was shooting my comeback film "Hot In The City".

"A little bit." I admired my tan. "But I've been shooting magazine layouts and it was easy to pick that up after four years." I looked at my face in the mirror and was marveled at how clear my skin looked. It's amazing what daily facials will do for your complexion.

"Making a movie will be easy for you too, and at least you'll know everybody you're working with. In fact, your first scene is with Tom Byron."

Good old Tom. It would be fun to see him again. I closed my eyes and pretended to fall asleep. I was scared shitless.

Somewhere on the freeway, I did fall asleep and woke up to Tina's voice. "Wake up little girl. You're home."

"I'll see you on the set in the morning." I grabbed my bag.

"Ten o'clock."

I walked to the elevators and wondered if I was doing the right thing by making a comeback.

The next morning I woke up at eight and laid in bed thinking about my love life.

There wasn't any, and hadn't been for a while.

My high hopes for Shadow had crashed when he turned out to be a total freak.

I saw Grant the other night and as cute as he was, the timing was off. Grant knew I was back in the business. Was that sadness in him that I detected? Did he feel sorry for me? As much as I would love to be with Grant, I had to figure out who I was first. I didn't want Grant or anybody to feel sorry for me. I wasn't pushed into returning, no gun was pointed at my head when I signed my contract, I genuinely wanted to make my comeback.

But why? What drove me to reenter the world of adult after four years? I didn't know who I was or where I was headed in life. I had a poor relationship with my parents, yet it wasn't about rebellion this second time around. It was about being independent and paying my bills at the same time. Could I have been independent from my father by working another job? Yes, but after working at Bullocks, the local department store, I quit after my first week. Taking orders from somebody at minimum wage wasn't my thing.

Grant looked so cute, if only he could have kept his promise to me when we were eighteen. He said he wanted to take care of me so I didn't have to make porno films. But I didn't have to make them, I chose to make them. How could I expect Grant to take care of me when I had to learn how to take care of myself first?

I knew a relationship with Grant, or anyone, wasn't in my immediate future. I wasn't in an emotional position to love somebody.

I had to learn how to completely love myself first. Where I was going today was my path in life.

I got out of bed and headed to the kitchen.

I sat at my kitchen table and thought about having sex with Tom Byron in three hours.

He wasn't so bad. In fact, he was adorable with that baby face. He was always reliable in a scene, never one to lose his hard on halfway through.

I went into the bathroom and turned on the shower. Stepping in, I wondered what my parents would think. Would they even find out? Maybe they would just think it was old footage and negatives being redistributed.

Yeah right.

I dried off, got dressed and headed out the door. Whatever was about to happen would be one hell of an adventure. It was just what my boring, humdrum life needed.

I pulled into the parking lot of the Video Exclusives' sound stage in Northridge and the memories flooded back. A crew of five were unloading equipment, two of the faces I even recognized from the mid-eighties.

"Hey! J.D." I yelled.

"Well Christy Canyon! It's really you!" J.D. gave me a big hug. "I thought Tina was bullshitting me when she said she hauled your ass out of retirement."

I smiled. "No. I had to shake up this business. Wanda told me there was a lull in girls." It felt good to be back.

J.D. took my wardrobe out of my trunk. "Hey, thanks for telling Tina you wanted me to be your director."

I did? "No problem. You're the best."

J.D. blushed. "Follow me into makeup."

I followed him down a hallway and saw a Harley Davidson in the middle of the soundstage to the left. Eeks! my first scene takes place on that. I felt my palms get all clammy.

"Here's Danielle. She's the best makeup girl around."

Maybe I wasn't ready for a comeback. I felt a little dizzy.

"I'll catch you later Christy. I'm lighting your first scene."

I felt faint at the thought of a sex scene with cameras, lighting and a full crew.

"Hi Christy, I'm Danielle. Do you want something to eat before I start on you?"

I shook my head yes and felt the color drain from my face.

"Great, follow me."

Like a zombie, I followed her down another hallway and saw a couch. Eeks! I think that's where my second scene is. "Where's Peter North?" I asked.

"Oh, he wont be in 'til later. You'll work with him second."

Oh God, did she really have to remind me? "How is Peter?" He was really cute actually and somehow talking about him made me feel comfortable. Like slipping into an old shoe.

Danielle smiled. "He's the same great guy."

"Here's the food. Meet me back in my room when you're done."

I said thanks, but Danielle was already gone. I walked up to the buffet table and saw two guys hunched down in a corner on the make believe kitchen set.

"Do you got a light dude?"

I knew that voice.

"Yeah, right here man."

I knew that voice too.

A flick of a lighter and a deep inhale followed.

I knew that smell.

"Tommy, is that you crouched down there?"

Both boys turned around.

Tom Byron gave me a glazed over smile. "Hey."

After not seeing me for four years that was all he had to say? Maybe he didn't recognize me even though I looked pretty much the same and he knew it was my movie. "It's me, Christy Canyon."

Without letting any smoke escape his mouth he managed to say, "Cool."

And I requested him for one of my sex scenes? "How are you?"

"Hey Christy." The second guy said.

Him I could do without. Why would Tina allow that junkie on her set? Where was Tina anyway?

"Hey Steve." I remembered him from the mid-eighties as the cocaine connection to the talent. Then, he was a great guy to know. Now, he was a horrid, foul memory.

"How have ya been Chris?"

I couldn't stand that nickname. "Great." Until I saw his drawn out, wrinkled before its time, face. "What are you doing here today?"

"Just visiting my good pal Tommy."

They both chuckled.

More like selling him something.

Tom finally coughed out the smoke and asked. "So, how have ya been?"

Just the same as two seconds ago when Steve asked. "Fine." Tom's innocent baby face from the mid-eighties was now bloated. "Just checking out the sets." His eyes that once sparkled, were now sleepy sockets. "What have you been doing?" His once trim, boyish physique was now supporting a baby beer belly.

He smiled. "Just working."

Even with his new look, there was still something cute about him. "That's good." In a hard type of way.

The three of us stood there without much to say. "Well, I'm going to get some breakfast guys."

Steve asked. "So, where do you live now?"

"Florida." I lied. I didn't want him to know anything about me.

Steve walked over to me and I felt the hair on my neck stand up. He was so toxic. "We should get together and party while you're in town."

What a complete loser. "I haven't done that for years Steve." I just wanted him gone. "Drugs are so out dated. In fact," I tried to conger up a good lie. "I'm into the Herbalife work out and diet regime now." I took a bite into my bagel that was loaded with cream cheese and wondered if that goofy company still existed. "I only allow purified foods and liquids into my system." I popped open a can of Dr. Pepper and took a big swig. "I take twenty herbal pills a day."

"Why?" His drug high was wearing off fast. "Isn't that soda bad for you?"

Buzz off idiot. "No. It's purified sugar." I took another sip and thought of an old wives tale. "Plus, it's filled with prune juice." At least I thought it was a wives tale.

"Purified sugar and prune juice." He repeated. Before he could ask another question, I heard Tina. "Where the fuck is Steve?" Her Samoan body stomped into the kitchen and I instinctively moved behind her for protection. Against what, I did not know. "What in the fuck are you doing on my set you worm?"

Go get him Tina.

Steve cowered, "I just wanted to say hi to Chris. I heard she was making a comeback."

Tina looked around for me and found me behind her left leg. "She doesn't want to see you." Her voice softened. "Do you Thumbelina?"

God I wished I could be mean like her, but "Uh huh," was all I could muster.

"Let me make this real clear to both of you." Tina pointed a bright red manicured index finger at the men. "One. Tom, no drugs are allowed on my set." Tina's middle finger pointed next and I noticed a big chip in her nail polish. "Two. Steve is not allowed on my set, ever." She stared at both of them. "Do I make myself clear."

"No problem." Tom said.

"Oh come on Tina, those days are behind me." Steve had the nerve to say, standing there weighing all of ninety pounds looking like a walking corpse.

"Do I need to make point two again?" Tina's nostrils were flaring. "Get off of my set NOW!"

Steve flinched. "Okay, let me just say goodbye to Tom."

Tina threw down her clipboard. "Don't make me hurt you." She took three strides towards him.

"Hey, is everything alright in there?" Jimmy, the soundman asked.

Steve's petite frame was no match for Tina's one hundred eighty five pound body. "I've got it under control Jimmy." And she sure did. Tina manhandled him through the hallway to the front door. Steve turned around to say one last parting word about Tom owing him some money, when Tina shoved her combat boot in Steve's rear punting him through the door and onto the street. "TOM!" Tina yelled.

I scurried into hair and makeup. Show time was over.

I sat in Danielle's chair reading my script. I read the same two lines over ten times and still couldn't remember them.

"Close your eyes, I'm going to use some hair spray."

I closed my eyes and wondered if I was doing the right thing. I opened my eyes and saw Tina standing in the doorway. "You look so beautiful Thumbelina."

I was doing the right thing. Wasn't I?

"Are you ready?"

"I guess so." I followed Tina down the hallway and thought about what my Geometry teacher use to always say to our class. He would put our lessons on the chalkboard, whip through the solution of finding out what "X" equaled and say, "Class, it's like giving candy to a baby." I was never sure what he meant by that, but I think he was trying to say Geometry was easy.

Handing me a cigarette Tina asked, "Are you nervous?"

Mr. Jones had a deep southern accent and I wondered what he was doing now. "Yeah, a little bit." I never did find out, or care, what "X" equaled. I just made sure I sat by Grant who let me cheat off his tests every week. Was Mr. Jones still teaching at the Catholic school I went to?

"You'll be fine honey." Tina smiled.

Or was it a Christian school. "I know. I'm just glad you're here." I managed to get straight "A's" in geometry even though I still had to use my fingers for simple multiplication. I never mastered the square root of anything but I did master the art of wearing low cut blouses.

Lights, camera, action. It was show time.

"Well, you two are pros at this so just do what you want to do." Tina took a look at the motorcycle. "Just give me three good positions and of course, let me have a minute warning before you come Tom." Tina stepped in a little closer to Tom and me. "Just be kinda careful with this bike." Tina pointed to a corner of the soundstage. "The owner is over there and he's really worried that it'll get damaged."

"Why is he even letting us use it?" I asked.

Tina shrugged her shoulders. "I think he's hard up for the hundred bucks."

I looked down at my cowboy boots. At least they weren't high heels.

"J.D." Tina yelled. "Were going to do their dialogue, Tom and Christy will get naked, then we'll shoot the hard-core stuff."

That's where I got nervous again. Hard-core sounded so hard-core.

"Sounds good to me." J.D. winked. "Are you nervous Christy?"

You better believe it. "No, not at all." I could see Ron standing a few feet back checking out his camera lens. "It's fun to be back." I felt even safer with Ron around me. It was almost like being in some odd time warp. I looked at Tom, Ron, J.D. and Tina and realized that not much had changed over my four-year hiatus.

A grip switched the set lights on, and my body started to feel their warmth. Somehow I remembered all two lines of my dialogue and then Tom's pants were around his ankles. I thought of how warm it felt in Hawaii with Tina last month. I wished there was more of a script so I didn't have to do what Tom whispered next.

"Give me head."

I looked at my arms and saw goose bumps. "Okay, lean back a little." Was it because I was cold two minutes ago and then the lights warmed me up?

Tina whispered from the sidelines, "Give him head for five minutes."

Or did I have goose bumps from nerves? I glanced at my watch so I knew when the five minutes were up. I squatted down and took Tom in my mouth. I felt his cock harden between my lips and thought about the next trip to Hawaii Tina and I were planning. Tom grunted so I figured I was doing something right. I made some over exaggerated slurping noises while giving him head and thought about how I fed the dolphins at our hotel. They were so cute and innocent when they jumped up and took the fish out of my hand.

Tom grabbed the back of my head and pushed it deeper on his thing. I

256

snapped back into the present and moved my head back. I hated it when guys pushed my mouth on them. I couldn't deep throat and I felt like gagging. In an effort to look sexy and give my mouth a break, I licked the tip of his dick and ran my hands up his legs. In truth, I just wanted to check the time on my watch. Four and a half minutes was good enough for me. I stood up and tried to remember Tom's name in the movie. "I want you to fuck me now." I couldn't remember it and I could care less. I just wanted to move along here.

Tom turned my body around. "Let's start off in this position."

Why not? One position down, two to go.

I felt Tom enter me from behind, and I thought of my new car. I moaned "oh yes," but my mind groaned, oh brother. I positioned my right foot on the glistening muffler for a better camera angel just as Tom reached around and squeezed my tits. His move startled me, and I lost my footing. I watched the heel of my boot slide across the entire muffler with a deep black line trailing it. I moaned a bit louder hoping the owner of this fine hog didn't see what I just did to his prize position. Tom turned my body around and began doing me standing, face to face. I told him how great he felt inside of me but my mind was in a boutique I was at yesterday. "Oh yeah, fuck me deeper." I was deciding which jacket I would buy tomorrow. I sat down on the edge of the seat and counted this as position number two. "God that feels so great inside of my pussy." I think I'll get the salmon colored jacket with the black fringe. Loud enough for the microphone two feet above me to pick up, I said, "Squeeze my tits." I panted for some good effect. Then again, that gray jacket with the horse's head was so cute. "Your cock feels so great." Did I already say that? "Do you like fucking me?" God I sounded so porno.

"Oh yeah baby. You feel so good." Tom grunted between strokes.

"Good because I'm going to come all over you." I looked into the side mirror and saw Tom's face. It was contorted and he looked like he was in pain. I pushed my hips faster and faster on Toms cock. "Oh yes." I threw in for some more sound effect. Tom and I were moving back and forth pretty fast and I wondered if the bike was going to topple over. "Harder." I groaned. Maybe if the bike fell over we could end the scene early. "Deeper." I moaned. That kickstand looked pretty small. "Faster." I begged.

Sensing that the bike may fall at any moment, Tom went into position number three without a word. He leaned my back against the left handlebar and continued.

I wondered what Tom was thinking of. What went through his mind during all of his sex scenes in the past decade? "This feels so great." I fibbed. I could feel the handlebar digging into my spine, and it hurt like hell. I wondered if Tom knew how many sex scenes he'd done throughout his career. It must have been around five or six hundred.

"Christy." Tina whispered. "Put your right foot on the front tire so the camera can see more."

I lifted my leg up, and noticed that Tom's pinched face was turning red. He looked so funny that I started to giggle. I covered it up by turning my face down, and moaned real loud. Tom began pumping me even faster, and again, I lost my balance on just one foot.

I reached behind me for support, and grabbed onto the first thing my hand connected with. I heard a loud snap. In my right hand was an Italian flag that had been perfectly placed between the handlebars. The flag that had once flown with such pride on the streets of LA was now an over sized toothpick clenched in the palm of my sweaty hand.

Tom just kept on going. Maybe nobody saw that. "Oh Tom, this is my favorite position." I hoped the owner didn't see that from where ever he was hiding on the set.

Tom put his lips by my ear. "That's not my name in this movie."

"What is it?"

He shrugged.

I changed the subject. "Oh God, I think I'm going to come again." I'm sure the guy could get it glued back on. I produced an orgasm and let the flag fall to the floor.

"I'm going to come now."

Well it's about time. "Oh good, come all over me."

I thought about my high school friends. Did they know I was back in the adult business? Grant did. What would they think?

Tom panted out the magic words. "Here I come." I didn't care what anybody thought.

Tom pulled out of me and began stroking himself.

But I did care what people thought of me. I wanted people to know that I was a regular girl that just happened to make porno films for a living.

Tom came all over me and I decided I deserved both jackets.

One sex scene down, two to go.

Now I knew what the male actors always wanted. It was what I needed as well. Fresh meat.

After my second sex scene of the day, I took a shower. I scrubbed away any traces of my scenes. My sweat, their sweat, dust from the sets, a streak of grease on my left shin and the come. I lathered up the bar of soap under the hot water and cleansed every inch of my skin.

"Don't get your face wet." Danielle yelled from the next room.

"I wont." I yelled back. Two scenes down, one to go.

Today was the tough day with shooting all three of my sex scenes. Tomorrow was just outside pick-up shots and some dialogue. Today was the day I had to get through. I rubbed the bar of soap back and forth between my breasts. Keep your mind focused. I thought back to the first time in 1984 when I shot my first video. A loop as Jim had called it. Everybody was telling me that it was just sex, relax, it's no big deal. I didn't understand what they meant five years ago. But today, maneuvering around on that motorcycle under a flood of lights and a room full of people, I understood it more. Today I was moving around for the camera, and for the fans to see everything that was going on. Five years ago I was fighting to survive at eighteen. I had no idea which way was up and which way was down. Five years ago, I was trying to figure out who I was. I never knew if I was coming or going. Five years ago I didn't understand why my parents threw me out. I took the weight of the world on my young shoulders. Five years ago I was discovering what sex was all about. Five years ago I found Jim and my life changed. It was sink or swim at eighteen and I swam.

Tom and I were just having sex. It was a paycheck to him and me. It meant paying his bills, buying a new car or maybe even saving up for his own house. I didn't know what it really was to him and I didn't care. Outside of this set, some other set, or a convention, I would never see Tom. He wasn't my friend; he was somebody I worked with.

To me, my paycheck meant freedom. Free from the restraints of my father. Free from the sick relationship that he had with Carol. Free to do what ever I wanted. My return into the business even let my mom be free. It was her perfect excuse to cut me off again. We had no relationship outside of a dinner once a month. She never forgave me for stealing Marvs credit card. She never forgave me for getting into the adult business. Maybe she never even forgave herself for picking Marv over me.

I turned off the water and Tina opened the shower door. "A fresh towel for my little star."

I took the towel and realized that Tina was a true friend. "Thanks." It was Tina who was always there for me.

"How are you doing today?" Tina asked.

Tina was the one who always came to my side. "Actually, I'm doing fine." And I was. Tina would never lead me down the wrong path. Tina understood where I was coming from. She was a rebel, just like me.

"Do you think you made the right decision Christy?"

There wasn't a shred of doubt in my mind. "Absolutely." My parents would accept me when they accepted themselves. I couldn't control them and they couldn't control me.

"Lunch is being served and that writer Mike is here to interview you for Hustler."

I shot a comeback layout last month for Hustler magazine. It was scheduled to hit the stores in November for their December issue. What would my mom and dad think when they saw it sitting on a shelf? "Great

…na, I'm starving." When and how would they find out I was back in the business? "Tell Mike I'm going to get dressed and get some lunch." I wondered how long we wouldn't speak this time. "I'll meet him in the office in fifteen minutes." Dad wanted to control me, Mom wanted to figure out what was wrong with me. "Tina, I love you so much." I didn't want anybody controlling me and I knew there was nothing wrong with me.

"Oh Christy, I love you too." Tina hugged me. "We're so lucky to have each other."

Dad couldn't control his own life and my mom needed to figure out what was wrong with her own situation in life. "I know we are."

Tina left and I stood alone in the dressing room. I was lucky to have Clair, Tina, Lois and Wanda in my life and in my corner. I could hear my father's voice. "You can pick your friends in life, but you can't pick your family." How true he was for a change. Mom and Dad were stuck with me as their daughter whether they liked it or not. They didn't have to agree with my life but I was a part of them. They didn't have to like me but I knew they loved me.

I pulled a pink satin robe out of my suitcase and put it on. Mike could shoot away on the questions, but no way was he getting a free show during our interview.

I brought my lunch plate into the office. "Hi Mike, I'm Christy."

He looked at me from the couch and held up his hand. "Testing, one, two, three." He pushed stop and then the rewind button on his tape recorder. "Hi Christy, it's so nice to meet you." This time he held out his hand to me. "Give me one second here." He pushed the silver play button and his voice boomed out, "Testing one, two, three." He pushed stop and rewound it again. "Always got to make sure it's working properly. Well, how about if we sit here."

I cinched the pink tie tighter around my waist and sat next to him on the couch. "This is perfect." I tucked my legs under me and balanced my Chinese buffet lunch on my knees. I speared two pieces of sweet and sour chicken on my fork and stuffed it in my mouth.

"Do you want to eat first?" Mike asked. I smiled trying to keep my mouth shut. "No, I'm just so hungry I had to eat a piece, but I'm ready, ask away."

"All right then." He pulled out a list of questions.

I picked up an egg roll and dipped it in the sweet red sauce.

He pushed the record button. "So, how does it feel to be back in the adult business after disappearing for four years?"

I could see the gooey red sauce beginning to drip off the tip of the roll and onto my plate. "Well," I took a bite and pretended to be mulling over his predictable question. "It feels really good to be back." God this sauce

260

was great. "I can't believe it's been four years since I've been on a set." I looked at my plate and counted two egg rolls left. "Time flies when you're having fun." The four years at my fathers office really seemed like ten years. I had never felt time drag like that before. "But now that I'm back on a set, it feels like nothing's changed." But it had changed. I had changed. I wasn't the naïve eighteen year old anymore. I wasn't blowing or screwing anybody they threw at me. This time around I had some say. This time around I earned a piece of the pie. I could feel myself zoning out in my own thoughts and gave Mike my full attention again. "It was fun working with Tom Byron this morning." I widened my eyes and smiled. "He's just as sexy as ever." I took a sip of iced tea and realized that I forgot to dump a packet of Sweet 'n Low in it.

Mike glanced at his notes and took out an 8x10 photo. "How was your sex scene with Johnny?" He starred at Johnny's naked body. "He's the new guy." A smile spread across Mike's pink lips and lily-white face.

I looked down at my plate and began twisting some lo mien around my fork. "Yeah, I think this was his first video." My left boob began falling out from my robe. "I think the scene with Johnny is going to be a soft-core one." I brought the fork up to my mouth and watched Mike's face. He was engrossed with Johnny's photo.

Mike's eyes shot up at me. "Why?" He made sure the microphone was close to me "Tell me about Johnny."

I shoved the noodles in my mouth. "Well."

Johnny and I were on the couch, exchanging our dialogue. I was excited about working with Johnny and was thankful that the lines were at a minimum. He was new, fresh and about to be mine in a few moments. I could see his hard on under his jeans.

"You are so beautiful." Johnny said. It wasn't part of the script; it was a feeling between us since our soft-core magazine layout last week for Ron.

I smiled at him. "Thank you." Under the hot lights and people around us, it was still just Johnny and I on the set. I told Tina that I wanted to work with him in my comeback film.

"No problem Christy." Tina said. "Part of our deal is that you get to pick the talent."

So now I was about to finish off what I started at Ron's. I began rubbing his crotch, feeling the outline of his hard cock. "I can't wait to feel you inside me."

Johnny began rubbing my boobs. "I can't wait to finally get inside of you." His hands fumbled around and began to undress me.

"Take your pants off." I whispered. He was so hard, that I didn't want to un-zip his pants. What if I got the zipper got stuck on him. "Now Johnny." I couldn't wait to feel his cock in my hands.

261

Johnny was out of his pants in seconds flat. His ding-a-ling was standing at full attention.

My hands had a mind of their own and reached between his legs to touch him. His hard cock felt like silk between my fingers.

Johnny finished undressing me, and pressed his bare skin into mine. I could feel his heart racing and his member pulsating. I just wanted to slide him inside of me, but this was a movie set which needed foreplay. Ten minutes from now he would be inside me, right where I wanted him. Johnny began kissing me, sliding his tongue into my mouth while his hands explored my chest.

"I can't wait to make love to you." He whispered in my ear.

Make love on a porno set? "I can't wait either." To fuck your brains out.

Johnny squeezed my ass and pulled my body in even closer to his.

"Move back!" Tina yelled. "We need to see Christy's hands wrapped around your cock."

Johnny froze. "What?" He stopped touching my body and took a step back. The poor bastard looked dazed and confused.

"It's a God damn porno movie, not a Playboy layout." Tina inhaled deeply on her cigarette. "Just pick up where you left off, but stand back so the camera can pick up the action."

"What did I do wrong?" He asked me.

I smiled trying to look sexy, "Oh nothing really." I was trying to keep that spark between us. "We just need to stand back a few inches." But I knew what was coming.

Johnny bent in to kiss me when Tina yelled. "Action, take two." Johnny jumped and mumbled, "Why are there so many hot lights?"

Funny how right before Tina broke in, he didn't even notice the lights. "Kiss me Johnny." I looked down and saw that his once full erection was deflating by the second. Screw the kiss. I got on my knees and took what was left of him into my mouth. I pulled out every trick I could think of, but I felt him getting softer by the second.

Johnny had beads of sweat rolling down his face.

"What's the problem here?" Tina was standing next to us, and I felt the final inch of him recoil.

I stood up and remembered why nobody wanted to use a new guy on a set. "Well, you interrupted my concentration." Johnny tried to cover up his privates with a hand. A finger would have done the trick.

"This is a porn set, not a spelling bee." Tina spat. "Alright everybody." Tina made a scene of looking at her watch. "Lets give the talent a few minutes."

The lights were turned off and the crew shuffled off the set.

Johnny and I sat on the couch and began to kiss. Two minutes into it, I looked down and saw no action in his crotch area. I couldn't even see the tip of it. His dick was hiding in his mass of curly blonde pubic hair. I guided his hand onto my boob in a last ditch effort. Maybe if he touched me for a few minutes, which was all the time that he had right now, it would spark him up again.

He touched me for a minute but his eyes were on the ground. "I don't understand what happened." Johnny put his face between his hands. "I had no problem at Vogel's, but now…"

But I knew what happened. Ron's magazine shoot was just us, with Ron sashaying around, snapping a photo here and there. We barely even noticed he was there. Besides hearing Ron say "Ooh, that's nice," every so often, he was as quiet as a church mouse. Cut now to Tina and a full crew.

"And that Tina didn't have to be so nasty about it."

He obviously didn't know Tina. "I know, but just try to pretend nobody's on the set with us." Suddenly I was sick of this over grown Baby-Huey.

The lights were turned on and voices filled the room. Primarily Tina's voice. "Are we ready yet?" She took one look at Johnny and said to J.D. "Looks like we'll be shooting this scene soft-core." Tina looked around and saw Danielle. "Get me a glass of milk with a pack of sugar mixed in it, and a straw for the come-shot." Tina shot a scowl at Johnny. "Give me some soft-core footage at least."

Twenty minutes later and three non-hard-core positions later, Tina stepped in with a straw and a glass of milk. "Are you ready Thumbelina?" She smiled, took a sip of milk and shot it out of the straw onto my skin. The camera stayed close on my face, chest and stomach. "Oh, yeah, that feels so good." It took all of my acting abilities not to laugh. "Mmmm" I rubbed the liquid on my body and then licked my fingers one by one. "Oh, you taste so sweet."

"It's a wrap!" Tina yelled. "Time for lunch."

I got up and headed for the shower. On my way, I could hear Tina telling Johnny why he was only getting half of his pay. "There was no penetration Johnny. You're lucky I'm producing this and not my husband." She opened her fanny pack. "He wouldn't pay you a dime."

Johnny was about to say something, then shut his trap.

Tina pulled out a few twenties. "Once you sign the release, I'll give you the cash."

"Do you have a pen?"

I never saw or heard about Johnny again.

Mike shook his head back and forth. "Oh my, what a shame. He's such a good looking man and this business could use a few more men who look like this." Mike seemed saddened at the thought of no more Johnny in

263

the adult business. Mike and I both knew that no erection meant no future. Word would spread like wildfire.

I went to take the last bite of food and Mike asked, "So, what did you do during your four-year hiatus?"

I looked down and saw that both of my boobs were showing now. "I worked at my father's office." I didn't bother covering up. Mike could care less. He was more into Johnny's gender.

"What does your father do?"

"He's an accountant." As the words came out, I realized that I didn't want to be truthful about my family. The fans didn't earn that. They got to see me having sex on film but I wouldn't give them everything. I had to keep something for myself even if it was a set of parents who wrote me off. I had to protect my mom and dad. "He's a CPA really." Even though they weren't there to protect me. "He has a great big office in Century City." I couldn't subject their personal lives to the public because I decided to get in the adult business.

"You worked in Century City every day? It's beautiful there."

"Oh it sure is," I couldn't even remember the last time I had been to Century City, but I continued with the whopper of a lie, "a big penthouse office with a sweeping view." May as well pump up my fathers business in the process. He actually had a two-room office overlooking an alley, above a Mediterranean restaurant deep in the San Fernando Valley.

Mike went on about my father. "Did he teach you how to do accounting work?"

"Oh sure, he's an accounting whiz." I didn't think my father was an accountant legally. Last year he screwed up so badly on a client's tax return that they had him investigated. It seems Pops hadn't renewed his license in over twenty years. "My dad sure taught me a lot in those four short years." Dad paid some twenty-year-old kid to take the current tax course under his name. Eight weeks later, Dads new license was framed and hung on his office wall. "My parents and I are really close."

"That's great to hear."

And it was great to say, even though it wasn't true.

My holidays were going to be spent with Tina and her family in Indiana.

31

After shooting my comeback film "Hot In The City", I could feel the onset of a bladder infection. This non-sexually transmitted infection occurs when a girl has too much sex, after not having sex for a while. Prior to this movie, I had not had sex in six months. There went my super slut status.

Two hard-core scenes later, my bladder was screaming for antibiotics.

I popped a second antibiotic in my mouth, and headed out the door for a forty-five minute drive to Lancaster, Ca. to shoot a hard-core magazine layout with Rocco Siffredi. How unlucky can a girl get? I finally got to have sex with Rocco, and I couldn't enjoy it.

I had pre-warned Rocco the night before that he would have to take the brunt of the work upon himself, just sticking the tip inside me for a camera shot here and there.

Like the trooper he was, he didn't rely on me to keep him hard throughout the four-hour shoot. He'd seen it before, and he'd see it again. Rocco was a true professional.

"Christy," his voice reeked of pure Italian sexuality, "I was looking forward to having some great sex with you today."

"So was I Rocco." Buttering up his ego I tossed in, "You're so cute, I'll make sure I have you in my next movie."

Looking down at his raging hard on, I made a mental note to tell Tina that I didn't want to work with him. A few strokes of his big one, and I could already feel a second bladder infection coming on.

Contrary to some beliefs, bigger is not always better. Well, my beliefs at least.

But, he was cute, gorgeous actually. Oh well, twenty four hours from now, this entire shoot would be a blur in both of our memories.

Driving home, I stopped by my mailbox to pick up my fan club letters, before hitting the supermarket for some yummy pre-prepared food, paying of course, five times the amount than I would if I cooked the same thing myself. I never did master the art of cooking.

I pulled into the parking lot of my favorite gourmet market and found a space right in front.

Standing on the corner, near the three magazine stands, was a girl in her twenties, already looking like a haggard woman in her late forties. Her tattered cardboard sign read that she and her five children were hungry and needed money. "PLEASE HELP" were in larger letters at the bottom. Unless she started having children around the age of eleven, I highly doubted she had five children, let alone even one.

I had noticed in the past six months, that a new breed of homeless people were popping up on street corners all around Los Angeles. Each had a big cardboard sign with lettering in big black markers telling drivers why we needed to give them our hard-earned money. Just last week I recalled seeing a young man standing on the freeway off ramp with a sign that read "Vietnam Vet. Please help." Vietnam Vet at that young age? Oh sure, and I'm Dorothy visiting from Oz.

I remember when I was sixteen and use to hang out in Westwood on Friday and Saturday nights. It was the "in" place to be as a teenager in the early eighties, until a Spike Lee movie opened up one night, and rival gangs shot and killed each other. Westwood was never the same small, safe community. Anyway, I recalled the homeless there in 1982. They worked for their money on the streets. One lady, dressed as a gypsy, had two cats draped in beautifully ornate capes of gold and green. If you gave her cat a dollar, it would step on a small lever, and your horoscope would pop out.

I sat in my car, watching the lady bum shove her sign in people's faces before they even had a chance to get out of their cars. Four out of five people shook their heads no. It was that one out of five that amazed me. If they had so much extra money to dole out, give some to the animal shelters, or the Red Cross.

Moving along in my memory to 1985. The hottest place to be for shopping and dining was an outdoor mall in Santa Monica called the Third Street Promenade. Men dressed up as mimes and robots entertained the crowds for their money. A group of boys would break-dance to a large ghetto blaster. The amazed audiences who gathered around the talented young boys were happy to fill their hat with money. They earned it.

I kept my eyes on the lady bum, trotting from one end of the parking lot to the next, searching so diligently for a free hand out. After somebody used one of the three pay phones or bought a magazine from one of the newspaper stands in the parking lot, she religiously checked the change slot, always coming up empty fingered. Filthy fingers to boot.

In 1987, my roommate Keri and I decided to go to New York. Neither one of us had ever been. We had saved a portion of our paychecks for six months, and finally boarded the big bird to the Big Apple. Walking down Madison Avenue late at night, a lone man played the saxophone. Keri and I stopped to listen to the beautiful music coming from his throat and through the instrument. It was the most moving sound, and I felt tears in my eyes. His heart and soul came through his piece. Perhaps a song he played to a long lost love I'll never know. His open saxophone case lay at his feet. I dug in my purse, and added a five-dollar bill to his collection.

Why did people want a free handout now?

I made sure I had my payday of twenty-five hundred cash from today's work tucked safely in the side zipper of my purse. I worked for a

266

living, why shouldn't she? I got out of my car, locked the doors by remote control, and set the second alarm on my Porsche. I worked hard for my car, why can't she work?

As I walked towards the glass front doors, I kept my eyes on the ground not wanting any contact with her. Too late, she spotted a fresh customer. I could see her feet running towards me. I recognized her new Nike's. I had just seen the same pair two weeks ago at Footlocker to the tune of seventy-five dollars.

Her graveled voice interrupted my thoughts. "Hey Lady."

I clutched my purse tighter to my body and looked up from the pavement. I hated being called a lady. It sounded so prim and proper. A woman or a girl I am, but never a lady.

"Do you have any spare change?"

I've got more than that I thought. "No." I felt my skin crawl at the sight of her so near me. Her arms were black and blue. Red swollen track marks popped out from the veins on her inner arms. She was a common street junkie. Her problem, not mine. But it was my problem, wasn't it? She was invading my space.

"Not even a dime?" Her vacant eyes and chapped lips pleaded.

I couldn't remember if she saw me getting out of my car, so I thought I better play it safe. "Well, maybe after I go shopping I'll see what I've got." Smile. Didn't want to come out to a keyed-up car.

"Thanks Lady."

Get out of my life loser.

Pushing my cart down the produce aisle, I picked a basket of red, plump delicious strawberries at eight ninety-nine. Raspberries at this time of the year? Yep, for $5.99 a basket, there sure were. I placed the small green plastic baskets in my cart.

Next stop, the salad bar at seven forty-nine per pound.

Four and a half minutes later I carried off a fifteen-dollar salad. Who had the time and desire to wash and chop all of these delicious greens, hard-boiled eggs, chunks of chicken and even crabmeat? Not me.

My handful of items rang in at a little over sixty dollars and change, which I put right in my change purse. It was my change, not hers. I began to wheel my cart to the front of the store, and there she was outside. I could see her. The lady bum was hunched over, her back to the parking lot. I stopped to watch her next move.

She reached deep inside the front right pocket, of her worn out brown corduroy pants, and pulled out a wad of cash. I walked closer to the window with my cart of groceries and saw twenties, tens and fives. She was too stoned to realize I was only two feet behind her, behind the glass window, counting right along with her. Her grand total, three hundred five dollars. She shoved the stack back into her pocket, then dug the fortune out of her left pocket. All one dollar bills, but plenty of them. She was sure organized, just like a business. Something about seeing her with so much unearned money, begging for more, enraged me beyond belief.

I did a wheelie with my cart, and found the manager, dutifully at his podium, still smiling at each customer after several hours on his feet, on the job.

My cart came to a halt five inches from him.

"May I help you?" He asked.

I did a quick scan of the wooden plaques on the wall and picked out his proud face smiling down at me from a color photo glued to the center. Bruce it read, was the manager of the month. "Yes you may. I was wondering Bruce, if your fine establishment condoned people harassing your customers in the parking lot for money?" A pure look of concern spread across my face, wrinkled brow and all.

Bruce straightened to his full height of six feet, and readjusted his blue and red tie. "Why no we don't." The smile had disappeared from his face. "Has somebody been bothering you?"

"Yes, some girl out there said she needed my change for booze or drugs or something, I can't remember."

"No ma'am, we do not allow that. This is private property." He fumed. "I do apologize, and will handle this situation." He picked up the telephone mounted above his station, and punched in a three-digit code. "Thank you for bringing this to my attention."

"You're welcome." I turned my cart, and saw a security guard nearing the manager.

I walked out the double doors, and on cue, her radar picked up on me. "Excuse,"

"No! Leave me alone."

She recoiled like a sewer rat.

I reached my car, got comfortable in the plush black leather seat, locked my doors and turned on the stereo. I sat back and began to open up my fan mail while waiting to watch the security guard shoo her off the property like an unwanted cockroach. The large tan manila envelope was stamped "photos! Do not bend!" in big bold red lettering. I tore open the top of the envelope, and took out a glossy 8x10 of a man, stark naked, with a black leather whip tucked under his left armpit. His deep dark skin was oiled from head to toe. His facial features were chiseled to perfection; high cheekbones, deep set chocolate brown eyes looking right at me, and full pouted lips, opened ever so slightly. His arms and legs muscular, not an ounce of fat could be seen. His ding-a-ling, as hard as a rock, was nearing his kneecaps. This body part reminded me that it was time to take another antibiotic. I found a bottle of water in my grocery bag, and popped a pill in my mouth. Inspecting every inch of this funny photo sent to me, made me forget the reason I was on a stakeout. I looked in my rear view mirror, and saw the security guard talking to the girl. His finger was pointing her in the direction of the next block.

I looked back down at the photo in my lap, fascinated that somebody would send me their naked photo, so big, so colorful and oh so proud. I lifted it up, and a note fell on my lap.

"Christy, I want to be lovin' on you real soon. Danté" with his phone number underneath. I gathered the note and the photo and shoved it back in the envelope.

I looked back in the rear view mirror, and saw the girl gathering up her life from under a tree. A worn out green backpack, two trash bags stuffed, and her hand made sign.

I sat in the car and contemplated my next move. My eyes went from the envelope to the beggar. She settled kitty corner to the market in front of a gas station.

No offense to Danté, but that phone call wouldn't be coming.

I started my car, and eased out of the parking lot turning left. I crossed the intersection, and unrolled my passenger side window. Her sign was up, and I slowed my car, stopping at the curb in front of her.

She did not remember my face from our previous encounters, and gave me her blank smile. I in return, gave her the tan manila envelope. "Here, I thought you might need this." I slid it through the open window.

"Oh I do, I do. God bless you."

I pulled away from the curb and parked two cars away from her, watching for her reaction in my rear view mirror.

She thrust her hand deep inside of the envelope and pulled out the photo. Her eyes and face stared for a minute. Not a muscle moved. The naked photo of Danté must have finally penetrated her pickled brain, because her facial expression finally changed. Her eyes and lips opened wide, alive with shock, and then disgust. With more energy than I had seen, she crumpled the pornographic photo and chucked it in the gutter.

For the second time in ten minutes, she picked up her belongings and headed elsewhere.

I couldn't fathom why people thought that they deserved a free handout in life.

That very photo of Danté, was the first of many nude photos sent to me. Each and every photo found a special, unsuspecting recipient.

Whether people liked my line of work or not, was irrelevant to me. It was legal, and I paid taxes on every dime I earned.

The good thing was, I never saw her in my neighborhood again.

The bad thing was, plenty more followed her in the years to come.

32

I had been back in the adult business for six months now. As much fun, and as lucrative as it was, I knew that my personal gravy train would not last forever. Whether I would choose to quit the business, or the business would tire of me, I knew this line of work definitely had a time limit.

The question was what talents did I have? None. Okay, next question. What did I like? Clothing.

The following day, I found the top three fashion schools in Southern California, and set up interviews with each.

My favorite of the three, was a private school in downtown LA called "Otis Parsons". The cost of tuition was $12,500 a year. Not a problem. The problem was that they required transcripts from high school.

Because I dropped out of high school one week before graduation, I felt that this was going to bite me in the ass. Hard. The "C" average grade, when I did happen to attend, was not impressive either. Too bad a social life at school didn't earn me anything. I would have gotten straight "A's".

So there I sat, at my kitchen table, staring at the one section that I left blank on my application. Maybe they wouldn't notice. Yeah right, it stuck out like a sore thumb. I licked the envelope, attached a cute stamp, and said a prayer as I dropped my future into the mailbox.

The following week, I left my house at 10 a.m. for my 11 a.m. second interview with Otis Parsons. This was the college I was determined to be accepted to.

I made one quick detour to my bank.

At 11:05 a.m., I was called into the administrative office. I sat across from the Dean with my knees knocking and hands trembling.

"Miss Canyon, I have been looking over your high school transcripts." Lynn put the manila file folder down, took off her tortoise-shell glasses, and rubbed her temples.

I froze. She had my pathetic transcripts on her desk. I could feel the sweat pooling under the arms of my baby pink silk shirt. "Oh, you do?" I squeaked out. "I couldn't find mine at home."

"Well, we called over there, and they had them on microfilm."

Damn that technology I thought.

Lynn continued, "Is there a reason that you chose not to complete twelfth grade?" Her sweet, enthusiastic disposition from our first interview was now ruffled, as if I was a total waste of her time.

"There is a reason. I was having some trouble at home, and I had to move out." A big lump was gaining speed in my throat. "It started when my mom got remarried to this guy and." Oh boy, I felt the first teardrop sliding down my cheek before it hit my hand that was resting on her desk. I lowered my head. Where do I even start? How far back does this go? Too far, she's a Dean, not a therapist. I heard Lynn shuffling papers on her desk, and told myself to pull it together. If you want it, you'll get it. Stop blubbering you big baby and go to phase-II fast.

I lifted my head and looked at Lynn, who had her glasses firmly back on the bridge of her nose. My file was still open, which I took to mean that I still had a shot.

"Let me ask you this Christy. Why do you think you can pull it off at our school, when you couldn't even complete high school? College is tough and takes determination." I noticed a bit more of that warmth was back in her voice.

"Because my life is different now. I want to learn and I want to go to college. Here."

"Maybe you should start off at a junior college for a year, get your feet wet, complete the three courses you need for a diploma, and then try us again."

I refused to take no for an answer, and no way was I going to take cooking, Spanish II and health again. "No. I've decided that I will attend my two years of school here for my AA degree."

Lynn folded her arms across her chest, and tapped the tip of her silver pen on my transcripts. "We want students here who are committed to us, committed to learning. Without your completion of even high school, I have no way of knowing if you can follow through with college."

"I do. I have a way."

Lynn cocked her head, and blonde bob hairdo to the left. "How? How can you prove to me, and our school, that you will give it your all?"

"Because I have a cashiers check in my purse made out to the school for my full tuition."

Her head snapped back to the center. "You're willing to pay for one whole year in advance?"

"No, actually," I dug in my purse and pulled out my ace in the hole. "It's actually for both years. I hope $25,000 will cover it."

Her hand was definitely quicker than my eye. I could already feel the sting of a paper cut begin.

I'm not sure where her red marker materialized from, but it checked off the accepted box. "Welcome to our family." Lynn stood up and shook my hand. "Classes begin in three weeks. If you see Vanessa in room 402, she will furnish you with a list of supplies that you will need for your first quarter."

I shook her hand back. "Thank you Lynn. You don't know how much this means to me." And she didn't.

Driving home, I realized just how powerful money was. It bought you anything and everything you wanted.

Almost.

33

It was Friday night and Tina and I were getting ready to go out.

Tina put on her Rolling Stones T-shirt. "Bill said that CC Deville is going to meet us at the China Club tonight."

"Tina, where's your red lipstick?" I wished Bill were going to be there. I had a crush on Tina's singing coach, but Tina had a crush on him too. "What about Bill? Is he going to be there as well?" I knew that if Tina had a crush on Bill, even though she was married, he was hands off. CC was in the famous rock band Poison, not really my type. I tended to form crushes on men like Bill who were more shy and unassuming.

Tina dug into her purse, "Here it is." She handed me the lipstick. "No, I doubt it. You know him, he's happier staying home every night. He doesn't like the club scene."

A homebody, just my type. "How does Bill know CC?" I didn't really care about CC; I just wanted to hear more about Bill.

Bill worked on one of Poison's albums and I think he told them that he was friends with us. CC got so excited; he's a big fan of yours. So, when I asked Bill to go out with us tonight, he told CC where we were going."

"Oh that'll be fun." I tried to think of what he looked like from the cassette cover that Tina had. From what I remembered, he had bleach blonde hair and wore more makeup than I did. "Tina, where's your Guns 'n' Roses T-shirt?"

Tina riffled through her stack of T-shirts. "Here it is."

I put the shirt on and took one last look. "Okay, lets go."

Driving into Hollywood, Tina cranked up the Poison cassette. "CC is so cute, I can't believe we're going to meet him tonight."

We pulled up to valet the car and Tina took out a ten-dollar bill. "We're going to be the cutest girls here." She handed the guy the money. "Park it close, will you?"

The money disappeared into his front pocket. "Of course I will."

We walked through the VIP entrance, avoiding the line of hopefuls waiting to be hand picked by the bouncer to get in the club. "I love being us Christy."

I loved being me, but I wasn't sure about the "us" part lately. Over the past two months I had noticed a change in Tina. Ever since I started college, she had become so possessive over me and with our time together. She cut down my new set of school friends every chance she got.

Within moments of stepping into the club, a burley, bald, security guard stopped us. "Mr. Deville would like to see you."

273

They were playing my favorite song. "Cool, tell him we'll be on the dance floor."

"He is in the VIP lounge."

"Cool, tell him we'll be on the dance floor." I couldn't stand it when people expected me to go to them via a bodyguard. Why couldn't CC just come up to me? "Let's dance." I grabbed Tina's arm.

After four minutes on the dance floor, I felt a tap on my shoulder. "Hi Christy, I'm CC."

Attaboy, I knew you could do it on your own. "We have the same initials." He was really cute up close. A bit heavy handed on the black eye liner though.

"Hi, I'm Tina." She began dancing close to him. "Is Bill with you?"

Bill? My ears perked up and I tried to move closer to CC to hear his answer but Tina's body blocked me. I moved to the right and so did she. I scooted to the left, and she moved left two steps as well. Was she purposely trying to block me from him? I could see his white head of hair surfacing over Tina's shoulder every few seconds to try to talk to me. Our eyes would connect for a second before Tina's big body blocked us. Tina began pressing her body against his smaller frame. Her wide hips connected with his stomach, due to the difference in height, and she began grinding her body against his as hard as she could. It was too much for the boy. One too many hip thrusts from Tina sent CC flying across the dance floor. I wasn't attracted to him, but I was not going to let Tina take control. He was after all my fan, not hers. I walked over to CC and held out my hand. He grabbed it, with a bit of shock and fear in his eyes and hoisted himself off the wooden dance floor. "What's with her?" He asked?

I shrugged my shoulders. "I think she's a big fan of yours, she has your posters all over her bedroom walls." She didn't, but I felt like fibbing to make her look the geek she was acting like. I didn't know what had gotten into Tina lately. It seemed as though any guy who showed an interest in me she suddenly wanted for herself.

"She has posters of me hanging up?" He looked over my shoulder at her. "Isn't she a bit old for that?"

"And she cut out all of the other band members, so it would just be you on the posters." I was starting to get a really bad feeling about my friendship with Tina.

"Oh God, she's coming over here." There was actually terror in his voice, not to mention the sour, stale alcohol stench on his breath. He grabbed my hand, "Come on, let's go to the VIP section."

I was following him the short distance when I heard her. "Hey, where do you two think you're going without me?"

CC kept pulling my hand and walking, but I stopped for Tina. "There you are." Like I had lost her or something. "We're going to the VIP lounge."

"Oh goody! Let's get some drinks." Her eyes never left CC's face.

Tina had been drinking quite a bit lately as well. "I'll just have a bottle of water."

"You're no fun." She was using that stupid baby voice again. "What do you want CC?"

As if he needed another drink. He could barely keep his intoxicated eyes open. "I'll have another rum and coke."

"That's what I drink too!"

Since when, I thought? She was a vodka girl these days. Straight from the bottle.

Tina left to order the drinks, and CC and I sat down on the dark blue couch. "What's up with your friend?"

That's what I would like to know. "She's just obsessed with you." Suddenly I wanted to be home in bed watching TV. I wondered what Bill was doing right now.

"Shit man, she's not one of those stalker types is she?"

I looked at him, not that his eyes could focus much, and just half smiled.

He scooted even closer to me on the couch and motioned for his bodyguard to sit on the other side of him.

Tina came back with our drinks, "Hey, where am I supposed to sit?"

CC pointed to a footstool across the table, I kept smiling, and the bodyguard folded his arms across his chest keeping a close eye on her.

"Here Christy, I got you a Long Island Iced Tea."

I didn't see my bottle of Evian water anywhere. Bitch. I set my iced tea down in front of CC, which he drained in a few minutes. "So CC..." Tina sat on the small stool and her knees jetted out like a grasshopper. "When can we see you rehearse?" She tried to scoot her stool closer to him, but the bodyguard stuck out his combat boot preventing her to get too close.

CC snuggled into my body. "Would you like to see us Christy?"

I opened my mouth to answer and Tina's voice said, "She would love to."

CC propped his feet on the table. "How do you like my genuine alligator skin boots?" He admired them for a moment. "They cost me five grand."

Five thousand dollars for a pair of boots? What a fool. "I've never seen a purple alligator before." I looked down at my own boots. Fifty-nine dollars I paid for these white leather babies at a close out sale last year.

Tina reached out to touch his boots. "Those are awesome CC. Where did you get them? I want to get a pair."

"Dude, there ain't no such thing as a purple alligator." He touched the toe of his right boot and looked up for a second, lost in a hazy thought. "At least I didn't think there were." He pulled his boot close to his face. "I think somebody must have dyed them."

Gee, ya think?

"CC!" Oh brother, Tina's baby voice was back. "You didn't answer me, where did you get them?"

He shrugged his shoulders. "Don't know. I told my manager I wanted a pair, and presto," He tried to snap his fingers, "The next day he gave them to me."

I was sure that was where half of the five grand went, right into the manager's pocket.

"These boots here are my pride and joy." He took his feet off the table.

Tina drained the last of her drink. "Anybody want more?"

CC drank the last of his. "Sure, I'll have another double."

An hour later, and many drinks between them, I was parched and ready to go home. CC was slumping down in the couch cushions almost looking like he could do a somersault onto the dance floor at any moment.

"Let's go." They were both boring me, and between both their alcoholic breaths, I think I felt a contact high begin.

The bodyguard stood first, I stood second. CC swayed to his feet and Tina shot up and made her move to be near him. She put her arm around him. "This was so much fun."

CC put his arm around her for balance. "It was?" His reply came out in a question. I wondered how much he would even remember in the morning. Tina wrapped her big Samoan arm around his waist and CC held on to her body for dear life, his overpriced boots barely touched the ground. I think the toes were actually scraping against the concrete floor.

"I'll go get the car," the bodyguard said. He must have thought CC was finally interested in Tina, as his face was nestled into her bosom.

We made it outside and Tina propped CC's body between the wall and herself. "Kiss me good night CC." Her face was an inch from his.

He opened his eyes. "Man, I've got to take a leak."

"Kiss me first." Tina demanded.

"I've got to go real bad." He began moving up and down.

Tina put a hand on each of his shoulders preventing him from escaping. "CC, I want you to kiss me."

"Tina, he's turning blue." Why was she acting like this?

"I'm going to piss in my pants!"

That wouldn't be good for his leather pants, I thought.

Apparently, even in his drunk stage, CC thought the same thing. With his right hand, he managed to unzip his pants, and pull out the head of his penis.

"Uh, Tina." Oh screw Tina, let him piss all over her.

"Now CC, kiss me." Tina closed the one-inch gap between them, just as urine started to stream out. his body dropped a few inches with the relief, and Tina ended up smooching the wall behind him. CC pissed all over his genuine, purple alligator skin boots. The yellow and purple colors met, and formed a small stream heading southbound on Gower Street.

Tina released her hands from his shoulders. "You pissed on my jeans and shoes!" She screamed.

"Fuck that felt good." CC zipped his pants back up, or so he thought. He did manage to zip up the warm air, just an inch away from the zipper.

Tina backed up, and looked at the urine spreading on her jeans.

CC asked, "Where's Jimmy? I need to get home, I don't feel too good."

I looked at CC's boots, which now had a white, lavender and purple tie-dye look to them.

What a mess those two were.

Jimmy, who I assumed was the bodyguard, rounded the corner and honked twice. CC stepped in his puddle of urine and fell head first into the back seat.

The eager valet pulled Tina's Corvette around. "I hope you ladies had a lovely evening." He was smiling from ear to ear in hopes of another big bill.

Tina bumped into his hand that was holding the door open for her. I was apparently persona-non-gratis to him. He stifled a yelp as she slammed the door shut in his once happy face.

The ten-minute drive home was in silence and I was so happy to see my building. "That was," what was tonight? "Different."

"Are you kidding?" Tina ejected the Poison cassette, which caught her diamond wedding ring and ripped the thin cassette tape. "He's an asshole."

Takes one to know one. "Talk to you tomorrow."

I climbed into bed and wondered what was happening to my best friend.

The following month, Tina and I seemed to see less and less of each other. I was busy at school with finals and Tina started hanging around a new group of people, an unsavory bunch if you asked me.

"They're really good people Christy, they just get a bad wrap because they're bikers. Hold on a second." Tina muffled the phone, but not very well. "Yea, I've got two hundred in my wallet. Give it to Chico for my share."

Was she buying drugs? "Oh, I'm sure they're good people." Good for nothing that is. "But I can't go to the Outlaw's Bar tonight," or any night, "Sarah and I have to finish our final project this weekend."

"You're no fun any more Christy. All you do is go to school, do homework and hang out with your new set of friends." Tina made a sniffing noise.

"Bless you," I knew it wasn't a sneeze.

"I didn't, what? Oh that. I think I have allergies."

Oh sure, I used to use that excuse five years ago. It's funny how when you stop snorting cocaine, the old allergies seem to disappear. "Uh huh." I began putting my school supplies on the kitchen table. "Well Tina, are you still going to Lisa's birthday party with me?"

Please say no. "Yes."

Shit.

"When is that again?"

For the tenth time in a week I told her it was Monday night. "You really don't have to go if you don't want to. It's just going to be about six of my school friends. It will probably bore you to tears. I'm not really looking forward to it," but I really couldn't wait. "I just have to go because we all go to school together." And because I'm excited as hell to go.

"No, I guess I can hang with a bunch of school chicks for a night."

"Well, I don't want you to feel like you have to." I loved my new set of friends, and I was beginning to hate one very old friend.

"Alright, have fun tonight Tina."

"Yeah, you try and have fun too. Later."

Much later I hoped.

Tina never showed up on Monday night, thank goodness.

I called her Tuesday afternoon and she was sound asleep.

"Tina, are you okay? It's two in the afternoon."

"I'm sleeping, I'll call you later."

Three days later, she finally surfaced. "He's, he's…"

"Tina, are you okay?" But I knew she wasn't. She hadn't been for the past two months and it was only getting worse.

"No. Mark and I are…" She was crying uncontrollably.

"I'll come right over."

"Thanks."

On my drive to Tina's, I thought about where our, once so tight, friendship fell apart. It was the day I started school. Before college, Tina and I were together twenty-four hours a day. We would stay up until three in the morning playing double solitaire, drinking hot chocolate and playing ding-dong-ditch in the neighborhood. We slept 'til noon, went shopping, got massages and ate out with Mark every night. Not a bad life, but I couldn't do it forever.

She didn't understand that going to school didn't mean I loved her any less. I, unlike her, didn't have a multimillionaire husband to fall back on. I couldn't and didn't want to make fuck films forever. I only had myself, which meant I had to create something for me to fall back on.

Tina's door was open. "Tina." I stepped in and closed the door behind me. I had to hold onto the doorknob for support. Her beautiful condo looked like it had been ransacked. Clothing was strewn everywhere, ashtrays overflowed with various brands of cigarettes, dirty dishes were piled on the coffee table and it stunk to high heaven.

I began to walk towards her bedroom. "Tina, where are you?" I pushed her bedroom door open, noticing a hole had been punched through it. "Tina." An inch of sunlight was streaming in through a slit in the curtain, and I could see Tina shove a plate under her bed.

She wiped her nose with the sleeve of her flannel top. "Mark left me."

I turned on the light and she yelled at me for the first time ever. "Turn the fucking light off God Damn it!"

"What happened?" But I could see what happened. She had gone back to drugs with her new set of "friends". Yep, they're real good people.

"Well, Mark said he had to work late one night so I had some friends over." She was eyeing that plate sticking out from under her bed. "We got a little drunk and the next thing I knew everybody left except for Kicker."

I didn't know who Kicker was, but it didn't sound good. "Did Kicker kick that hole in your bedroom door?"

"What?"

I don't think she even knew her door had a big hole in it. "Never mind."

"So anyway, at about eleven, I called Mark, and he was just sitting down to eat dinner." She was fingering a rip in her comforter.

I noticed a big cold sore under her left nostril. "So what happened?" God she was a loser.

"Kicker and I started to mess around, and then Mark..." She took a swig of Jack Daniels from a bottle that she pulled from under her pillow.

"Mark called and Kicker answered and," she started to cry. "Hung up."

There was no need to ask what she and Kicker were doing. "Have you talked to Mark since?"

"No. He won't take my calls." Her eyes narrowed at me. "And you," she gulped down another big sip. "You." She was now pointing the bottle at me. "This is all your fault." The bottle was moving back and forth, the alcohol splashing on her sheets. "If you hadn't left me for your new set of friends, your new stuck up school girl bitch cunt friends, this wouldn't have happened." Her voice was getting higher with each word. "I did everything for you. I got you that convertible Porsche, I got you the paycheck you wanted and the royalties and this is the fucking thanks I get. You ignore me and now look what happened." Gulp, gulp, she continued swigging from the pintsized bottle. "And don't forget about those two free first class trips to Hawaii you took. Let's see your new friends do that for you."

This spoiled rotten ungrateful bitch had some nerve. "For the one Porsche Mark bought me, he bought ten with the money my films made for him." I flung the curtains wide open. Come on in Mr. Sunshine. "For every royalty check I receive, his is ten times higher." A quick flick of a switch and the rack of one hundred watt floods above her were shining ever so bright. "For every Hawaii trip he sent _us_ on, he could have taken a three week European holiday with the money my naked ass has made for him." I opened the window to feel and smell some fresh air. "So don't you call me a user Tina. Mark made out pretty fucking great in the deal."

Tina was cowering in bed but still had a little pep left in her. "Well." She was squinting up at me, mascara smeared under her eyes. "All I have to do is tell Mark not to renew your contract next week." She looked so pleased with herself for threatening me. "We are after all your bread and butter."

What a pig she was. "Then that's your choice. But don't forget, while you may be my bread and butter I am your steak and lobster." We locked eyes across her sty and right then and there, I had made my own decision about work. Go to plan B fast. "You did this to yourself." I looked around the room. "You could have done anything you wanted. When you wanted to learn how to act, Mark sent you to the best acting coach." I looked down and saw one of my shirts and grabbed it. "When you wanted to become a singer, Mark sent you to the best voice coach." It was that or getting earplugs. "When you wanted to become a chef," for all of one week, "Mark enrolled you in the finest culinary school around." I saw that tube of lipstick I liked so much and slid it into my pocket. "Your problem is, you don't know the meaning of a dollar. It's just handed to you."

She gloated. "So that's it, you're just jealous of me."

That little comment cost her a pair of sunglasses I saw on the floor to my left. I looked around her room and back at her. Drunk in bed at three-thirty with a pile of coke under it. "Girl, I wouldn't trade places with you for a million bucks." I'll make it without you.

"You're own parents won't even talk to you. They don't even love you." That was a low blow.

Yes they do. "Goodbye Tina." I stepped over the piles of crap on her floor and opened the front door. My hands were trembling with a mixture of rage and sadness. I had to call Lois.

I heard her size ten feet hit the carpet with a loud thud. "Wait Thumbelina, I didn't mean that. Don't leave me, please."

I stepped outside and closed her front door. I took a deep breath of the fresh air.

I had just closed the door on a once great relationship. It was a wonderful era whose time had come to an end. A very awful, ugly end.

I drove straight to Video Exclusives.

"Hi Judy, can I pick up my royalty check today?" I smiled at the accountant. "I'm a little short this month." Had Tina reached her first?

"Sure, I don't think that will be a problem. Just give me a few minutes to figure it out."

"No problem." I sat down and pretended to call Tina. "Hi! Yeah, Judy is figuring it out right now and then I'll be over." I smiled at Judy who was as slow as molasses. "Tina say's hello and to put a rush on it. We have a facial appointment in thirty minutes."

"That girl!" Judy huffed. "She always wants something ten minutes ago."

I smiled again and shrugged my shoulders. "You know Tina!" I thought I did. "Okay Tina, I'll be there as soon as I'm done here." I paused for effect. "I'll hurry, I swear." I hung up and jumped every time the extension rang in Judy's office.

"I'll never finish figuring your check out on Tina time."

I froze. What did that mean? No check today?

"Let me just write you a check for nine thousand, and we'll figure out the difference next month."

There wasn't going to be a next month for us. "Perfect."

Judy handed me my check. "If Tina calls, tell her I'm on my way over." To the bank that is.

I cashed what I knew would be my final royalty check from Video Exclusives. Sometimes you just have to cut your losses and move on.

Which is exactly what I did when I left the bank. I drove right over to the Vivid headquarters.

"Is Steve in?" I asked the nice lady at the reception desk.

"Are you Christy Canyon?"

"Yes."

"I'm Yvonne, I spoke to you about a year ago."

"I remember but then I ended up with V.E." I instantly liked Yvonne.

"So how's it going there?"

"Well, my contract is up and I was going to talk to Steve about signing with Vivid."

She looked at her desk calendar. "Does he know you're coming?"

"No." I looked around and didn't see any badges, sign in and out sheets, or security guards. Maybe I should have called first. "Should I make an appointment?" I thought back to the rigamarole I had to go through last year when I went to that awful Cabalerro.

"No! He's in right now, let me just tell him that you're here."

She buzzed Steve, and I walked over to a wall unit that served as the Vivid Girl's mailboxes. Hyapatia Lee, Jamie Summers, and Barbara Dare.

The first box had a gum label that had been torn off.

Yvonne hung up the phone. "Steve said to go right in."

I pointed to the first box. "Whose name used to be on this one?

"Oh, that was Tori Welles, but she quit last month."

I looked around and saw three office doors. "Where's his office?"

"Let me show you."

I followed Yvonne around the corner. "Hi Steve."

"Hi Christy." He smiled. "Sit down."

I sat down and looked around. No security monitors or bulletproof windows. No steel enforced door with a code panel to lock and unlock it. Just a regular guy sitting in a regular office.

"So are you finally ready to be a Vivid girl?"

One week later I shot my first Vivid film, "A Portrait Of Christy." A fresh white gum label was on the first mailbox. My mailbox.

Two weeks later, while I was having a slumber party at my place with two of my school friends, the phone rang. "Save me a piece of pepperoni pizza." I hobbled to the telephone with cotton balls stuck between my freshly painted toes. "Hello." Maybe it was that cute guy Anna and I met last night at The Roxbury.

"Christy?"

What did she want? "Yeah."

"It sounds like you're having a party there."

I didn't say anything.

"It's just that I hear music and voices in the background."

"What's up?" I looked in my living room from the kitchen and saw Lisa putting a mud mask on Anna. "You're next Christy." Lisa said.

I held up a finger. "Give me a minute."

"I was wondering if we could get together and talk."

"About what Tina?" I had nothing to say to her. Nothing nice that is.

"About our friendship."

"What friendship?"

She started to cry. "I miss you so much. I didn't mean anything when I said all of those nasty things that day. I was just in a bad way."

"You know what the problem is when you say something nasty like that Tina?" I looked at the clock and realized our movie on HBO was going to start in ten minutes and I still didn't have my mask on.

She was sniffling. "No, what?" She blew her nose.

"You can't take it back. It will always be there."

"But I didn't mean any of it. I know you're with Vivid now, and I'm not even angry about that." She started to whimper again. "In fact I'm glad. Now we can just be best friends again and work won't get in the way."

Lisa was putting some hair conditioner on Anna's hair.

282

"Work never got in the way, you did." And now you're getting in the way of my facial and hair treatment.

"I spoke to Mark about your future royalty checks, and he has agreed to still pay you every month."

Yes, but at what price? That I had to be her friend? I sure didn't want or need the money that badly. "Thanks but no thanks." I wanted a clean break from her.

"Oh great, so now you're just going to cut me out?"

"If I cut my parents out of my life, for not treating me with respect, what makes you think you're so special Tina?" You fucking bitch I would have been your friend for life. "Don't ever call me again."

The following day I changed my phone number.

34

The airplane tires hit the pavement at LAX airport and I was home sweet home. I had been gone for one week signing in Texas at bookstores promoting my latest Vivid release. From Waco, to San Antonio I sat for four hours a day signing and meeting my fans. This was such a nice change from making videos. I could wear clothes and nobody touched me other than putting their arm around my shoulders, or waist if I deemed them cute enough, for a snapshot. I loved to travel, I loved the attention, I loved the twenty-four hour room service, and I loved the daily housekeeping. But lately, I didn't love the thought of making films. Had I outgrown that stage in my life?

I looked through my stack of mail wondering if I could go through with making my next video in ten days. Of course I could, I was a professional. Maybe when my contract was up in six months I would quit, but for now I had to fulfill my obligations. What exactly the level of my obligation was, I wasn't sure. Not being a quitter was one reason and not disappointing Steve was another. Somehow, that didn't seem like enough for me anymore.

I read a postcard half way through my mail reminding me to bring Ninja into the vet's office for his yearly shots. I thought about what day next week I was free when I saw the return address on the next envelope. I knew her writing and felt my heart stop before it began pounding at double speed. I let the stack of bills, junk mail and the latest issue of National Enquirer fall to the ground. I stepped on a twenty percent discount coupon for the local drycleaner and made my way to the couch. My head felt light and I had to hold onto the back for support as I lowered myself onto the cushions. I stared at her perfect writing on the baby blue stationary. Did Clair know Mom was going to send me a letter? No, she would have told me. Or maybe warned me. I stared at the envelope and felt my heart beating fast. Was it good news or bad news? What ever it was, it was the first time my mom had made contact with me in over three years.

I turned the envelope over and stuck my index finger under a corner of the flap. I sat in the silence of my apartment and wondered if I should call Clair or Wanda. What if it was a nasty letter? I would want somebody to tell me they loved me right away. I slid my finger down the length of the envelope and looked at my phone. The message light on my answering machine was blinking to the rhythm of my heartbeat, fast and anxious. I took out the folded single sheet of paper and put the envelope on the coffee table. I didn't need to call anybody. At this point in my life, what was the

284

worst my mom could write? I unfolded the sheet and my eyes blurred for a second until they focused in on the first line.

"Dear Christy,"
At least I knew I was still a dear, so I read on.
"I just want you to know that no matter what, I love you. You will always be my baby."
Love Always,
Momma

There was no I miss you, call me, or let's get together. But it was all right there between the lines. Mom was making the first step.

Sitting still on my couch, I re-read her letter twenty times. I wondered if Marv or Clair knew she wrote to me. I could call Clair and ask her, or call Wanda and ask her what I should do, or even Steve. Steve knew how to handle everything. I looked at my suitcase in the hallway, the mail scattered across the Spanish tiles and my kitty Ninja making his way over to me from behind the curtain. For now, I was going to keep this my secret, my triumph and my victory. My mother was finally accepting who I was. The question I asked myself was, now what do I do?

I got up and made myself a pot of coffee. While it was dripping, at what seemed an extra slow pace, I un-zipped my suitcase and threw my first load of laundry in the washer. Next stop; shower. While I was drying my hair, I thought about what my dad would have said to me. *"Christy, the ball is in your court."* And for one of the very few times in life, my dad was right. The next step was mine.

My arm got tired of drying my hair so I stopped for a coffee break. I sat on the couch, sipped my coffee laden with vanilla cream, turned on the TV and thought about my week in Texas. If I decided not to make films anymore, I could certainly survive on my royalty checks, personal appearance fees and my fan club. My fan club with its cast of characters kept me entertained. Sometimes my brother-in-law would read the letters to me in the voice he thought went with their letter.

Bud was a man from Oklahoma who took the time to write a ten-page letter about the Monster Truck rally he was in last week. He included a roll of photos of him standing by his fine truck in all sorts of positions, similar to one's I've done for girlie magazines. He was so proud of his truck that had been jacked up twenty feet in the air.

George, from Alaska, decided to send me what he considered a rare delicacy in the world. A jar of pig's feet.

Stan was a used car salesman who claimed to once be on top of the world financially until his company went belly-up due to a minor bookkeeping problem. He owed Uncle Sam nearly one million dollars, and somehow it was his partner's fault. His six-page letters told me his woes of how the car company repossessed his cherry red Ferrari late one night, his million dollar house was sold at an auction and the final straw was his wife left him for another woman. Stan ended up filing for bankruptcy and would appreciate any free videos or posters I could send him.

There were always a handful of letters from people telling me God would save my soul from the business I was in, if only I had faith. I was always perplexed by how these types acquired my fan club address as it was only printed in porn magazines. I think their faith was on the same centerfold where I was stark naked, spread eagle.

Cheri was a girl who wrote in always asking me for a pair of my heels, preferably in a size twelve. Somehow I knew Cheri had a five o'clock shadow and was wearing Dockers at the time "she" wrote to me. I would have sent the damn shoes to him, but I wear a size eight and a half!

Then I realized that I was avoiding the real issue of thinking about my mom.

I finished the last of my coffee and went to my writing desk. I opened the middle drawer and looked at my stationary. I decided against using Ms. Piggy, or the stationary with cows jumping across the top and slid out a piece of mint green paper with a matching envelope.

I sat at the desk and stared at the paper. It was clean, fresh and stayed empty for twenty minutes. What I needed was another cup of coffee and a cigarette.

I sat back down and thought about how I felt. I was content with my life yet there was always that piece missing. My mom. A chunk actually, my dad was missing as well. My life wasn't ideal. *"Dear Mom,"* but who had idealism? *"I miss you,"* I could have held out forever I tell you, *"and no matter what, I'll always love you too."* but I didn't want to. I missed her madly. *"I loved getting your letter,"* but I refused to have anybody in my life who looked down on me. *"and when you're ready to accept me for everything I am,"* Family or not. *"then I would love to see you."* Three years seemed like a good amount of time to me. *"In my therapist's office."* I think we needed mediation. *"I love you, Christy."*

I would love to see my mom, but I knew it had to be done with the aid of Lois.

I sat at my desk and re-read my letter a dozen times. I carefully folded the stationary and slid it in the envelope.

I punched in Clair's number.

"Clair, did you know Mom was going to send me a letter?"

"She said she was thinking of it. Why? What did she write?"

I recited it out of memory and my letter back to Mom as well. "Do you think she'll call?" Suddenly I felt insecure. What if my mom changed her mind? What if her letter was just a fluke or a passing fancy? I had grown accustomed to the idea of being orphaned and I didn't think I could take another round of my mom shutting me out. "Maybe I shouldn't send this letter to her." I held my breath for Clair's answer. Clair would be honest with me.

"I know she'll call, just send her the letter."

"I'll let you know what happens. I love you."

"I love you too."

I looked outside my window and saw the sun setting. Where had the last three hours gone since I got home? I looked at the mint green envelope and sealed it shut with a swipe of my tongue. I suddenly felt drained. I rummaged through my top drawer and found a stamp with the American flag on it.

"Momma will be right back Ninja." I grabbed my keys and headed to the mailbox on the corner.

I climbed into bed by nine and wondered when my mom would get it. I fell asleep thinking about a guy in Dallas, Texas three nights ago. He asked me if I was talking to him in my last video when I said, "I want you," into the camera. Didn't he understand it was just a movie? No, he was a freak. I told him it was part of the script, and that I was saying it to my co-star, a very female Jamie Summers, who couldn't possibly be any more different than him.

He stood there clutching his autographed 8x10 and video of me with tears forming in his feral cat brown eyes. "You mean, you weren't talking to me in that movie?" His eyes began to focus and that wasn't a good thing.

I was in no mood for this. "No. I wasn't talking to you." I loved my fans when they kept reality in check. "I was playing a part in a movie." But every so often, I met a fan who's perception of fantasy and reality crossed wires. "I didn't even know you until five seconds ago so how could I have been talking to you?"

"So why did you make me buy this video?"

"I didn't make you do anything. I was most likely at home in California when you bought this." One look to Shorty, the 6'5" bouncer and the nearing-the-danger-zone-fan was escorted out of the adult bookstore.

How pathetic is your life when a porn store kicks you out?

Tuesday afternoon my phone rang. "Hello."

"It's your Mommy! When can we go see Lois? I miss you Spot."

That was my nickname when I was a kid because my shirts always had food spots on them. "I'll call her right now. I miss you too."

The next day, my mom and I hugged in the hallway outside of Lois's office.

Neither Mom nor I wanted to re-hash the past twenty-five years. What was done was done and it was time to move forward. Our relationship shifted into something stronger than it had ever been. We learned to respect, trust and be supportive of each other. I learned to acknowledge Marv as my stepfather and she learned to accept my past, present and future.

Speaking of which, I had to shoot next week.

The script was called "Sex" starring Christy Canyon. I pulled up to the location on the first day of the shoot and felt my insides turn.

The P.A. met me at my car. "Let me get your wardrobe for you."

I thought about my mom. I wanted to be having lunch with her right now. "Thanks Paul, it's in the trunk." I wanted to be anywhere but here. "Is breakfast still out?" Maybe I should just forget my work ethics and leave.

"Yeah, and it's a real treat today." Paul rolled his eyes, "P.T. sprang for enough Egg McMuffins for everybody." Paul popped my trunk open. "We don't have to share today."

"What about hash-browns?" Maybe that grease would comfort me.

"Yeah right! Dream on Christy." Paul threw my bag over his shoulder and went inside.

I stood on the street high in the Hollywood Hills over looking Sunset Blvd., and knew I would never last the following two months to fulfill my two-year contract. I tried to focus on lasting for the next six hours. How bad could it be? I would just go on automatic pilot. My sex scene today was a four-way with two other girls and Mike Horner. With so many people involved, I would just try and gets lost under a limb. Maybe I could stake out a chair in the corner and just masturbate. P.T. never wasted much footage on one of my sex scenes since I bored him silly. The new Vivid contract girls had to endure hours in a sex scene if P.T. fancied them. Mine were shot and in the can within a thirty minute time frame. P.T. told me the viewer preferred teasing and a lot of "T and A" over the hard-core stuff. I couldn't disagree more with him, but who was I to argue with the man. I even tried to get the scenes down to fifteen minutes, changing positions in record time, but he said we needed at least thirty minutes of footage. He seemed just as disappointed as I was.

"Christy," Paul yelled from the front door, " you better hurry up if you're hungry. Tom Byron is eyeing the last McMuffin."

I locked my car. "I'm coming!"

"You will be in about one hour!" Paul laughed at his own joke and I looked at my car for a fast escape.

While in hair and make-up, P.T. came in to tell me that Peter North couldn't make it tomorrow and that my sex scene was going to be with a new guy named Larry White. "You'll love him. He's a really great guy who's married to Crystal, the girl you're having sex with today."

My heart sank. At least I knew Peter and felt comfortable with him. "Well, what does Larry look like?" Maybe I could handle change even in my fragile state. "Is he here?" If I could just finish this movie, I would be home free. I could tell Steve this was my last and at least I would have completed this part of my career with a clear conscience.

"Sure, he's just getting a copy of the script and then I'll bring him in." P.T. smiled at me and I could see traces of an Egg McMuffin jammed between his teeth and gums. "We're lucky he dropped Crystal off right after Peter called." He got a far away look in his eyes and I knew he was going to get philosophical on me. "It's funny how things work out in the world."

"P.T.?" A male's voice broke in. "I would like to meet my co-star."

Kent, the make-up artist was in the middle of gluing on my fake lashes. "Don't open your eyes yet."

I stuck out my hand blindly, "Nice to meet you Larry." Maybe he was cute, after all, his wife was adorable.

"You too Ms. Canyon."

The hair stood up on my neck. I hated being called Ms., it made me sound so old and superior.

"I've been watching your films since I was in high school. I use to steal them from my father's collection."

Eyelash glue or not, my eyes flew open. "How old are you?" I took one look at him, and wished Kent would glue my eyes shut forever.

"Twenty-two." He smiled and I felt my McMuffin rise.

"I'm only twenty-six." I wouldn't fuck this guy on my drunkest night. "You make me sound so old by saying that."

"I'm sorry Ms. Canyon, I wasn't trying to insinuate anything, I'm just such a fan of yours and I can't believe I get to work with you tomorrow."

Good, don't believe it, because no way in hell are you touching me. "Right," was all I could say. Think Christy, think. Get out of this mess. Larry seemed like a nice enough guy, it's just, well, he wasn't my type. He must have weighed 98 pounds soaking wet. One wrap of my Armenian legs around him and I think his back would snap in two. And those red pimples covering his face were making me ill.

Kent saved the moment. "I have to finish you Christy. They need you on the set in ten minutes and your eyelashes are on your cheeks."

Larry backed out of the room. "I'll see you on the set Christy."

I bolted up, "What do you mean Larry? Are you also in this scene?"

He smiled from the doorway, "No, but I want to see you live." He blushed, "My wife gets you today and I get you tomorrow, how much better does life get?"

It's got to be better than this bleak reality. "Not much!" Maybe death.

Twenty minutes later, I stood in the middle of the living room with my three co-stars, while P.T. gave us a breakdown. "Christy and Crystal should be together on the staircase." P.T. gave Crystal a good leer and I knew he had a crush on her. Shit, that meant a long scene.

"You don't think one of us should play with herself in that chair over there?" I asked with high hopes of being the chosen one.

P.T. looked around the room. "What chair?"

"Over there." I pointed to the far left corner.

"That's in the other room, it wont even be in the shot."

"Well, do you want me there?"

P.T. looked like he needed a strong hit of pot. "The staircase will be fine."

I looked at the maroon jumpsuit I was wearing and knew I would never wear it again. "Okay." I could still run. "Staircase." My eyes were glued to the front door.

"Uh, Christy, the staircase is directly behind you." P.T. said.

"Sure." I turned around and saw Larry crouched behind a coffee table for prime spot viewing smiling from ear to ear. "Stairs." I began walking towards them, each step feeling like one of those dreams where your feet move but you don't feel like you're going anywhere. Unfortunately, I was moving. I was at the staircase, one foot from the pip-squeak Larry who was giving me the thumbs up. Ugh!

P.T. whispered to the cameraman and everything felt serene. I leaned against the rail while Crystal tried to strike up a conversation with me. I heard her whisper something about her husband watching my film "W-Pink" when he was in high school. I could have smacked her, but I felt too disconnected from everything. My mind and body felt like they were floating above this scene and I was watching everything from above. Why was I here?

"ACTION!" P.T. yelled.

I snapped back into reality and tried to remember my dialogue. Crystal just asked me something and I realized I never once bothered to read the script so I just changed the subject. "I love your outfit." I smiled at her confused pixie face. "Where did you get it?"

She looked around the room for P.T. who was nowhere to be found and stammered, "At Sears."

Did those stores still exist? "Really, I didn't see that last time I was there." Which was about twenty-two years ago when I broke the iron and had to buy a new one with my allowance "Well, let's get you out of that sexy outfit." What the fuck, let's get this over with.

Crystal smiled and undressed. "What about your outfit?" She teased.

290

"Oh, I got this at Betsy Johnson last week." I touched the velvet fabric and marveled at the deal I got on it. I was about to tell her it was on sale when I saw the confused look on her face.

"I meant, shouldn't you get naked also?"

I stared at her naked body and felt protective over my body. "Oh sure." I no longer wanted to share it with her. "Take it off for me." Or anybody.

Crystal tugged at the fabric unable to figure out how my outfit came off. She started on my left shoulder, which I raised an inch to make it hard on her. "Help me out here." She whispered with a smile plastered on her face for the camera that began zooming in on us.

"Fine." I stared at her face and body and thought about how she reminded me of a blow up doll. "Touch me." I slid her hand over my breasts, savoring the time before I had to take off my bra and panties. "Right there." Her face was blank, like one of the dolls that are boxed up, sitting on a shelf waiting to be blown up. "Mmmmm." Blank and stupid looking.

"Ooh, you feel so nice." She cooed for the camera. How would she know what I felt like? Her hand was on the silk fabric, not my skin. "I love your tits." She said while trying to free one and put her mouth on it. I turned my face around, so I didn't have to watch, and ended up eyeball to eyeball with Larry who looked like he was about to spank the monkey. Looking at her was the better of the two, which wasn't saying much, so I closed my eyes and said, "That feels nice."

"What does?" She was a foot away from me, picking out which dildo she was going to use on me.

I looked over the railing and saw Mike Horner going in for the first position with Nikki Dial. "Don't use any lube on that thing." Maybe when it was his turn to do me, it would be near the end of the scene and five minutes of footage would be enough.

"No lube at all?" She giggled. "Are you *that* turned on?"

I unhooked my bra and let it slide to the ground. "No, they give me a yeast infection." I slid out of my undies and chucked them across the room. "Come on, let's get this over with."

I felt the tip slide inside of me and said, "Okay, it's your turn."

"But,"

"Bend over for me." I pulled her hair to let her know who was in charge here. She positioned her little ass at me and in it went. I began sliding it in and out of her, looking around the room for P.T. He was nowhere to be seen and the camera was still on the couch. I saw Crystal bent over the rail with the dildo inside of her and felt bad. I really shattered her illusions of working with the great legend, me, Christy Canyon. I let go of her hair and began kissing her neck. "Does this feel okay?" It wasn't her fault I checked out mentally from making films the one time she got to work with me. I could see the camera from my peripheral vision panning over to us. "The camera is on us." I whispered in her ear.

She started moving her hips back and forth. "That feels so great in my pussy." She said loud enough for the mic to pick up on.

I smiled fighting back tears. "Good." What was wrong with me? I thought of a joke my mom told me yesterday and began to giggle. "Turn around for me." I looked at her face and began to laugh while fucking her with the dildo.

She kept a plastered smile on her face and asked, "What's so funny?"

"Just a joke I heard yesterday." Poor thing thought I was laughing at her. "I'll tell you later." I think I was on the verge of hysteria. If I didn't laugh, I would cry.

"Stop laughing God Damn it." P.T. hissed which only made me laugh harder.

"Sorry." I buried my face in Crystal's hair and smelled Herbal Essence shampoo. "I'm so sorry Crystal, let me just laugh in your hair." I whispered. "I don't know what's gotten into me." But I did know. I had finished this chapter of my life.

"Switch positions everybody." P.T. said. "Christy, you on the couch with Mike."

That was all it was, one door closing. I straddled Mike and thought about my future. I loved Vivid, I loved the owner and I loved making films prior to today. Mike bent me over the couch and I let a few moans escape. I had to quit while I was ahead. I had always preserved my sanity because I knew my limits in this business. I never did anything I felt uncomfortable with and now I recognized that I had reached my breaking point. If I didn't listen to my inner guidance system, all hell would break loose. "I'm going to come." I panted at the microphone above me. Steve wouldn't care, for every Vivid girl who quit, ten more were waiting to sign along the dotted line.

"Me too." Mike said and pulled out of me.

I turned my head away from Mike and looked at the front door while he came all over me.

P.T. looked at his shooting board. "You're done for the day Christy. Be here by eight-thirty in the morning. Tomorrow you have two sex scenes."

"Great. I'll see you in the a.m." Of what year, I didn't know.

I grabbed my wardrobe and got in my car. I turned the car on and took one last look at the house. Paul was standing outside smoking a cigarette, talking to Rocco. I think I was supposed to have sex with him tomorrow. I put my car in first gear and lowered the emergency break.

"Christy, beautiful Christy." Rocco was waving at me and walking over to my car. "I can't believe after all this time we finally get to work together tomorrow."

"It's been a couple years since that magazine we did together."

Rocco looked at me and I realized he didn't know what I was talking about.

"See you Rocco." Just not tomorrow. I waved and pulled away. I held it together and called Wanda when I got to the bottom of the hill.

"Hello."

"Wanda." I started to cry.

"Christy? What's wrong?"

"Can I come over?"

"Of course, are you okay."

"Yeah, but I don't want to make movies anymore." I talked to Wanda on my car phone, the big clunky kind from the early nineties, for the ten minute drive. "I'm outside, I'll be right up." I replaced the phone in the cradle and headed to her unit, feeling better already.

Wanda opened the door and gave me a big hug. "It's only normal that you would outgrow that stage in your life."

"It is?"

"Of course. You don't want to make films forever. You grow up and move on. That's natural and healthy. It would be unhealthy *not* to want to move on in life."

I was healthy and normal. "Can I call Steve from here?" Oh great, how do I tell Steve that now that I'm normal and healthy, I can't finish a movie?

"Of course." Wanda handed me a glass of iced-tea.

"What should I tell him?" I looked in my phone book and got his home number. "Hey, will you call him for me? I'll take you out for Sushi dinner if you tell him I quit."

"No I won't call him. Part of growing up is taking responsibility for yourself."

I punched in his number. "Really?"

"Hello." Steve answered.

"Steve." My voice squeaked. I felt bad that I was about to screw up his movie. "It's Christy."

"What's wrong?"

"I can't finish the movie. I just can't do it anymore." I thought about my nearly two years with Vivid and felt a loss. I wasn't able to make movies anymore, yet I felt sadness that a part of my life had ended today. I just couldn't do it anymore.

Wanda held my hand.

293

"Are you okay? Did something happen to you today on the set?" Steve asked.

"No. Everybody was great, my head just isn't into it anymore."

"Christy, you never have to do anything in life you don't want to do, especially making a film."

"You're not mad at me? I shot one scene, but I just can't go back tomorrow and finish. I'll pay you for anything you're going to lose today because of my quitting."

"Don't be absurd. What did you do today?" His wheels were turning.

"A sex scene for the end of the film."

"Perfect. Now, instead of starring Christy Canyon, we'll print on the box, featuring Christy Canyon."

He always had an answer. "You are so nice."

"Come by next week and if you still want to do personal appearances, I'll keep you busy with those."

"I would love to do those. I just don't want to have sex on camera again." The thought of sex on a set made me cry again. "I love you so much. Steve." It was the end of my two-year contract with Vivid.

"Above all else Christy, you're my friend."

"For life." I hung up and Wanda hugged me.

"See Christy, everything works out."

"I'll still buy you a Sushi dinner. I'm starving."

The following four months were spent with my mom, sister and traveling out of town once a month.

I loved my life and I loved being with my mom and Clair. We were unbreakable now. During the time my mom and I were apart, we just became stronger as people. I had to look at it that way and never be angry at one choice I made and knowing me, will make. Life is just a constant change I thought. With every step I took, with every opportunity I chose or declined, it was all just a part of life. I took and learned from everything I did and never resented one day.

I was in Boston getting ready to sign autographs for the night when my mom called. "Honey, I found the perfect house for you to buy."

I had been looking for a few weeks, finding nothing. "Where?"

"Four houses away from me and it's adorable inside. I heard through the neighborhood grapevine that it will be going on the market Sunday."

Today was Wednesday. "I wont be home until Monday morning."

"I know you're going to love it. It needs a little work but if you can get it before it hits the market, you can save on the agents fee."

"Really?" I hadn't lived in a house since I moved out at seventeen. "How do you know?" I had outgrown my condo six months ago.

"Well, I spoke to the owner and she said if you want it before it's listed, she'll deduct the agent's fee from the selling price."

"How much does she want for it?"

My mom told me the price and I did a quick calculation in my head of what my payments would be. "Do you think I can sell my condo soon?"

"Of course, it's such a cute place, but I want you by me."

I didn't want it to be any other way either. "Tell her I'll take it."

"Oh, you're going to love it honey, trust me."

And I did trust her. "I'll sign the paper work Monday evening."

Monday evening I was the proud owner of a new house that needed to be updated into the nineties. The "Brady Bunch" look had to go.

Clair, Mom and I walked through the empty rooms. "It's all just cosmetic stuff honey, any handyman can fix this up."

A handyman with a bulldozer I thought. "It's going to be perfect." And I knew it would be. I was right by my momma.

The following week I found a contractor. "Well," Bob surveyed the job. "It's going to take me about six months to complete this, but when I'm done with it, you're going to have one sharp house." He smiled and I thought about how cute he was in those work boots and tool belt. "I'm going to write you up an itemized proposal and then give me a call when you get it and look it over." He smiled again and threw a wink in as well.

Sixty days later, with the house deed in my hand, I hired Bob to remodel my house.

As Steve promised, he kept me busy with personal appearances every two weeks. I still had five unreleased movies in the can, which Vivid decided to spread out over the next year.

At signings, fans would ask me what my latest movie was.

"Have you seen this one?" I would hold up whichever video was closest to me.

The fan would crease his brow and take a good long look at the box cover. "This one here your latest?" He would ask reaching for his money.

I would look at the box cover from "A Portrait of Christy". "Have you seen it?"

"No."

"Then it's new!" Even if it was shot two years ago, it would be new to him. "Do you want me to sign it for you?"

"I would be honored. Make it out to Joey."

In between my signings when I was at home, I would pick out new toilets, sinks, alarm systems and appliances for my house.

"Construction is going a little slower than I thought." Bob informed me three months into the project.

"How much slower?" I thought about the two mortgages I was paying every month.

"Well, when we tore down a bedroom wall, I noticed you had rag-style wiring, so I decided to update it. You don't want your house to burn down on you girl." He pointed to the bathroom wall. "That there was old school wiring."

"Oh." I tried to remember if I approved that. "Did you send me a proposal on that?"

"Naw, I did it for nothing."

He was so cute. "Thanks." I wondered why he never asked me out.

"No problem, but it's the little extras like that that are putting me behind about a month."

I wondered what else he had done without telling me or charging me. "Don't worry about it." I wondered if he knew who I was.

He smiled. "Oh but it's going to cost you."

I froze. "Really?" What did this creep have in mind? "What do you mean?" Suddenly I went on defense. Maybe he knew who I was and thought I was loose or something.

"Well," He leaned against my new shower door. "I wouldn't mind a lunch at my favorite restaurant."

I relaxed and smiled. "You've got it." He was just one of those nice guys that finally found a way to ask me out. "So tell me, what's your favorite restaurant?"

"Micky-D's suits me just fine."

"Where's that?"

Bob looked at me like I was from another planet. "Golden arches, McDonalds. Come on girl, don't tell me you don't know what Micky-D's is." He rubbed his fingerprints off the shower door with his Bud Light T-shirt.

"McDonalds? I'll take you anywhere though." With McDonalds being his favorite, I felt safe saying that. "What about Spago or Tony Roma's?" I could just see Bob with a full size slab of ribs and a baked potato with all the trimmings in front of him.

Now it was his turn to look confused.

"I'll pick out a place and surprise you when I get home from San Diego next week."

"Boy, you sure do travel a lot." He adjusted a towel rack he had just installed. "What do you do?"

And there was my answer. "I sell computer parts." Bob had no idea who I was.

Four days later, I checked into the Hyatt Hotel in the heart of San Diego. I was going to sign at the convention center the following day promoting a new line of snow boards and a poorly made but somewhat sporty looking clothing line that went with it. It was nice to be promoting myself on a poster and a glossy 8x10 in clothing for a change, yet a part of me felt awkward signing at a non-porno show. Would my fans be there or just young surf and athletic types that didn't know me from other 80's icons like Cindi Lauper or The Go-Go's? When I signed at a show or a bookstore, I always felt I was in charge. Everybody that went to see me at a signing was there for me, even those stray guys who pretended to be looking at the wall of dildos in the back. But I didn't know what was in store for me tomorrow.

Why did I get the feeling I was going to feel like a baby-huey?

The owner of the snowboard company knocked on my door. "Christy, it's me. Lon."

Lon was a nice enough guy. "Come in." Just drunk as a skunk all the time. "Are those the posters I'll be signing?" I couldn't wait to see the final product. We shot this ad campaign six months ago, giving Lon more than enough time to pull it together for the unveiling of his boards at this convention.

"Simmer down now. All in good time." He giggled

His good time was just about up.

"Are you hungry?" He asked.

I smiled. "No. I'm pretty spent from the plane ride." I couldn't wait to see what room service had to offer.

Lon looked up to the ceiling and squinted his eyes. I never knew what this man was thinking or what would come out of his mouth. "It's only about a thirty minute flight I thought."

With the strong tail winds we had, it took twelve and a half minutes. "It was something like that but I get jet lag easily." Lon always seemed to be working at half speed. "I'll help you unroll these."

Lon waved me away. "I can do it."

Lon unrolled the stack of posters and held down two opposite corners. The two corners that he wasn't holding down rolled inward, giving me a fine view of my naval.

I looked around the room and saw a crystal ashtray and vase. I grabbed both pieces of crystal. "Let me put these on the other two corners." I took a look at my bellybutton on the poster and wondered if I should get it pierced.

I placed the crystal pieces in two corners while Lon held the other two down. "It's so," I took a step back and squinted my eyes. "It's so beautiful, but I think it's a little fuzzy." I did a quick calculation in my head of how much these would fetch in the fan club. Fuzzy or not, it was marketable.

"Well, my friend who took the photos that day had the wrong type of film. It came out perfectly for the 8x10's, but when we blew it up, you got a little distorted."

I took a good look at my eyes on the poster and wondered if they were really that close in real life. "I thought he was a photographer."

Lon reached for his flask again and my poster image vanished. "Well." He tipped his head back and I could see his Adam's apple bobbing with each gulp. "He was in the early to mid seventies." He plugged the flask and put it back in his pocket. For now. "He took some photos at several Grateful Dead concerts and one of those hippie Woodstem things."

"Do you mean Woodstock?" Somehow I could never see Lon's blue blood at a Woodstock event wearing moccasins and passing a doobie around.

Lon scowled, "Whatever those hippie gathering places are called. All of that free love and shit." Lon began laughing. "Mike and I had some good times back then." He shook his head from side to side smiling at some foggy memory from several decades ago. "Then he grew up on me and got a real job as an attorney." Lon wasn't smiling anymore. "But he still likes to fuck around with his camera every so often." Lon had his hands on the back of the oak desk chair, his knuckles stark white. "He ended up getting married and popping out a few kids."

Who cared? This whole scene reminded me of some off beat David Lynch movie. "Oh well, the posters look fine."

Lon snapped back to the present decade. "They're fine."

I just wanted him out of my room before he started balling about something that took place when I was about two years old. "Well, what time do we work tomorrow?"

Lon shook his watch from side to side several times before looking at it. "Ten. I'll pick you up at nine forty five."

I eyed the mini bar basket overflowing with sweets and nuts. "See ya later." I opened the door. "Bye."

He chuckled and started to say something but I shut the door in his face. My stomach was grumbling.

I slid the chain in place and wondered how people like him survived this crazy world.

I pulled out the pack of Famous Amos chocolate chip cookies and a jar of macadamia nuts from the basket. I sat on my king-sized bed, turned the television on and called room service.

One hour later, after a picnic on my bed, I fell asleep watching Jay Leno.

I heard the phone ringing in my dream. The shrill noise wouldn't go away and it was interrupting my, much needed, beauty sleep. I rolled over and saw the red neon numbers. It was Seven-ten. I was due another twenty-five minutes of sleep and somebody was going to pay dearly for this. Most likely Lon. My voice ready to scream, I answered, "Hello."

"Honey?"

I sat up in bed. "Momma?"

"I'm on too." Clair said. "We're on three way."

The hairs on the back of my neck stood up. "Hi you guys." As much as they loved and missed me, I knew this wasn't a social call at this ungodly hour. "What's going on?"

Mom started. "We hate to call you this early when you're away at work."

Oh God, did my new house burn down? I tried to think of what sort of coverage that mile a minute talking insurance salesman wrangled me into. "No, my alarm was going to go off in a few minutes anyway." I closed my eyes and prayed that my animals were okay. "Is everything fine at home?" Maybe that old goat Marv finally keeled over. And where was room service with my pot of coffee? Then I remembered I ordered it to be delivered at seven thirty five.

"He's going to be fine." Clair sniffled a little.

Oh God, my heart stopped. My sweet baby boy Roscoe was hurt. I had just adopted him from the pound six months before. I took a deep breath and felt tears rolling down my face. The thought of that beautiful brindle dog in pain was too much for me to imagine. "What happened?" I was crying into the phone by now. "Is he going to be okay?"

"Honey," Mom said, "He's going to be fine. He just gave us all a good scare last night."

The sign above his cage said he was a Lab mix, but as he grew over the months, his head squared off and his brown eyes took on the shape of slivered almonds. "Tell me what happened you guys. I have to know." And I ended up with a beautiful Pit bull that would protect me with his life. "I can be home in two hours." He was the best damn dog I had ever had.

"He's going to be fine, he's in the recovery ward and keeps saying over and over that he has to see you." Mom said.

My hand stopped reaching for the Kleenex half way. Roscoe can't talk.

Clair took over now. "The doctor said he had a heart attack." She started crying again which made me cry even more. I just didn't know whom we were crying about.

"You guys, who had a heart attack?" God I was so confused and desperately needed the pot of caffeine.

"Daddy!" Clair said. "Dad had a heart attack yesterday right in front of me. He kept telling me that his left arm was numb and I thought he was lying just to get a shoulder massage out of me. But then he grabbed his heart." Clair couldn't talk anymore and I couldn't see straight.

My father died. Almost. When was the last time I spoke to him? He nearly died last night and I couldn't even remember why we stopped talking. He was mad at me about quitting his office and going back into the adult business.

"Christy? Are you there?"

Was that Mom or Clair's voice? "I have to pack up the car." The last time I spoke to him was nearly three years ago.

"I have to come home right now." But I didn't have a car to pack up. "I have to call the airlines and change my flight or rent a car or something." I always fancied myself a cool, even headed person under pressure. Not now. "What should I do?" The walls of my suite were closing in on me and I heard a pounding noise in my ears.

"Oh honey, we hate to tell you this over the phone, but we thought you had to know."

"Momma, my head hurts, it's pounding."

"Room service." Somebody screamed.

Coffee. "Hold on, I have to get the door." I ran to the door, flung it open and took a nosedive back to the phone sitting on the bed. "Sorry about that you guys."

"I've been knocking on your door for five minutes." The silly looking man in a maroon polyester monkey suit informed me. "I almost left."

As if this was my fucking problem. "I think the planes take off every hour from here." I moved my hand in the air, indicating that I wanted to sign the check.

"Don't come home yet. His doctor said he'll be in recovery and pretty doped up for the next few days. There is nothing you can do except work and keep busy. Believe me, if he wasn't going to pull through I would let you know."

The waiter slid the brown padded checkbook in front of me. "If you can just fill it out and sign the bottom for me please." He smiled and his silver tooth in front made me sad, so I added an extra five bucks of gratuity, on top of the eighteen percent the hotel already calculated into the total.

His worn out brown eyes became as large as my coffee cup saucer. "Oh thank you Miss."

I waved goodbye and thought about how Lon's five bucks made somebody so happy.

"I don't know if I can get through today." I poured a cup of coffee and added tons of cream. "What if he doesn't make it?" And then something my mom, or was it Clair said, hit me. "Was he really asking for me?"

The thought of my father asking for me after his operation made me cry all over again causing the hot coffee to bubble up in my throat and burn like hell going back down. "I miss him so much!" I sobbed. "Is he really going to live?" Why had I let so many years go by? Pride, defiance, and bullheaded came to mind, but being a stubborn mule stood out the most.

"Of course he'll pull through." Mom's voice soothed Clair and me who were crying in unison. "This is just going to have to be a wake up call for him. His doctor said he will need to drop eighty pounds, start exercising, start eating healthy and lower his stress level. Come on girls, you know your dad is as strong as a bull."

And built like one too I thought. "Can I have his number and call him at the hospital?"

Mom gave me his number. "He'll be sleeping now, so try him later this afternoon and if he's awake, the nurse will put you through."

"Mom and I are going to be there at five today, so if you can, call around then."

Memories of my father filled every cell in my brain. "Can we see him tomorrow when I get home?" Even the not so great memories, which didn't seem so bad now. "I miss him so much." It didn't matter anymore what type of a father he had been growing up. The past was the past and I chose to live in the present. He loved me and did the best he could in life. He just didn't know any other way of being a parent and that was fine with me. He loved me and I loved him. He never beat us or sexually abused us.

"Of course we can. What time does your plane land?" Mom asked.

He just forgot about us once and a while. "I'm supposed to land at noon but I'm going to see if we can get on an earlier flight." Everyone has a story. Some children may have had it easier growing up than I did, but I knew a lot more must have had it a lot worse. "I love you two so much and I'll call you with my new flight information." I wanted to see my father as soon as possible.

I hung up the phone and poured another cup of coffee. I sat in bed staring at the television, which was turned off. Lon would be here in two hours. Now what? How could I smile and sign for three hours without talking to my father first. I got out of bed and turned the shower on. Because I had to get through the day, the show must go on.

I put my make up on and stared at the phone. It was nine thirty. I put on the shorts and T-shirt Lon gave me with his company logo on the front. Nine forty. I picked up the phone and called Lon's room. "I hope you don't mind, but I'm running fifteen minutes late. I'll sign fifteen minutes later than I'm scheduled to make up for it."

"What's the problem?"

You have no idea. "Girlie things." Who's going to be dumb enough to argue with that?

"I'll see you then." Lon hung up.

Not even Lon is that dumb. "Thanks so much."

I hung up and stared at the number my mom gave me. What do I say to a father I haven't spoken to in so long? I picked up the receiver and punched in the number. Should I tell him I quit the adult business and became a secretary somewhere?

"How may I direct your call?"

No. I wasn't going to lie to my dad. He would just have to accept me once and for all for who I was whether he liked it or not. "Yes, room 402 please." After all, I accepted him for who he was. My father.

"Please hold."

I listened to an instrumental version of an old Kenny Loggins' song and wondered how many extensions I would have to go through to get my father. If I even got him. It was only nine fifty, hours away from when I was supposed to call, but I had to try. I had to hear my father's voice.

A female voice answered. "Room 402."

My heart stopped and I could feel the palms of my hands sweating. "Uh yes, my name is Christy and I would like to speak to my father." Was that one of his girlfriends who answered? I wondered how many girlfriends he had.

"Oh Christy, I've heard so much about you. He's awake but groggy from all the medication."

I didn't want to know what she had heard about me. I just wanted to scream at her to put my father on. "May I speak to him?"

"Well, he's not coherent, but I'll see if he's awake enough to say hello."

Speed it up who ever you are. "Thank you."

I could hear her voice speaking to my father and I was envious she was with him and I wasn't. "Your daughter is on the phone."

"Huh? Who?" I heard his voice in the background and I felt tears in my eyes.

"It's your daughter Christy."

It sounded like the phone dropped, but then I heard his beautiful voice. "Monkey? Is that you?" Dad's voice sounded weak, yet it sounded like a mega-phone had just gone off in my brain. I was talking to my dad.

"It's me Daddy. I love you so much and I'm so sorry I'm not with you right now." I began crying. Crying for the years that we lost, crying for the years ahead that I would never let slip away again. "I miss you Daddy."

"I miss you too baby and I love you." He was fading in and out.

"I'm going to see you tomorrow." And every day for the rest of my life I thought.

"What time will you be here?" He whispered.

"I'll be there at noon, just in time for lunch."

"Honey? Do you know a girl by the name of Nina Hartley?"

Doped up or not, where did that come from? "Yes." I hesitated. "I know her." Very intimately actually.

302

"Is she a nice girl?"

"She's very nice."

"She has the nicest hind quarters I've ever seen."

Maybe he was hallucinating from the medication and thinking about a racehorse he once owned.

"I would like to meet her one day."

"Who, Nina?" Could he have known her for something other than a porn video?

"Yes, but Daddy's tired now."

As if I would send her right over. "Dad?"

"Huh?" He was fading fast now.

"Don't ever scare us like this again." I blew my nose in a tissue.

"I'm proud of you Christy. You're a leader and a survivor in this world."

My heart soared. "You made me who I am and I love you Daddy."

But all I heard was a deep inhale followed by a snore.

I was going home to my family.

Epilogue

Six months later…

"Hey Steve, I wanted to ask you something."

"Sure, what's going on?" He put his slinky down.

"How do the Vivid girls like dancing at the strip clubs?"

"I thought you said you would never do that?"

"You don't think I should dance?" His word and opinions meant everything to me.

"No, I'm not saying that. The girls love touring and they make a fortune. It's just you've always been so adamant about not stripping." Steve looked at me and cocked his head. "Are you okay financially? Do you need an advance on royalties?"

"No, no, not at all. It's just that after moving and buying furniture and all that stuff," I thought of the two new Gucci purses as well. "I dipped below my safety line in my savings account." There was also that stunning new diamond bracelet I just had to treat myself to last week. Oh, and that new set of French luggage. "So I was thinking that if I just danced for a week I'd be back up to where I felt safe."

"Well, if you're really interested, try it for a week. In fact," Steve began flipping through his Rolodex, "Let's call the agent right now. His name's Dave and all of the Vivid girls go through him. He's really honest from what they say." Steve punched in the Canadian phone number. "Dave, Steve here. Christy Canyon is in my office and she wanted to ask you about booking a gig. No, I'm not joking, let me put her on speaker." Steve pushed the speaker button and wrote something down on a piece of paper.

"Christy? Is that really you?" A man's voice boomed through the speaker.

"Uh-huh." I read Steve's note that he passed to me. "I think I want to dance for a week." I looked at Steve and gave him the okay sign.

"You have no idea how many clubs have been requesting you."

"Really?" They actually asked for me?

Steve crossed off the first figure he wrote down and wrote in a new dollar amount along with two airline tickets.

"Oh yeah, at least three clubs a day." Dave said.

Steve added two rooms on my list to tell Dave.

Suddenly, I was excited to try out this dancing thing. "So when do you think I can get a booking." Who should I bring as my bodyguard?

"Well, lets get some things figured out." I could hear papers shuffling over the speaker. "Okay, for starters, what do you want to ask for the

304

week? Let me back up here a minute. A week of dancing consists of six days, four shows a day. Normally, you have one afternoon show, and three at night."

"I talked to Amber Lynn and she kind of explained things to me."

"Amber?" His once happy voice became somber. "That woman has made me go bald." There was an uncomfortable silence on the phone 'til Steve broke in. "I want Christy at your best club."

"Of course Steve, of course." More papers were shuffled around on his end. "I have the perfect club to put you in at. The owner called yesterday begging me to find you."

The thought of traveling excited me. "Where is his club?" I had visions of Boston, New York or even Hawaii!

"It's in a town called Reading, Pennsylvania."

I looked at Steve and cocked my head; Steve just shrugged.

The Statue of Liberty flew out the window along with the white sandy beaches of Hawaii. "Where's that?"

"A few hours outside Pittsburgh."

"Oh." I so wanted to see the Windy City again.

Sensing my disappointment, Dave continued talking faster. "I sent Hyapatia Lee, Barbara Dare and Nina Hartley in the past two months. All three of them said they made a fortune there. They needed a brinks truck for all the money they made." He laughed at his own joke.

Money? And tons of it? My eyes lit up. "I'll try it."

Dave breathed a sigh of relief. "Now, the other Vivid girls get a fee per week in the ballpark of five thousand, plus one ticket and one room."

I looked at Steve and froze.

Steve shook his head no and pointed to his notes.

"That's great." For them I thought.

"Okay, so I'll put you down for the same."

"But I want ten thousand a week, two tickets and two rooms."

There was silence on Dave's end.

"You know Dave, I spoke to Ginger Lynn about this too, and she said she goes through a guy named Adam. Do you two work together?" I knew they didn't, but no way was I worth less than Ginger or Amber. "Ginger said..."

Dave interrupted me. "It doesn't matter what Ginger said. I shouldn't have any problem getting you that rate." Dave sounded depleted now. "Why don't you send me some promo and give me a number where I can call you later."

I gave him my home number. "I go to college every Monday and Tuesday but I have a quarter break in two weeks. So maybe book that week for me and then if I like it, I'll go out for four days only."

"Oh, okay, but if you go out for four days, you realize that your fee will be pro-rated."

"That's okay, school is my priority."

"Good for you, what are you taking?"

He sounded genuinely interested, but I was already bored with this conversation. I wanted him to hang up and get me a booking. "Marketing." Plus, I had to figure out whom I was going to bring with me.

"Oh marketing is a good thing to know."

"Okay, call me when you have it booked. Bye."

Steve hit the off button while Dave was saying something. "Do you have costumes Christy?"

"What?"

"Costumes to dance in. The girls all have extensive costumes that they strip out of."

I remembered Amber showing me her costumes once; A plethora of gowns in sequins, feathers and rhinestone. She said each costume cost several thousand dollars. I thought about what I had tucked away in my closets. An old prom dress, a dress I wore to a movie premier seven years ago and a lace skirt and top I use to wear when my roommate Kari and I went out to clubs in Hollywood. "Yeah, I got plenty of stuff." Shit was more like it. My goal was to save as much money as I could. I may end up detesting stripping after one week, and then it would just be a waste of good money.

"Keep me posted." Steve began working again. His mission was accomplished.

"Thanks Steve." Steve was more than just an employer to the Vivid girls. He was a father, brother, banker, trouble-shooter, therapist and the list goes on.

"Anytime."

And I knew he meant it.

I got home an hour later and my message light was blinking. "Christy, Dave here. I have you scheduled at Al's Diamond Cabaret in two weeks. Call me when you get home so I can give you all the details."

I froze. Dave got me a job so fast. Did I really want to strip? I looked around at my beautiful house and thought about my paycheck for a week of dancing. But I couldn't dance; I would look like a fool. I didn't have one ounce of rhythm in my blood. I hit the play button again, maybe I heard him wrong. Dave's voice came through loud and clear, especially the part where he said Big Al agreed to pay me ten thousand dollars for six days of work. I saw the bank balance on my latest savings account statement. Did the fans care if I knew how to dance? Somehow, I knew that they didn't really care how I slithered and shimmied out of my clothing. I recalled what Amber said at dinner last week. "They just want to see tits and pussy." Speaking of clothing, I ran to my room to see if I had donated my old prom dress to Goodwill yet. I found it shoved in the back of my closet along with the coral blue and black gown I wore to Ginger's movie premier in 1985. Scouring my shelves, I finally found the lace skirt and top behind a pile of sweaters.

I laid out the three dance costumes on my bed. That should be enough for twenty-four shows. I peeled the plastic dry cleaning bag off of my prom dress and a portion of the fabric came off with it. Oh well, those clubs were dark weren't they? I sat on the edge of my bed and realized I had never even been to a strip club before.

Shoes - I guess girls dance in high heels. I put on a pair of four-inch pumps and danced around my bed. Walking in these shoes was one thing, but dancing in them? I held onto the brass footboard of my bed for dear life as I felt my ankles give. I eyed a sensible pair of two-inch pumps in my closet. Perfect.

My doorbell startled me. I looked at the clock, right on time as always.

I opened my door and let my personal trainer in. "Hey Joe, come in." I closed the door and a light bulb turned on in my brain. "How would you like to go on the road with me? I need a bodyguard."

He shrugged his shoulders. "Sure, why not."

I told him how much I could pay him. "Now it's at a strip club you know." He did a very rare thing. Joe smiled. "When do we leave?"

"In two weeks."

Since you can't get enough of me, use this form to reorder another copy of "Lights, Camera, Sex!"

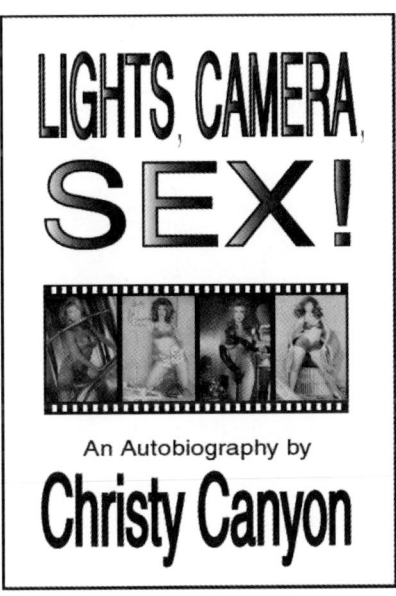

Make check payable to: Christy Canyon
13547 Ventura Blvd. #218
Sherman Oaks, CA 91423

I WOULD LIKE TO ORDER_____BOOK(S).

NAME_____

ADDRESS_____

CITY,STATE,ZIP_____

$19.95 US ($22.95 CANADA) ($26.95 EUROPE/JAPAN)
California Residents add 8.25% Sales Tax

ALL ORDERS WITH THIS COUPON WILL RECEIVE FREE SHIPPING
AND HANDLING.

If you're interested in—and I know you are—helping my favorite charity, here's your chance

This wonderful foundation rescues any and every animal. If you can find it in your heart and checkbook, please send any donation to:

Villalobos Rescue Center
P.O. Box 1544
Canyon Country, CA 91386

Make checks payable to: Villalobos Rescue Center.

Villalobos has been written about in the Los Angeles Times as the leading rescue center. They have also been praised by LA County Animal Shelters for their ability to rescue, train and adopt out hard to place animals.

Don't forget to spay and neuter your pets and always adopt from your local shelter.

violated/abused "It's only a"
LOOP

By november I had been
shooting for two months. Had
posed for every mens magazine:
Penthouse, Hustler, High Society
and every other newspaper
stand and monthly
subscription available! my life
was wonderful. Thru modeling
I found my courage, strength,
self confidence and independence
again. My bills were paid, and
a car
that started every morning and
several thousand dollars in
my bank account. I felt
safe and secure for the first
time in over a year. nobody
could hurt me, touch me, tell
me what to do or take anything
away from me. Everything I
owned was bought and paid for
by me.

I was shooting with a new
photographer today. I had never
heard of him and couldn't
recall any of my girlfriends
mentioning his name before.
my pay today was 1200. this
must be a two layout day.

312

slice of balogney, dun w/ n.
over a month

"Savage Fury" ~~IIII~~

It was the beginning of April.
I was booked for the following
Three ~~days~~ days on Video Exclusives
big budget production, "Savage
Fury."

I was so tired. My body was
exhausted, depleted, ~~plumb worn out.~~
& drained
~~It was so drained.~~ My brain
couldn't function, it was empty
of any thought other than ~~it's~~
the immediate activity. In front of me.
I was plumb worn out ~~and~~
over worked. & over fucked.
~~I got out of bed & hit~~
~~the shower.~~
I rolled over and touched
Michaels shoulder. "I have to
get up & go to work."
~~It w~~ The red neon lights on my clock
read 9:30. I wanted to fall
back asleep. I understood why
bears hibernated for so long.
One night of sleep wasn't
enough for me anymore.
My body craved weeks of endless
sleep.

Photo courtesy of Vivid Video.

Christy Canyon was born and raised in Southern California and is currently working on her second autobiography. Her dancing adventures (and there are plenty of them) will be in her sequel due out next year, "Danger, Curves Ahead." This book will take you behind the scenes into strip clubs across the world, several marriages, another comeback into adult films and so much more.

Visit my website at: www.Christycanyon.com

For information on my fan club, send a self-addressed envelope to:
Christy Canyon
13547 Ventura Blvd. #218
Sherman Oaks CA 91423

Check out my one of-a-kind auctions on Ebay, under seller name:
Christycanyon11

For official Christy Canyon T-shirts, sweatshirts, coffee cups and hats online go to CaféPress at:

http://www.cafeshops.com/ccanyon